D1572134

The Last Jews on Iberian Soil

Published with the cooperation of the

CENTER FOR MEDIEVAL AND RENAISSANCE STUDIES

University of California, Los Angeles

The Last Jews on Iberian Soil

Navarrese Jewry 1479/1498

BENJAMIN R. GAMPEL

University of California Press
Berkeley • Los Angeles • Oxford

University of California Press
Berkeley and Los Angeles, California

University of California Press, Ltd.
Oxford, England

Copyright © 1989 by
The Regents of the University of California

Library of Congress Cataloging-in-Publication Data

Gampel, Benjamin R.
 The last Jews on Iberian soil: Navarrese Jewry, 1479 to 1498 /
Benjamin R. Gampel.
  p. cm.
 Bibliography: p.
 Includes index.
 ISBN 0-520-06509-3 (alk. paper)
  1. Jews—Navarre (Kingdom)—History. 2. Jews—Spain—Navarre—
History. 3. Navarre (Spain)—Ethnic relations. I. Title.
DS135.S75N384 1989
946'.52004924—dc19   89-30582
                                                              CIP

Printed in the United States of America

1   2   3   4   5   6   7   8   9

The paper used in this publication meets the minimum requirements of American
National Standard for Information Sciences—Permanence of Paper for Printed
Library Materials, ANSI Z39.48–1984 ∞

To Miriam, with love

Contents

Preface

This is my first scholarly book and as such the trail of my indebtedness is long. I begin with my parents Reema and Reuben Gampel who passed on to me their love for things Jewish, and with my father whose continual fascination with Jewish history was contagious. My first formal course in Jewish history, though, was as an undergraduate at Brooklyn College and to this day I remember being mesmerized by David Berger's classes. My graduate career at Columbia University was distinguished by the lectures of my first mentor, Zvi Ankori, who, more than any other teacher, shaped my vision of what history was and what the writing of Jewish history should be. Ismar Schorsch, then my teacher and now my senior colleague and the Chancellor of The Jewish Theological Seminary of America, initiated me in the art of writing a historical essay. Yet all this does not necessarily lead to the last generation of Navarrese Jews. For that, I must credit especially a pivotal conversation I had with Yosef Hayim Yerushalmi, then of Harvard University, in a darkened restaurant at the Copley Plaza Hotel in Boston. It was there that an anxious graduate student was seeking a dissertation topic and it was Professor Yerushalmi who, among his many other suggestions, pronounced: "And what about Navarre"?

What about it indeed? So off I was to Pamplona, Tudela, and other wonderful Navarrese cities, where the natural graciousness of the Spaniards and the help and support of so many archivists proved crucial in my finding the hundreds of documents on Jewish life in this medieval kingdom. Some stand out: Don Florencio Idoate and Don Jesús Imas of the Archivo General de Navarra in Pamplona and Don Julio Segura, archivist, friend, and generous host, who directs the Archivo Municipal and the Archivo de Protocolos in Tudela. It was Julio (I am sure he will permit me this familiarity) who first alerted me to the value of Tudela's notarial archives. And he spent much personal time making sure the documents were at my disposal and were photocopied as requested. Other archivists and their personnel: Don José Goñi Gaztambide

of the Archivo Catedral in Pamplona and Don Santiago Portero of
the Archivo Catedral in Tudela and Pacxi Gonzalez, intrepid micro-
filmist (and fine photographer) of the Archivo General in Pamplona. And how I remember my wife Miriam at my side five of the
months I was there! Six A.M. bus rides to the city of Tudela so she
could paginate the notarial registers that I cite so frequently in this
book. As I often said, her work is sure to have a more lasting impact
than mine. I already see scholarly articles quoting these sources—
with Miriam's page numbers.

Back to the United States with thousands of documents, a need
to sort all this out, and fortunately, many friends, colleagues, and
family members—here I proudly single out Miriam's parents Rabbi
Herschel and Pnina Schacter—with helpful encouragement and advice. Among them, my very dear friend Jeff Gurock, with his un-
flagging support (and Pamela Gurock's food), who turned out to
be the "first reader" of my dissertation. But this work would not
have come to fruition without the fortuitous arrival of Yosef Yerushalmi at Columbia University as the Salo Wittmayer Baron Professor of Jewish History just as my first chapter was completed. From
him I learned and understood the medieval Sephardi experience; his
wisdom informs my thoughts to this day. Practically, he read every
chapter with care. And so too John Mundy, eminent medievalist,
who was willing to read my footnotes and correct them.

My thanks too to the various foundations who give young scholars the money needed to complete their work at this early and
nonremunerative stage of their careers. I am especially grateful to
The Memorial Foundation for Jewish Culture and The National
Foundation for Jewish Culture.

During the last few years, I have allowed this work to age and
so the volume before you is the fruit of some last mellowing reflec-
tions. I was aided during this period by a grant from the United
States–Spanish Joint Committee for Cultural and Educational
Cooperation.

It has also been my good fortune to work with some wonderful
people at the University of California Press. I would like to thank
Stanley Holwitz, Shirley Warren, and especially Genise Schnitman,
who put in many long and arduous hours fine-combing and im-
proving the style and flow of the manuscript.

I end this personal saga with Miriam. She knows and I know—
and now our daughter Hannah Leah does too—how she brought
all this to pass.

6 Heshvan 5748
17 October 1988

Introduction

"One day in the month of March" 1498, according to the Christian notary, Juhan Martínez Cabero, King Johan and Queen Catalina expelled all professing Jews from their kingdom of Navarre. By the very next day, no Jews were to be found—at least not officially—anywhere in the Iberian peninsula. Their Castilian and Aragonese coreligionists had already been expelled six years earlier by Ferdinand and Isabella, and during the first week of December 1496 the Jews of Portugal too had been ordered to either convert or leave the kingdom.

Throughout their long history, Jews had often faced the sudden dissolution of their age-old settlements. The catastrophe that befell European Jewry in the twentieth century set before contemporary historians the urgent task of understanding how such disasters could have occurred. They have sought, among other goals, to uncover the root causes of these events and to detail the Jewish reaction to their unfolding. One of the issues that has assumed crucial import in these deliberations is the nature of the Jews' awareness of an approaching catastrophe. What is being judged is not only the Jews' political sagacity but their communal health. Are they able to respond constructively to events that threaten to undermine their existence as a group? Do the Jews of the diaspora manifest a "blindness" to such threats "that is nothing short of proverbial," as one modern historian would have it?[1]

To respond to these questions (they are implicit charges, actually) requires first of all that a study be undertaken of a Jewish community in the years prior to its dissolution. It could then be determined whether those years were filled with socioeconomic turmoil and political defeat or instead (deceptive) tranquility and material success. In addition, one could ascertain whether the governments under which the Jews lived had clear policies toward them and determine if the Jews were so enfeebled as to be unwilling to recognize the untenability of their position.

Late fifteenth-century Iberian Jewry has already been subject to

such searching inquiry. Indeed, the investigation may well have
started in the years following the expulsion, when none other than
one of the exiles, Don Isaac Abravanel, the illustrious rabbi and
statesman who was a financier at the court of Ferdinand and Isabella, reported—probably to silence his detractors—that the expulsion order took even the Jewish courtiers by surprise. Indeed, as
Don Isaac observed about the years just before the expulsion, the
Jews seemed to be secure and prosperous. Is Abravanel's remark,
however, to be taken as the self-serving apologia of one who was
blind to the reality of his people's status in Castile and Aragon? Or
was he honestly expressing the shock of proud Iberian Jews, those
self-described "exiles of Jerusalem that are in Sepharad," who had
lived comfortably on peninsular soil for over a thousand years?[2]

The charges of ostrich-like behavior that may have been leveled
at the Castilian and Aragonese courtiers, and at the Jewish populations generally, take on greater force when directed at the Jews of
the small Pyrenean kingdom of Navarre. After all, they had witnessed the expulsion of the Jews at the order of Ferdinand and
Isabella in 1492 and had seen the Catholic Monarchs meddle in the
internal affairs of Portugal by forcing the expulsion of its Jews in
1496—how could they have been taken by surprise?

Until recently, examinations of late fifteenth-century Iberian
Jews have tended to lavish their attention on the communities of
Castile and Aragon, while those of Portugal and Navarre have been
neglected.[3] Understandably, the dissolution of the most prosperous
and distinguished of the Jewish communities has attracted the most
scholarship. Yet the Iberian peninsula in the late Middle Ages was
home to four Christian polities, and a thorough examination of all
the kingdoms' Jewries is needed to understand its Jews. Although
the story of Navarrese Jews did at times mirror that of their coreligionists in the neighboring kingdoms, forces peculiar to the Pyrenean kingdom shaped the lives of its Jewish inhabitants.

The study of the Navarrese kingdom itself has been furthered in
the last two decades by a younger generation of university-trained
scholars. They have eschewed the concerns of the amateur native-
born chroniclers who wrote in the late nineteenth and early twentieth centuries, who, charming and often informative as they are,
pursued their own parochial interests when recording the medieval
history of the modern-day province. Oddly enough, however, the
last years of Navarre's independent history as a kingdom have not

been adequately scrutinized by this new cadre of university-trained historians, perhaps in part because of the overshadowing presence of the landmark nineteenth-century study by the historian Prosper Boissonade.[4] A study of the last generation of Navarrese Jewry, therefore, whose dates not surprisingly coincide more or less with the final years of the kingdom, also illuminates the gradual weakening of this independent Pyrenean polity and the concomitant emergence of the powerful political entity engineered by Ferdinand and Isabella.

Just as the history of Navarrese Jews ends with the demise of the kingdom, the saga of this Jewry probably began almost from Navarre's very birth. A short review of the early days of Navarre's Jewry will provide important background, and thanks to the pioneering work of the nineteenth-century historian Meyer Kayserling and the recent research of Béatrice Leroy, the task is made much easier.[5] In northern Christian Iberia of the tenth and eleventh centuries, as in the largely agricultural areas across western Europe, Jews were to be found in the role of generators of commercial enterprise. The *fueros* (legal charters) of Nájera and Jaca testify to the growth of the Jewish population and reflect the desire of the Christian rulers to increase their population and the variety of social classes represented in it, thereby creating new sources of revenue.

Although opportunities were expanding and Jews were immigrating, these new Jewish communities could not be compared either numerically or culturally with the larger Jewish *aljamas* (communities) under Islamic rule. When local authorities invited the poet Moshe ibn Ezra to settle in Estella, Yehudah ha-Levi wondered how Moshe could live "among the tongue tied." Ibn Ezra sadly agreed. But the poverty of Jewish life in the north came to an end as the Christian conquests of the twelfth and thirteenth centuries created new political and economic opportunities.

When Alfonso I, king of Aragon and Navarre, conquered Tudela in 1119, the city already possessed a distinguished Jewish community. Its strength was reflected in the negotiations between the Tudelan Jews and Alfonso. The Jews had left the city when the Christians entered and only returned when given a royal promise of various rights, including those mentioned in the *fuero* of Nájera. Fifty years later, in 1170, Sancho VI of Navarre conceded to them the fortified area overlooking the city; that he did so is testimony to both the social value and military importance of the Jews. Sancho also granted the Tudelan Jews a cemetery and strengthened their legal and economic position.

Such were the rights of the Jews in Navarre—and generally, throughout the newly expanding Christian kingdoms. The Jews were a welcome urban element, trained both in crafts and trade. In these preponderantly agricultural societies, the presence of Jews was valued highly, and here in Iberia they were appreciated even more in view of the Christians' hostility toward the conquered Muslims.

While the kingdoms of Portugal, Castile, and Aragon embarked on their main peninsular conquests in the thirteenth century, Navarre was cut off from further expansion by its triumphant neighbors. Still, its Jews enjoyed many of the privileges gained by their coreligionists in the other kingdoms. Under Sancho VII el Fuerte, son of Sancho VI, the prosperity of the Jews continued unabated.

Navarre would not continue to enjoy uninterrupted dynastic succession. When Sancho died in 1234, Navarre fell to French domination when Sancho's nephew Thibaut, count of Champagne, inherited the throne. Changes of dynasty were generally disastrous for peninsular Jews, for anti-Jewish violence often accompanied the transitions. Jews were closely allied with established royal governments, and when there were lapses in royal power, anti-monarchic and anti-Jewish sentiments raged.

Not only the dynastic shift proved troublesome for the Jews; French influence also proved baneful over the long run. Navarrese Jewry under Thibaut did not suffer fiscal ruin or expulsion as did northern French Jews, but the community did feel the anti-Jewish attitudes and policies of the French sovereigns.

Thibaut IV (Teobaldo I to the Navarrese) tolerated the Jews— unlike his contemporary Louis IX—yet in 1238 he did confiscate Jewish-owned property (and some property owned by non-Jews) to fund a military expedition to Palestine. Exactly thirty years later, his son Teobaldo II went further, not only confiscating much of the property of the Jews, but also imprisoning them so that the ransom money could be used for a joint crusade with his father-in-law, Louis IX. Still, during this period the Jews generally lived at peace within the kingdom, engaged in their regular daily activities.

Another crisis emerged—again at a moment of weak royal control. When Teobaldo II's brother, King Enrique I, died in 1274, he left an underage daughter in line for the throne. The long-smoldering antipathy of local Navarrese for their French overlords erupted in Navarre—most virulently in Pamplona. The residents of the boroughs of San Cernin and San Nicolás took revenge on those of the nearby Navarrería, wreaking havoc and killing many citizens, and in the process almost destroying the Jewish community there. Philippe the Fair (later king of France), who had married Enrique's daughter Juana, compounded the Jews' difficulties in 1277 by issuing restrictions on moneylenders, preventing them from promptly and fully collecting on their loans. In 1299 he ordered that, as per the ordinance of Louis IX in 1254, Jewish moneylenders could collect only the capital on their outstanding loans.

The period of French domination brought other difficulties for Navarrese Jews. Even the Shepherd's Crusade of the 1320s, which inflicted damage on both Aragonese and Navarrese Jews, seemed minor compared to the outbreaks of violence that erupted in 1328 on the death of Charles IV, king of both Navarre and France, which marked the end of the Capetian dynasty. Hundreds of Jews were killed, mostly in Estella and its surrounding district. The Jews resisted militarily, as they had against the Pastoreaux, again without success.

Under Felipe III of Navarre, Count of Evreux, the Jewish community slowly recovered. Some of those responsible for the massacre were punished, and the ordinance of St. Louis banning usury was annulled. Jews rose to prominence in the court as financiers and tax farmers and distinguished themselves in commerce.

Other difficulties arose, however: The plague and the spillover from the Castilian civil war dramatically reduced the number of Navarrese Jews. Unable to conduct business, and thus to pay their taxes, Jews in substantial numbers left the kingdom. Carlos II attempted to stem the tide by trying to enforce a long-standing regulation that prevented Christians and Muslims from purchasing Jewish-held property. Already in 1370 his wife Juana was enticing Castilian Jews, much persecuted in their kingdom's civil war, to emigrate to Navarre with the promise of a dramatically reduced tax burden.

Quite fortuitously for Navarrese Jewry, Carlos III, a capable monarch intent on centralizing royal power, came to the throne in 1387. The situation in Navarre was comparable to that of Portugal, where the monarchy was strong, and the Jews were protected from the pogroms of 1391, which traumatized the Jewries of both Castile and Aragon. Navarrese Jews at the turn of the fifteenth century were able to rebuild their commercial and industrial life, and Jewish financiers, physicians, and political advisers were visible at the royal court. Troubled times returned, however, when the dreaded plague broke out again. As in the disaster of 1379 and 1380, the outbreaks in the early fifteenth century depleted the Navarrese population.

Little is known of the situation of the Jews in the middle years of the fifteenth century. In 1435, Juan II, infante of Aragon, and king of Navarre by virtue of his marriage to Queen Blanca, daughter of Carlos III, reduced the debts of Tudelan Jews and encouraged them to return to his kingdom. Navarre was soon beset by civil war, however, when Blanca died and Juan II did not transfer his power to their twenty-year-old son Carlos. Civil war raged intermittently in Navarre up to and even after Carlos' death in 1461, as partisans of the two rivals fought for control of the kingdom. Although as a rule Jews do not fare well in such times of upheaval for this moment in history, all that is known is that in 1469 Leonor, daughter of Juan II and Blanca and governor of the kingdom, ordered the Jews of Pamplona to return to their *judería* and rebuild their homes. Both this order and yet another invitation to Castilian Jews to emigrate to Navarre may have been calculated to boost the assets of the royal patrimony.

Juan II died in 1479 and Navarre embarked on a period of independence that would come to an end with the invasion of the troops of Ferdinand of Aragon in 1512. These years, however, were filled with constant machinations by both Castile-Aragon and France to control the Pyrenean kingdom or at least influence its policies. Navarre was also beset by internal tensions, a legacy of the civil war of mid-century much exploited by the forces on both sides of the Pyrenees.

The fortunes of Navarrese Jewry from 1479 until their expulsion in 1498 were bound up with this domestic and international turmoil. A brief discussion of the pertinent political data is therefore essential.[6] When Juan II died, Leonor, who was his daughter and Ferdinand of Aragon's sister, became queen. The monarchy was allied with the Agramontes party, whose leader in 1479 was Mosén Pierres de Peralta. The Beaumonteses, led by Luis, conde de Lerín, were backed by Castile. Both groups controlled parts of the kingdom: Agramonteses at times ruled the cities of Tudela, Olite, and Sangüesa, for example, whereas Beaumonteses were invariably in charge of Pamplona, Viana, Estella, and Puente la Reina.

Leonor died on 12 February 1479, less than a month after ascending the throne, and her eleven-year-old grandson, Francisco Febo of the House of Foix, inherited the kingdom. His mother Magdalena was named regent and was supported by the Agramontes party and her brother, King Louis XI of France. Ferdinand, aided by his garrisons led by Juan de Ribera, threw his weight behind the Beaumonteses. Magdalena, caught in a delicate situation, attempted to balance both their concerns and desires: Castile-Aragon's dream of peninsular hegemony and France's wish to extend its power beyond the Pyrenees—an eventuality Ferdinand would never permit.

Civil war erupted again in 1480, and although Francisco Febo was crowned in 1481 in the Agramontes city of Tudela, before long he had to escape to his French dominions on the other side of the Pyrenees. The next year was devoted to choosing a wife for Francisco Febo. The intrigues by both France and Castile-Aragon were put to an end with the young monarch's death on 29 January 1483.

Franciso Febo's sister Catalina, then three years old, inherited the crown and Magdalena remained regent. The energy devoted to searching for Francisco's future consort was now directed toward cultivating young Catalina's marriage prospects. Meanwhile, Louis XI died on August 30 and Charles VIII, Magdalena's cousin, became the new king of France. At this juncture, Magdalena decided that it was less a threat to Navarre for Catalina to marry a Frenchman than to accede to the wishes of Castile-Aragon, especially since Juan de Foix (viscount of Narbonne), pretender to the Navarrese throne, was being promoted by France to pressure the Navarrese to accede to its wishes. On 14 June 1484, Catalina married seven-year-old Juan de Albret, who came with much territory and a father, Alaín de Albret, with his own foreign-policy designs.

Castile-Aragon, much upset with Magdalena's choice, encouraged the Beaumonteses in their depredations, allied itself with the city of Tudela, and sent Juan de Ribera to occupy some Navarrese fortresses and the western border city of Viana. In May 1485, Magdalena had to sign a treaty with the Beaumonteses in the city of

Pau. By 1488, the Navarrese monarchs were subordinate to Castile-Aragon, which in the treaty of Valencia received further promises of loyalty from the Navarrese.

The "Castilian protectorate" continued unchallenged through the 1490s, for Charles VIII's designs on Italy persuaded France to allow Castile-Aragon free reign in Navarre in exchange for a hands-off policy in Italy. In 1492, Castile-Aragon made overtures to Magdalena and Alaín, because with the conquest of Granada completed, it had turned its eyes to Rosellón and needed Navarrese aid. Navarre granted Castile-Aragon the right to control the appointment of those in charge of Navarre's fortresses in exchange for its support against any French designs.

By 1494, with Castile-Aragon's position in Navarre secure, the civil war was brought to a halt, and Johan and Catalina were finally permitted to enter the Navarrese kingdom and to be crowned in Pamplona. In the waning years of the century, the Castilian-Aragonese protectorate was further strengthened. Magdalena died in January 1495, however, and Alaín, now in sole charge of the foreign policy of Navarre, attempted a rapprochement with France. Castile-Aragon reacted by reoccupying Navarrese fortresses and instigating the resumption of the civil war. In the meantime, Charles VIII returned from Italy in July 1495 and renewed his designs on his small Pyrenean neighbor.

In February 1497, Charles VIII and Ferdinand negotiated a treaty and counted Navarre among their allies. Ferdinand, however, incensed by a pact between Navarre and France at Tarbes in September 1497, sent Juan de Ribera and his troops to threaten Navarre. France, interested again in Italy, offered Navarre to Ferdinand in exchange for renunciation of its rights to Milan, Naples, and Genoa. Although this proposal was rejected, by 1498 Castile-Aragon and France were discussing how to dismember the many states in the Albrets' possession. Still, Ferdinand menaced the Navarrese frontier during these years, arousing the concern of its monarchs.

The nineteen tumultuous years from 1479 to 1498 in Navarrese history were also the last years of Jewish life in this Pyrenean kingdom. Whereas Navarre's diplomatic history can be confidently traced, it is much more difficult to explore the life of its Jewry in its last two decades of formal existence. The usual literary works left behind by rabbis, poets, and philosophers that might shed light on this last generation are almost totally absent. Fortunately, there exists a variety of unpublished sources in the cities, towns, and villages of the modern-day province of Navarre, and the tale of these Jews therefore can still be told.

The major repository of information about the medieval kingdom of Navarre is the Archivo General de Navarra, located in Pamplona, the former royal capital and now the administrative seat of the province. Not only the royal decrees and tax records are to be found in the AGN—albeit with spotty coverage, owing to the turbulence that marked the years 1479 to 1498—the minutes of the royal chancellery from late 1494 to early 1495 are available as well. Occasional documents from the collections of Navarrese monasteries and convents are extant in the AGN also.[7]

Most of the material that describes the daily life of the Jews was found in Tudela, the second largest city of Navarre. Its municipal archive (Archivo Municipal de Tudela) boasts a rich collection of documents, including a ledger of receipts and expenses whose first volume commences with the year 1480. The city's major treasure is the notarial archive (Archivo de Protocolos de Tudela), which has recently been made available to scholars, thanks to the efforts of its indefatigable archivist, Julio Segura. For the years 1479 to 1498 alone, I was able to consult twenty-four notarial registers from thirteen notaries. Although these notarial documents do not furnish a narrative recording of events, they do provide the foundation for understanding the day-to-day activities of the Jews of Tudela, especially in their relations with non-Jews in the society. Materials from Jewish notaries have generally not been preserved, with some tantalizing exceptions, which include a few marriage contracts and related legal documents.[8]

The collection of the Tudelan cathedral archive (Archivo Catedral de Tudela) contains lists of rentals and a volume of notarial acts that complements the documentation in the other city repositories. Other archives elsewhere in Navarre also provided materials, the most significant being the municipal archives of Corella and Pamplona (Archivo Municipal de Corella, Archivo Municipal de Pamplona).[9]

Through this confluence of royal, municipal, cathedral, and notarial sources, the daily life of the Navarrese Jews can be recreated and their changing political fortunes explored. [To minimize the confusion that can be caused by the inventiveness of medieval spelling, I have given in the text the most common or preferred spelling of personal names and foreign terms. When a name or term is spelled differently in a source document, I have so indicated in a parenthetical note in the relevant footnote.] What arises from the documents are chapters on the Jewish settlements and their population, an analysis of their rich economic life, and a description of the activities and structure of their communities. The sources also provide materials for another picture of this Jewry, quite different from the portrait of socioeconomic success. The available information has been reconstructed in this study to reveal the life of New Christian converts from Judaism; the attempt of the Castilian-Aragonese Inquisition to enter Navarre and the unsuccessful resistance to this venture; the struggle of the Jewish refugees of Castile and Aragon to settle within Navarre in 1492; and, finally, the road leading to the "expulsion" of the Navarrese Jews.

The Jews of Navarre were the last Jews on Iberian soil. Their story, gleaned largely from these archival sources, is told in these pages.

1. Everyday Life

CANTABRIAN
SEA

ULTRAPUERTOS

San Juan de Pie
del Puerto

LAS
MONTAÑAS

CASTILE

SANGÜESA

Pamplona

Puente la Reina
● Monreal

● Estella

ESTELLA

Sangüesa

Lerín   Tafalla ●   Aybar
● Los Arcos

OLITE

● Viana   ● Olite

ARAGON

● Villafranca
Milagro
● Valtierra
● Arguedas

LA RIBERA

● Corella
Cintruénigo   ● Tudela

Cascante ● Buñuel
● Cortes

0   30 kms

Map 1. Navarre: The Six Merindades (districts)

1. Settlements and Population

Navarrese Jewry throughout its history lived mainly in five of the six *merindades* (administrative districts) that constituted the kingdom in the fifteenth century. As in the preceding years, during 1479 to 1498 the northernmost precinct of Ultrapuertos—probably because it lacked an important urban center—rarely showed Jews in its records. In the areas that historically recorded a pattern of Jewish presence, no major demographic change can be detected for the last two decades of Jewish life in the Pyrenean kingdom.[1]

To determine precisely where Jews resided is a difficult task. Careful combing of the archives for indications of Jewish habitation can prove the existence of Jews or Jewish communities but it is not sufficient to ascertain the exact number of Jewish settlements. Not only is the documentation incomplete; the extant sources have inherent biases. Royal sources indicate only areas of Jewish habitation that were under control of the monarchs. Since those sources are mainly related to tax-gathering matters, they do not include locales where Jews might have been unable, for whatever reasons, to render their imposts. Moreover, few documents from other landholders—such as noblemen, churches, religious orders, and the like—are extant.

For the purposes of this study, when a single Jew appeared in the records as an inhabitant of a locale (not merely as an owner or renter of property) I have considered that site to be an area of Jewish settlement. The major source of information for sites of Jewish habitation is a tax record prepared for the newly crowned monarchs in 1494, data complemented by a report issued just the next year, which detailed the property of the conde de Lerín, the leader of the Beaumonteses, the anti-royal faction in the civil war. Ferdinand and Isabella ordered the compilation of this information. They had promised to bring the conde to their own kingdom, for they wished to remove him from the center of the political agitation in Navarre. The account of his assets was prepared so that Ferdinand and Isabella could give him equivalent property and thus secure his agreement with the deal.[2]

The list of the conde de Lerín's assets includes the number of Jews living under his rule and the taxes that they rendered. It is therefore biased and partial in the same way as the royal records. Fortunately, however, the information from these two sources can be corroborated against and augmented by references in other sources of this period, the most fruitful of which are the notarial records.

In the late fifteenth century, as in years past, the southern and western *merindades* of la Ribera, Olite, and Estella contained the largest number of Jewish communities in Navarre. Jews made their homes not only in the important cities of Tudela, Olite, Tafalla, and Estella, but also settled in the smaller towns of the southern and western *merindades*. In the north-central and eastern districts of Pamplona and Sangüesa, the Jews lived for the most part in the capital cities which were also named Pamplona and Sangüesa.[3]

It can be cautiously advanced that although the pattern of Navarrese Jewish settlement did not change greatly from the fourteenth century to the fifteenth, new Jewish settlements appeared at nine locations, while an identical number of locations lost their Jewish population. There were Jewish communities during the last two decades of the fifteenth century in Mendabia, Muniain, and Uxanavilla in the *merindad* of Estella; Murillo el Fruyto, Caparroso, and Miraglo in the district of Olite; and Fitero, Montagudo, and Cintruénigo in the area of Tudela. For the last two decades of the fifteenth century, the sources make no mention of Jews in these former areas of Jewish settlement: Murillo de las Limas, Cadreita, Valtierra, Buñuel, and Murchante in Tudela; Sesma and Cárcar in Estella; Artajona in Olite; and Monreal in Sangüesa. These demographic changes were surely the result of the turbulent events of the fifteenth century. Outbreaks of the plague, the wars with Castile, and the seemingly unending civil strife affected Jews along with the rest of the inhabitants of Navarre.[4]

Despite ecclesiastical and governmental pronouncements intended to isolate the Jews, not all Navarrese Jews lived in quarters specifically designated for their residence—some lived amongst their Christian and Muslim neighbors. *Juderías* (Jewish quarters) originally were created for the Jews' security, yet in Pamplona and Tudela in the late fifteenth century, Jews resided both within and without their local *juderías*. The southern town of Corella apparently contained no specifically Jewish area during this period, and the Jews were to be found in all the *barrios* (neighborhoods) of the village. This uncommonly high degree of residential integration troubled Johan and Catalina, the Navarrese sovereigns, and in 1488 they ordered that the Jews remove themselves to the neighborhood called Parte Casa, where the synagogue was located. Their order did not indicate that this was a primarily Jewish section, only that it ought to become one.[5]

The paucity of historiographical treatments of the cities and villages of Navarre makes it difficult to determine the location of individual Jews' residence and of communal institutions within the centers of Navarrese population in the late fifteenth century. Here an attempt is made, based on the sources of this period, to determine where Jews lived within the Navarrese centers. The overwhelming percentage of documentation comes from reports on property taxes recorded in the royal accounts of these years and from details of abutments of property included in notarial documents, listed when one parcel or an adjacent one was bought, sold, or transferred.[6]

These sources, and occasionally others, such as the royal directive concerning Corella, touch on property connected to Jews or the Jewish community, but the quality of data they provide is often uneven. The information that one Jew may have tax-farmed certain lands for a municipality or a church, that another received the house of a Christian or a Muslim as loan collateral, or that another Jew purchased an orchard or vineyard does not help us determine where Jews *lived* within that locale. Even in areas where for which there is information on houses owned by Jews, there often does not exist sufficient documentation to enable the researcher to identify clear patterns of Jewish habitation.

Still, sites of Jewish residence in the villages of Cascante and Puente la Reina and the cities of Olite and Viana can be partially determined, and for Pamplona and Tudela, located with greater precision. Because the sources are mainly of Christian provenance, they reinforce the impression that Jews lived interspersed among their Christian neighbors, especially in the smaller centers of population. And so it was in Cascante, a town less than ten kilometers southwest of Tudela, where Jews made their homes in the neighborhood of Pontarrón. The records indicate that Jews had owned houses there as far back as 1306, and the Nazir family, whose members Ezmel and Yento figure prominently in the late fifteenth century, appear in the local documentation throughout the fourteenth and fifteenth centuries. In Pontarrón, the Jews' homes directly abutted the walls of the village and, in a few cases, the neighborhood's communal road.[7]

The same pattern can be observed in Puente la Reina, where the Jews lived in the section of town called the "Nabarreria," and their homes located between the wall of the town and its major thoroughfare. This highway ended in the famous Roman bridge (hence the village's name) that crossed the Arga river and was part of the pilgrims' road to Santiago. Indeed, the Jews shared their quarter not only with the Church of the Crucifix but also with the hospital for pilgrims erected near the church in 1448.[8] As in Puente la Reina, the Jews of Olite lived in a corner of the town—in this case, the northeastern—near the neighborhood's main thoroughfare: the road leading to Tafalla.[9] The northwestern corner of the town of Viana probably contained the "sinagoga de los judios," whose administrators rented two houses in the same neighborhood, where the local castle was also located.[10]

The Jewish quarter of Pamplona was located within the *barrio* of the Navarrería, the original nucleus of the Navarrese capital. The *judería*'s southern and eastern borders were the city walls, and the quarter was separated from the rest of the Navarrería by a fortified fence.[11] Its major neighbor to the north was the orchard of the canons and to the west, the convent of San Agustín.[12] The Jews had lived in this area before the destruction of their quarters in 1276 and were relocated there after the Jewish sector was ordered rebuilt in 1336. They remained in this southeast corner of the Navarrería even after 1423 and the union of the three separate walled settlements that constituted Pamplona in the Middle Ages.[13]

There were three gateways to the *judería*: Two were openings in the city wall; the other was a portal in the palisade that separated the neighborhood from the rest of the city. The sector's eastern gate is called in the sources the "portal de garcia marra," and the opening in the southern wall is called the "portal de la fuent vieia." The "portal de la judería" connected the quarter with the Rua del Alfériz of the Navarrería.[14]

Many Jews lived in this street in 1469, when Leonor, then the "princesa primogenita, heredera de Navarra," commanded the

Jews to reside within the gates of the *judería* and prohibited them from living among the Christians in the Rua del Alfériz. The Jewish quarter was in dilapidated condition and its inhabitants had been forced to seek housing elsewhere. Leonor therefore also ordered that the houses of the *judería* belonging to the royal patrimony be repaired.[15]

It is highly unlikely that all the Pamplonese Jews were able to return to the *judería* following the issuance of the 1469 edict, although according to the royal accounts (*comptos*) of 1494, all Jews lived within the boundaries of their quarter. So did the previous *comptos* of Pamplona, however, even during those years for which we have documentation proving otherwise. The royal tax registers are misleading, for they follow prescribed formulas that do not immediately or sensitively reflect alterations in residential patterns. Furthermore, rents must be paid even when a house is not being used or is uninhabitable. Nonetheless, these registers are the major sources we have for information about the *judería* of Pamplona, and it is to these we now turn.[16]

According to the *compto* of 1494, the sole extant register from the last quarter of the fifteenth century,[17] the "houses and squares" of the Jewish quarter occupied over forty thousand square *codos*.[18] Within this area, three sections are identified. The first was located in the southeast corner of the quarter, near the Portal de Garcia Marra and extending "up to" the orchard of the canons.[19] If we assume that the tax rate for all homes was identical and that there were no exemptions, this section was apparently the smallest. There were fourteen households settled there, all occupying separate houses, which appear to have been larger than those in the other districts.[20] Within its precincts was the synagogue; indeed, in a fifteenth-century document, the area was called the "barrio de la sinagoga mayor."[21]

The second *barrio,* the largest one, contained the greatest number of houses (twenty-nine), and eight of these were subdivided to allow living quarters for twelve more households. This section was described as being near the canons' enclosure, "which is the major road of the juderia." That street began at the portal of the Navarrería and ran through the quarter to the southern part of the city wall and its Portal de la Fuent Vieia. The houses straddled both sides of the northern section of this street, the units divided almost equally on each side.[22]

This neighborhood originally had some substantial houses, nearly all of them subdivided by the late fifteenth century. The only home of appreciable size that remained was the house of Çaçon Alborge, which had been owned by a famous fourteenth-century Navarrese Jew, the royal physician and chief rabbi, Juçe Orabuena. Two houses of prayer were situated in this *barrio,* both located in houses that were privately owned by Semuel Alffaça and Salamon Levi. Although Alffaça's house was the larger, it was called in previous years the "oraçion menor." Therefore the synagogue of Pamplona was called "great"; it was, in comparison with the two smaller *casas de oración.*[23]

The location of the third Jewish section as described in the 1494 tax ledger is unclear. Fortunately, fourteenth-century records indicate that this *barrio,* which contained the smallest dwellings, was bounded on the west by the weaver's district and that it was situated near the Portal de la Fuent Vieia. Twenty-four houses are listed in the documentation and seven of them were subdivided, yielding ten additional units. Only two sizeable houses existed intact; both were owned by the Alborge family, one of whose members possessed the largest dwelling in the second district.[24]

Jewish communal institutions were located in the *judería;* the private home of Yento Camin, located in the second district, was used in the late fifteenth century by the "confraria de la teba," an association in charge of communal prayer. A smaller building in the same *barrio* was the communal property of the Jews and served as the hospital of the Jewish quarter. At least three Jewish-owned shops were located right near the portal in the city's southern wall.[25]

Some of the communal property of the Jews was situated beyond the confines of the quarter's boundaries. The cemetery was located outside the city's walls and could be reached by a road which ran from the Portal de Garcia Marra. Its grounds were also referred to as the "vineyard of the king," and it was surrounded by both Christian-owned vineyards and ones in which Jews labored.[26]

Although there was no clearly demarcated Jewish quarter as in Pamplona, in the fifteenth century the northwestern section of Tudela, where the medieval castle was located, was home to most of this city's Jewish population. During the Islamic period and after the Christian conquest of the city in 1119, the Jewish quarter had been situated on the shores of the Ebro, just north of the Queiles river. In 1170, under orders from King Sancho VII (the Wise), the Jews of Tudela were evacuated to the castle to insure their safety from Christian attack.[27] According to notarial documents, which constitute the overwhelming majority of the sources on the residential patterns of Tudelan Jews, the Jews remained in the vicinity of the fortress—although no longer solely within its walls—through the end of the fifteenth century.[28]

The castle was built on the highest point overlooking the city and the Jewish quarter shared the hill on which it was situated. The *judería* extended into the valley (*planilla*) beneath the mount.[29] There were at least two synagogues in the neighborhood; the small synagogue may have directly abutted one of the walls of the fortress. The Jewish "brotherhood" (*confraría*) was also located on the slopes of the hill. The weaver's district was in the eastern sector of the *planilla,* near the "weaver's barrio" of the parish of San Miguel.[30]

Christians lived within the *judería* and Jews resided outside it, in the adjacent parishes of San Pedro, San Miguel, and San Salbador. The boundaries of the Jewish quarter were fluid; a number of buildings are said to be part of the *judería* in one document, and in others to be part of the Christian districts. Although there is no evidence that a wall surrounded the Jewish *barrio,* one of the sources refers to the "first portal of the juderia."[31]

Jews and their communal institutions owned and rented farm land, especially vineyards, outside the residential area of Tudela. This pattern of widespread Jewish ownership in Tudela was evident at least from the period of the Christian conquest. Most of the holdings were in Traslapuente, a large area on the left bank of the Ebro.[32] Jews also owned some property in the environs of the city near the western Puerta de Calahorra; in the south, adjacent to the roads leading to Borja and Saragossa; and alongside Christian-owned properties throughout the lands under Tudelan rule.[33]

Before any assessment can be made of the degree to which Jews were integrated into Navarrese society, however, it is important to pause and ask about the number of Jews in the Pyrenean kingdom. Although any attempt to calculate Jewish population figures in the Iberian kingdoms is fraught with methodological difficulties, the number of Jews who lived in the cities and towns of Navarre during the years 1479 to 1498 can be reasonably calculated using two valuable contemporary accounts. In 1494, the Navarrese monarchs ordered their treasurer, Johan de Bosquet, to collect a two-pound tax from each Jewish hearth in the kingdom. Bosquet duly recorded contributions from 633 *fuegos* (hearths). He registered 160 hearths in Tudela; 60 in Corella; and 50 in Cascante, which together with his findings from five other towns in the district of la Ribera amounted to a total of 363 *fuegos*. Additionally, he listed eight locations with Jewish residents in the district of Olite that totalled 103 hearths. The districts of Pamplona, Estella, and Sangüesa also contained 58, 52, and 57 *fuegos,* respectively, according to the royal treasurer.[34]

The second source, a 1495 report that parenthetically notes the number of Jews living in territories controlled by the chief domestic antagonist of the Navarrese monarchs, the conde de Lerín, lists seventy-seven Jews. The village of Lerín itself contained sixty-one of them. Assuming that the figures in this report give the number of hearths, not individuals, the Jewish *fuegos* in the kingdom of Navarre, according to information culled from both sources, numbered 710.[35]

Clearly, however, these two accounts do not convey a complete picture of Navarre's Jewish population. Both documents surely listed only those hearths whose owners were able to render the levied imposts. Moreover, not all areas in the kingdom were surveyed in the reports. Bosquet's report explicitly mentions sites under control of feudal lords for which no further information was available; and only one of these locations appears in the Lerín document of 1495.[36]

Although these problems preclude a precise determination of the number of Navarrese Jews, they should not prevent us from making some informed yet cautious assumptions. Our knowledge of medieval Jewish demography is scanty enough without consciously withholding conclusions for areas where there is some evidence, however flawed or limited. That said, we begin with the figure of 710 *fuegos*. Although it is difficult to say how many people on average shared each hearth, multiplying the number of hearths by five, a liberal coefficient, gives 3,550 taxpaying Navarrese Jews.[37] This number surely reflects the swelling of the Jewish population in the aftermath of the Castilian and Aragonese expulsions of 1492. The Jews represented approximately 3.5 percent of the general population of 100,000 Navarrese. The density of the Jewish population derived from these figures accords with the probable percentages of Jews in the kingdoms of Castile and Aragon in the late fifteenth century, and is comparable to the percentage of Jews in Navarre in the previous century.[38]

Although the Jewish population of the kingdom was small, the Jews' presence within Navarre's urban centers was significant. The next chapter examines the Jews' daily lives, with particular attention to their economic activities. As will be seen, the Jews, while displaying a unique economic profile, were enmeshed in the fabric of Navarrese society: The picture of their economic activities parallels, then, that of their patterns of residence.

2. Economic Activities

The Jews' economic activities, like their demographic distribution, reflect the *convivencia* that they enjoyed with Muslims and Christians—a prime feature of medieval Iberian culture. Jews were an integral part of the Navarrese economy, and during the last two decades of their formal existence in the Pyrenean kingdom, their occupations brought them into frequent contact with Christians and Muslims. Such connections were not severed even during these years of civil war and political instability.

This sunny picture of the Jews' involvement in the Navarrese economy resembles some of the portraits that have been sketched of Jewish economic success in late fifteenth-century Iberia. That Castilian and Aragonese Jews enjoyed a rosy economic profile is maintained even by scholars who have argued that the decision to expel them was already being considered by the Catholic Monarchs in the 1480s. Much of the description of the Jews' economic life during these last years has been impressionistic, however, based either on the Jews' supposed concentration in high-visibility financial positions or on random accounts of the amount of taxes paid by the Jewish communities. Until very recently, no one has methodically studied an Iberian kingdom's Jewry to determine its actual economic health and to test these various assessments. Now, however, an organized study of Portuguese Jews exists, but only scattered data are available on the most populous of Jewish communities, those of Castile.[1]

A composite picture of Navarrese Jews' economic activities cannot be assembled easily from the contemporary sources. While the documents record nearly six hundred Jews, any attempt to reconstruct their daily occupations is fraught with difficulty. Occupational descriptions are appended arbitrarily in ten percent of the documents, but these identifying tags generally do not jibe with the actual business activity described in the documents. Careful study of the Jews' business undertakings yields different categories than those suggested on the face of the documents. Nevertheless, these occupational tags are worth a glance, for they provide information that cannot be simply discarded.

According to the listed descriptions, the largest number of Jews were involved in clothing manufacture and trade. They are called tailors, hosiery makers, weavers, furriers, and curtain sewers. The next largest group consisted of members of the medical profession, and included thirteen *fisigos* or *medicos,* who possessed a general knowledge of medicine, and three *cirujanos* (surgeons), who were viewed as skilled artisans. Johan and Catalina, the Navarrese monarchs, considered Mastre Ossua, a Jew, as "our physician."

Although the majority of the documents are records of business transactions, only four Jews are listed as bookkeepers, stewards, or merchants. The makers of candles, pack saddles, lathes, and sieves could claim only one Jew apiece for their craft, while the silversmiths could count two Jews among their group. One barber, who possibly was a surgeon, and a lone "cotamallero" round out the list of Jewish occupations.[2]

The sources themselves point to the Jews being actively engaged in other activities. The purchase, sale, and rental of land; agriculture; artisanry; mercantile enterprises; and various forms of agency, including tax-farming, are frequently mentioned and appear to reflect the Jews' major concerns. Although we should not suppose that the activities recorded in the documents can be precisely equated with the totality of the Jews' economic activity, this information contains the most important data and its analysis must determine any reconstruction of the Jews' economic profile. First, however, it must also be noted that because Jewish documentation is lacking, we do not know of the community's internal economy—that is, what they bought and sold among themselves—but only of the Jews' economic interactions with Christians and Muslims.

Jews living in medieval Christian Iberia had always been able to possess land and they continued to do so right up until the late fifteenth-century expulsions. Like their peninsular coreligionists, Navarrese Jews in the last quarter of this century maintained their interest in landed property: not only owning their private dwellings, but also possessing vineyards, orchards, and grain-producing farms. And like their Muslim and Christian neighbors, Jews held land according to a variety of legal forms and conditions and had the obligation of maintaining the districts that encompassed their holdings.

Throughout the years covered in this study, Jews and Christians appear almost equally often in the roles of both buyers and sellers of landed property in the contracts involving members of the two communities; the Jews were the sellers in about fifty-two percent of the cases. Neither the influx of Castilian and Aragonese Jewish immigrants in 1492 nor the news of the impending expulsion in 1498 disturbed the remarkable equilibrium between Christians and Jews. Only one document exists wherein a Muslim sold property to a Jew: In April 1497, Amet Ayn of Cortes sold houses in a Muslim neighborhood to a local Jew. Probably, other such transactions would have been registered with Jewish and Muslim notaries, whose notebooks have not survived.[3]

The most common properties involved in the transactions were agricultural lands. Because Jewish agricultural activities centered on viticulture, transactions involving *vinyas* and *majuelos* (established and newly planted vineyards) appeared most often in the records. Fully fifty percent of non-residential land owned by Jews were labeled *vinyas* and about nine percent were classified as *majuelos*.[4] The considerable amount of harvested grapes and wine, and the taxes that Jews paid on their vineyards (to be discussed in the following chapter) also indicate the Jews' intense involvement in this kind of agriculture.

It was not simply the large wine-producing areas of southern Navarre that stimulated Jewish interest in viticulture, an occupation that consumed Navarrese Jews from the days of their earliest settlement in the Ebro region. Portuguese Jewry, as well as communities in Castile and Aragon, were active in this pursuit, largely because there were religious restrictions on the consumption of wine made by Gentiles or made from grapes harvested by non-Jews. Sale documents do not tell us to what extent Jews actually worked these lands—we know more about the involvement of Muslims and Christians—but it is clear that they participated in all aspects of viticulture, up through the final stages of wine production.[5]

House sales were the second most prevalent type of property transfer, amounting to twenty-four percent of such contracts, followed by transactions involving orchards and various parcels loosely labeled *pieças* and *landas*. Although evidence of Muslims tending orchards and growing cereals is clear and forthcoming, only records of taxes rendered by Jews on barley and other grains, as well as records of Jews' involvement in grain lending indicate what Jews raised on property designated as *pieças* and *landas*. The fact that Jews raised livestock can also be inferred from impost records and from the identification of some of their property as pens or enclosures (*corrales*). The sources also mention Jewish graziers raising lambs and kids in Ablitas.[6]

Jewish landowners, like Navarrese Christians and Muslims, were responsible for the repair and improvement of roads and irrigation canals in the districts where their parcels were located. Local rivers were not sufficient to irrigate all the agricultural lands of southern Navarre, and a maze of canals had been built to insure an adequate supply of water. The ordinances of the Traslapuente area of Tudela, dated 20 January 1478, ordered Jews and Christians to contribute to the irrigation of the land by building stone dams and sluice gates. And on 6 February 1494, three deputies of the Tudelan city council charged with the investigation of the roads in Traslapuente traveled to examine Mosse Malach's vineyard, which abutted the road to Exea de la Calçada. They passed favorably on his boundary markers, though not without criticism, and declared that they should be left in the same position. They also pronounced the road that ran past the vineyard to be in good condition.[7]

The inhabitants of Navarre, like those elsewhere in the peninsula, held parcels of land in three ways: (1) by absolute possession; (2) by a form of ownership whereby the property owner still owed fixed payments to a permanent owner; and (3) through rentals for a set number of years at a fixed annual price. Absolute ownership by Jews is evidenced by many contracts of purchase and sale. These documents generally describe the transacted parcel as being free and clear from all liens, *censes* (a kind of annual rent), debts and taxes, thereby indicating outright ownership.[8]

Prices do not appear to have varied much during the last quarter of the fifteenth century; at the lower end of the spectrum prices were especially stable. Seventy-five percent of the land acquired or sold by Jews was priced between ten and forty florins, the lowest priced at five florins and the highest, three hundred. *Majuelos* ran from eleven to thirty-five florins and houses from twenty-four to ninety. *Vinyas* ranged in price from seven to three hundred florins, according to the size and yield of the tracts.[9]

Some of the Jewish-held property was jointly owned by husband and wife, and when a man sold a parcel, he needed the legal consent of his wife. Such was also the practice among Christian couples. A Jewish woman could also engage in land transactions by herself, as when Astruga Sassalon sold a vineyard to Mayr Bendebut. When two sisters, Joya and Ester Falaquera, wished to sell land jointly owned by themselves and a legally underage sister, Jamila, they and Jamila's tutor had to sign the contract.[10]

Arbitration was sometimes necessary before a sale could be concluded. It took the help of two Muslims, Muça Orof and Muça Algitneli, to arrive at a fair price for houses that Pedro de Miranda wished to sell to Ysac Bancalero. On 4 September 1496, they decided on 24 golden florins, one of which Ysac was to pay them for their efforts. Outside arbitrators were probably used, because the parcel was owned by Pedro's wife, who lived in Borja, Aragon, which had been off-limits to Jews since the 1492 expulsion.[11]

There was legal recourse for property transactions to be reversed. After the elder Johan de Caxafort had sold a vineyard to Mayr Bendebut for twenty-five florins, de Caxafort's son returned the money to Bendebut, who then relinquished the property. In July 1497, Açach Çaraçaniel and his wife sold houses located in Cascante's "new district" to Julio de los Arcos and María Garçez. Julio died, and his widow María, together with Martín Garçez, as executors of the childrens' estate, relinquished the property to Rabí Sento, who is identified as the nephew of Açach Çaraçaniel. It can be assumed that the latter returned the sale price.[12]

Money did not always change hands when property was transferred; an exchange system also existed, whereby parcels were swapped. The tracts being judged to be of equal value, Johan de Salinas and Teresa de Santa Fuego could exchange their vineyard for a *pieça* of Açach Xani. When in 1484 Pascual de Lodosa gave up his *majuelo,* he received in return not only a *landa* belonging to Simuel Vençida but also fourteen florins and an ass. In 1487, Jacob Levi gave his *landa* and five florins for a vineyard belonging to Johan Ortiz.[13]

Jews also held lands that carried fossilized annual rents (*censes*) to ecclesiastical authorities and to the royal government, an arrangement that gave them yet another connection to these two ruling institutions of Navarrese society. Under this form of land tenure, a parcel was the Jew's to sell or rent, but he owed rent on the property to the local church. Originally, the church had owned the land outright, until it had sold its legal rights to the parcel on condition that an annual rent be paid in perpetuity. Many years later, the church was still owed this rental, even though the property may have passed through many hands.

When a Jew wished to transfer these lands, whether by sale or in any other fashion, he had to renounce his "annual and perpetual *cens*" to the owner institution. The owner, in turn, would grant a *cens* contract to the new "tenant" at the same price and generally with the same conditions. For example, when Juçe Çaraçaniel and his wife Reyna decided not to retain their possession of a vineyard in one of Tudela's districts, they relinquished their legal prerogative on the property to the precentor (*chantre*), vicar general, and canons of the church of Santa María. On the same day (22 April 1494), these church officials rented out the vineyard to Pedro de Pelayre for the annual sum of seven shillings, the amount that had been paid by the Jewish couple.[14]

The rents owed this Tudelan church were due either at Easter or on the festival of John the Baptist in June. The amounts were recorded in the *tabla,* a special account book in which payments by Jews were listed in a separate section.[15] From this ledger it appears that Jews held some of this church's property for most of the second half of the fifteenth century. For example, Mosse Falaquera leased at *cens* houses in the parish of San Pedro in Tudela in April 1451. The 1482 *tabla* recorded that these buildings were subsequently leased by a Jewish shoemaker named Arayny. A contract of lease (*relinquimiento*) of 1487 shows that "Arayny" was Salamon Arraheni, who died and left his underage daughter's business affairs in the hands of an executor, Jeuda Bennaçan. Bennaçan relinquished the houses to the church, which in turn (on the same day, in fact) rented the property to Mosse Albala and his wife for half a florin, the annual sum rendered by the previous tenants. In May 1496, the Albalas released the buildings to the church of Santa María. On the same day and for the identical *cens,* the church let the houses to a Christian couple, Ferrando de Castanyares and Gracia Martínez de Ciordia.[16]

Tudelan Jews also held property at *cens* from other ecclesiastical institutions both inside and outside the city. The *primiçieros* (collectors of the first fruits) of Tudela's parish church of San Miguel signed a *cens* contract with Abraham and Johet Levi for a stockyard at five groats (*groses*) per year, and Abraham Gamiz possessed houses in the Jewish quarter for which he paid half a florin annually to the prior of Santa María de Roncesvalles. This latter arrangement was concluded through an agent of the church who was a local Tudelan citizen.[17]

Most of the houses in the neighborhood of the Nabarrería of Puente de la Reina, where the Jewish community had established its residence, carried these rents, payable to the local monastery of Santo Crucufijo. The Jewish *censes* totaled approximately thirty-two groats, which was entered into the monastery's accounts by its prior, Fray Martín de Leach.[18]

Navarrese Jews possessed houses, shops, and agricultural lands that had annual *censes* payable to the royal government. The records of these rents in Corella, Tudela, and Pamplona were listed by their districts' tax collectors (*recibidores* of the *merindades*) in their accounts (*comptos*) and registers (*registros*). It is noted in the 1496 account of Corella that Dabit Constantin paid ten shillings (*sueldos*) for an orchard and house, and that "the Rabbi" and a Jew named Pollo remitted eleven shillings for a house. The Tudelan tax collector recorded in a section titled "Of Properties at Cens" the vineyards on which Jews paid rentals ranging in amount from twelve pence to twenty shillings. In one instance, a Jew paid six shillings *cens* on certain houses, although the land had been contracted from the royal government by the Jewish *aljama*.[19]

The Jewish quarter in Pamplona was officially owned by the king, and the Jews remitted an annual *cens* on the houses. The rate of rental was twelve pence per thirty square *codos*; the total *cens* on the seventy-five dwelling units amounted to 1357 shillings and fourteen pence. The many plazas in the quarter were held by Jews whose total annual *cens* was forty-one shillings and twelve pence.[20]

In contrast to the first two modes of land ownership and tenure, standard rentals (*logueros, tributos*) for a fixed time period were seldom negotiated by the Jews. It is not clear why this was the case. In one instance, when Johan de Sesma, as prebendary of the collegiate church of Santa María in Tudela, rented an orchard in Tudela's Mosquera district to Salamon Ortelano, it was only because de Sesma needed a tenant immediately and the Jew possessed a previous connection to the parcel. Even then, Ortelano did not sign a formal contract until more than a year later, when a document indicated he was to pay eleven florins per year for eight years and plant whatever fruit-bearing trees necessary to fill the orchard.[21]

Another rental from the Tudelan church of Santa María provides a further illustration of Jewish tenancy. On 5 October 1492, Yento Nazir of Cascante leased houses, vineyards, and wine-making equipment from the *maestreescuela* of the church, Don Miguel Garçeyz. Just the day before, Nazir had sold these same properties to Garçeyz in order to cover debts that were coming due. The church, not being able to till the land and run the vineyard, turned to the former owner of these properties, who clearly wished to continue possession. The period of the lease was for three years and gave Nazir, while tenant, the right to repurchase the parcels for 250 florins.[22]

Rent contracts remained in effect when the property changed hands. On 4 October 1493, Juliana de Magallon leased some houses to Mosse Mazal for an annual rent of four florins. Almost a year later, Juliana became ill and wrote in her will and testament that the property was to be given after her death to her cousin, Anton de Magallon. He could not, however, ignore the contracted rental and dispose of the property as he wished.[23]

The lands that Jews owned probably produced the raw materials for some of the items Jews traded in during these years. Foodstuffs were principal items of commerce during the Middle Ages, and Navarrese documents reveal that Jews, apparently as merchants of agricultural surplus, traded in oil, wine, fish, and grains. For example, in 1494, Jacob Macuren of Sangüesa purchased four hundreds-weight of oil (the record indicates that he defaulted on his payment), and the above-mentioned Yento Nazir of Cascante owned a wine-making operation by means of which he kept himself financially solvent. In 1492 Nazir's enterprise included a vineyard, wine presses, vats, and barrels of grape must. Nazir used this wine factory and its apparatus as a surety on his debts. Because Jews were allowed to use only wine produced by their coreligionists for their own consumption, ritual and otherwise, Nazir's trade may have been mainly with other Jews.[24]

Just as the documents reflecting the Jews' land ownership indicated involvement in agriculture and animal husbandry, so do the few sales contracts that have survived. For example, Simuel Benaçan paid fifty Aragonese shillings for a small riding horse in 1497, and Simuel Azamel bought two hundred rams shorn of their wool in 1494 for seven *reales* apiece. Although the documents do not provide a clue to why these Jews purchased the animals, the evi-

dence of the Jews' involvement in this trade is buttressed by an
order of the royal chancellery dated 19 November 1494. The order
directed the foreclosure of the property of Jacob Macuren for his
failure to pay Johan Miguel for the purchase of, among other items,
two beasts of burden.[25]

Besides trading in live animals, Jews sold skins and freshly killed
meat to Christian customers. In May 1495, Johan de Jubera and
his son purchased the skins of lamb and sheep from the *judería's*
abbatoir at thirty-five groats per dozen. De Jubera and his son declared in October of 1495 that they purchased "certain skins" from
Aym Çalama, for which they owed him twenty florins.[26]

Jews were also active in the purchase of hides. Habran Farag
of Tudela bought all the skins of male and female "gabineros"
killed both in the village slaughterhouses of Corella and in the
private stalls of the Jews and Christians from July 1495 to June
1496. He paid sixty florins in advance; the skins would cost seven
groats apiece. The "ar[r]endador" (here probably administrator) of
the slaughterhouse in Arguedas sold all his skins to Habran Mataron at twenty-six groats per dozen from Easter through September
1496 and at a much reduced rate of five groats per dozen through
Shrovetide 1497. Mataron advanced twenty-five florins and promised to remit the future installments according to the customs of
payment prevalent among the Tudelan butchers.[27]

Jews also participated in the wool trade, one of the major commercial enterprises of the Iberian peninsula. A contract of May
1497 shows that Habran Aboçach of Villafranca sold all the wool
of lambs, sheep, and baby lambs killed in the village's slaughterhouses to a Christian merchant from Tudela. This economic enterprise among Jews is also reflected in a payment ordered in 1481 by
Tudelan city officials to a messenger who had traveled to the Castilian border city of Logroño during a conflict over the importation
of woolen products.[28]

Navarrese Jews were involved in the sale of other materials used
for the manufacture of clothing, a conclusion supported by the high
percentage of Jews listed in the occupational descriptions as being
involved in the fabrication of clothing and in its trade, and accords
with the information we have for Navarrese Jews of the previous
century. In a declaration of obligation of December 1494, Mateo
de Segura acknowledged that he still owed Jehuda Bendebut twenty
florins on the sale of twenty-two *rouas* of hemp that he had pur-

chased for twenty-two groats apiece. The two parties arrived at a schedule of payments. In another such document of August 1490, Johan de Nadal promised fourteen florins to Juda Levi of Cascante for cloth that Nadal used to make some clothes for his wife.[29]

Jews' economic activities involving clothing and its accessories went beyond the manufacture and trade of textiles; Jews both manufactured and traded in jewelry, and Jewish silversmiths owned shops in Tudela and Pamplona (silversmithing was a traditional occupation among Navarrese Jews). In at least one case, trafficking in such objects brought complications. Ali el Pardo, an Aragonese Muslim from the border town of Borja, claimed that silver pieces and other jewelry had been stolen from him and that a silver belt had found its way into the hands of Yuçe Çaraçaniel of Tudela. "In order to avoid problems, friends intervened" between Çaraçaniel and el Pardo, and Rabí Mayr Bendebut and Mahoma Alozeria were appointed arbiters in the matter. During their investigations, witnesses testified under oath that Çaraçaniel had purchased the silver belt, silver bracelets, and other items and had, in turn, sold these objects; the silver belt was purchased by Muça Rabaniel, a Tudelan Muslim. After deliberation, the arbiters pointedly ordered the Jew to return all the jewelry to Ali el Pardo and to defray the expenses of their retrieval.[30]

Food, however, was the major item of trade during medieval times, and given Navarre's location near the Cantabrian Sea and its major ports, it is not surprising to observe that Jews were involved in the sale of fish. In the thirteenth century they were already participating heavily in this trade throughout the Iberian peninsula. Interestingly, while all the evidence for this trade among Navarrese Jews comes from Tudelan notarial registers, no contracts are extant. The activity is inferred from business connections among Jews, mule riders, and cart drivers—and all this from the books of just one local notary, Pedro Latorre.[31]

The practice seems to have been for Jewish dealers to purchase large quantities of fish from merchants who traveled from the north and to sell it in bulk to innkeepers and fishmongers. In one instance, from February to May 1494, Yuçe Hanbron of Tudela sold batches of salted cod to Christian innkeepers through specialized contracts of "deposito" and "comanda y deposito." In these agreements (see later in this chapter), the *ostalero* (innkeeper) acknowledged the receipt of the fish, measured in weight or in volume, and stated the amount of money he was to return to Hanbron at a specified date after the fish had been sold. This amount was identical to the price that had been listed for Hanbron's purchase of the cod. The profit was carefully obscured in the records in order to avoid possible censure; most likely, once the innkeeper sold enough fish to cover the stated price, he could keep the proceeds of the extra sales. As for Hanbron, he probably inflated the recorded purchase price to include the profit he wished to earn.[32]

Because, according to the contracts, the fish was delivered in advance of payment, the buyer had to appoint a guarantor. On 2 March 1495, Pedro de Salbatierra, himself an innkeeper, pledged his properties to guarantee the payment of twenty-two florins that Miguel Sánchez owed Mastre Yuçe Bendebut by Easter of that year, on fish he was to sell during Lent. A marginal note in Latorre's notebook declares that the sums were received during the same year and that Bendebut released both de Salbatierra and Sánchez from their obligation.[33]

In the Christian society of Navarre, the Lenten season and other periods of abstinence from meat created an important seasonal market for the sale of fish. One Jew who took advantage of this opportunity was Jehuda Bendebut of Tudela, who owned fish stalls in his native city and rented out these "tablas" to Christian fishmongers. On 26 October 1494, he leased a stall selling conger eel, cod, and sardines to Pedro Agostín and his wife, María Ortiz, from that day until the end of Lent in 1495. Bendebut supplied the fish for which, when the merchandise was sold, he would receive two groats for one thousand sardines; two *cornados* per pound of conger or cod; and for each batch (*carga*) of cod, he would be remitted twenty-six florins and four groats. Agostín and Ortiz promised to keep good accounts and to show the books to Bendebut; Bendebut agreed not to remove Agostín and Ortiz from their position in the shop. It took until March 1496 before Bendebut, satisfied with the proceeds, officially cancelled the contract.[34]

Bendebut also supplied fish to owners of Tudelan fish shops. In one case, Charles de la Rosa had contracted with Jehuda for the year 1495 and then sold his store to Johan de Vitoria. The new shopkeeper promised Bendebut that he would give an account and payment of all the salted fish (including conger, cod, sardines, and herring) that de la Rosa had sold. This was noted in Jehuda's and

Charles' books. In addition, he bound himself to complete the year-long contract with Bendebut.[35]

Like the innkeepers, the fishmongers required guarantors in some instances. Johan de Mendavia in May 1495 stood as *fiador* for Catalina de Tiebas for the assorted salted fish she received from Bendebut for sale in her own shop. It was over a year later, on 10 June 1496, that the account was settled.[36]

One aspect of mercantile activity, one essential to the functioning of the medieval economy, has not always been analyzed dispassionately by historians. It is precisely this economic function, however, that Jews in Europe filled during the later Middle Ages, including in Navarre, and it therefore needs to be discussed fully: Jewish commercial activity was not limited to actual sales; it included loans of money and material for profit. Through contracts of obligation, Jews lent and borrowed foodstuffs, textiles, and money to and from the Christian and Muslim inhabitants of the kingdom. These transfers in capital and goods and the Jews' involvement in this industry were integral to the efficient operation of the Navarrese economy.[37]

Here, unlike in the direct sale of foodstuffs, where Jews dealt with a variety of items, the Jews traded solely in grains—mostly wheat, but also barleys and rye. In every instance of these grain loans mentioned in the notarial documents in which Jews were one of the parties to the contract, Jews appear in the role of the lender. Most of these Jews lived in Tudela, and the majority of them were members of the Bendebut family. Seventy-five percent of the borrowers were individual Christians. Others included the village of Lerín, the *aljama* of Muslims of Ablitas, and a Corellan church. Most of the borrowers lived in the hinterland around Tudela, a few lived within the city. The occupation of most of them is not identified though a few are listed as *labradores,* probably not poor farmers but possibly absentee landowners of substantial farms.[38]

The average quantity of wheat lent was about fifty *robos*; over eighty percent of the quantities were between two and twenty-four *robos*. The most common was twelve *robos*. Most of the loans were contracted between February and July and contained the standard stipulation that they be repaid by St. Mary's day, August 15, of that year.[39]

It is probable, given the amounts and the dates of the contracts,

that the Jews were lending wheat to farmers for consumption purposes. The farmers' own supply was being used for seed in the
spring, and during the early summer months they were waiting
for the harvest. By mid-August, the borrowers felt confident that
enough would be harvested to repay their creditors. It is also possible that both the borrower and creditor were engaged in price
speculation, buying grain futures in the hope that when the debt
was repaid, the new price of the grain would be to their advantage.

No documents detail where the Jews acquired the grain. The
land that they owned probably could not have produced enough
wheat for loans but, as will be seen in the following chapter, Tudelan Jews did import into Navarre wheat, for which they paid royal
and municipal taxes. And a document of March 1497 shows that
one Jew, Yuçe Orabuena, rented a large silo for the storage of cereals in the border town of Ablitas.[40]

Jews lent the grain through a number of kinds of legal agreements. One of these was the *comanda,* a term that implies commission selling, but in fact such agreements were loan transactions.
Another kind was a contract of obligation, to which the seal of the
royal court was appended. These contracts, for which the government collected fees for appending its seal, while technically protect-
ing the creditor, proved also to be a safeguard for the consumer. At
any rate, while the term "loan" was rarely used in either of the two
procedures, the due date was noted, with the stipulation of penalties
if the wheat were not returned by then. These penalties, whether
found in *comandas, obligaçiones,* or any other type of contract,
ranged from five shillings to one florin daily on delinquent payments.
Ostensibly, if the wheat were returned on time, the borrower would
remit the same amount of grain he had received. In reality, for the
few repayments detailed in the documents, the grain was returned
between four and twenty-six months after the date due.[41]

There were varying procedures for recovering the outstanding
amounts. For example, on 1 February 1496, Salamon Bendebut appointed Simuel Mataron of Estella and Saul Aljamín of Lerín as his
agents to collect the three hundred *robos* of wheat from the councillors of the village of Lerín. Sometimes, under pressure from creditors, the borrower acknowledged the loan in front of a notary.
When María de Mirafuentes assumed the obligations of her husband and brother, she promised, before the notary Diego Martínez

de Soria, to pay Rabí Yento Chico 110 *robos* of wheat. When the debt was paid, the borrower requested an *albarán* (receipt).[42]

Borrowers and creditors, naturally enough, were not always of like mind regarding repayment. Mayr Bendebut of Tudela and three Christians from the village of Cabanillas, for example, agreed to arbitration to settle their differences. Bendebut argued that he was owed forty-four *robos* of wheat; the villagers claimed they already had paid. The arbiters ordered the Christians to pay thirty-six *robos*. By August 27 of that year, the villagers had complied and Bendebut formally relieved them of their obligation.[43]

After cereals, hemp (*cañamo*) was the material Jews most often lent to other Navarrese. As in the grain trade, in all the cases involving Jews discussed in the sources, the Jews were lenders. All the Jews mentioned in the documents were members of the Bendebut family of Tudela. Again, approximately three-quarters of the borrowers were Christians and the rest Muslims. The debtors were from Corella, Cascante, Valtierra, and Murchante; some of them had recently taken up residence in Tudela. The amounts borrowed ranged from just over two *rouas* to thirty; apparently, the hemp was borrowed for the making of garments for private use and local sales. More than half of the loans of *cañamo* were accompanied by loans of money and grain.[44]

The majority of these transactions during a ten-year period from 1487 to 1497, were described as outright obligations. Seals were attached to attest to the validity of the loan contract: One case is described as a "comanda and obligation," but, like the grain *comandas,* the transaction was really a loan. The obligations were negotiated at various months during the year and, unlike grain loans, were due at the end of November. Some payment schedules were stretched over a two-year period. Penalties on overdue payments ran from five groats to half a florin per day. Interest rates were never mentioned, and in a case in which hemp and money were loaned, only the money was lent at twenty percent per year.[45]

Capital transfers, however, were the most common loans that Jews negotiated and, indeed, were the most frequent type of business activity mentioned in the extant sources for the years 1479 to 1498. It need be noted at this juncture that the denunciations of usury by modern historians reflect Christian theological conceptions and thus have little to do with the Navarrese economy and the Jews' role within it. The accusations against the Jews as the most egregious usurers leveled by Navarrese Christians of the time will be discussed in the last chapter and treated as part of the anti-Jewish sentiment that aided in the royal decision to expel the Jews from the kingdom.[46]

Credit was part and parcel of many economic transactions such as sales, labor contracts, and commission agreements. For the following analysis, however, only contracts in which moneylending appears to be the central activity are examined. In those in which Jews were involved with Christians and Muslims, the Jews were the creditors in almost eighty-six percent of the cases. To be sure, Christians and even churches lent money at times, but for Pedro Latorre, a Tudelan notary in whose notebooks we find over half of the transactions involving Jews, that the Jew would be the creditor was taken for granted. In the one case in his register wherein a Jew, Yuçe Falaquera, borrowed twenty-one florins and five groats from a Christian merchant, Latorre's marginal note, instead of just containing the word "obligaçion," states clearly that the Jew was obligated to the Christian.[47]

The notarial registers of this period contain more than nine out of every ten of these loan documents, and all but one of the notebooks originated in Tudela. It is not surprising, then, that close to ninety percent of all the creditors listed in these sources lived in Tudela. Fifty-six percent of the creditors were from the Bendebut family; in twenty-five percent of the cases, the lender was Jehuda Bendebut.[48]

Jewish moneylending was then mainly in a few hands, as it had been in the previous century, but the Christian debtors were many, held a variety of occupations, and came from several different places within southern Navarre. Nearly a third were residents of Tudela and the rest spread over thirteen villages and towns. The most common occupation for the debtor, as reflected in the extant sources, was *labrador* (farmer or landowner), although merchants, cart-drivers, ropemakers, a squire (*escudero*), and a lord ("sennor de Ablitas") also appear as borrowers. When Jews were the debtors, they were mostly from Tudela, Pamplona, and Cascante. Their Christian creditors were also from these cities and villages and had various occupations; they included merchants, a squire, a student, and a cleric from the Sangüesan church of Santa María.[49]

Although there was a "bewildering monetary diversity" in the kingdom of Navarre during the fifteenth century, it is clear that the Jews were borrowing and lending middle-sized sums. The same was true in fourteenth-century Navarre and for Iberian Jewry as a whole in the last years of the fifteenth century. Over three-quarters of the loans in the documentation were listed in Navarrese currency; the average loan involved approximately twenty-nine and a half florins. If we ignore a few major loans at the high end of the price spectrum, the average principal was nineteen florins, and about half of the loans were for between ten and seventeen florins. It is the references in the documents to other economic activities—such as land sales or commission selling—that indicate that these loans could be used for smaller-scale contractual obligations. Thus the Jews were (a) furnishing the means, at the lower-middle end of the economic spectrum, for people to engage in commercial transactions, and (b) in this basically agricultural society, supplying money as the need arose, just as they had provided grain during lean times for consumption purposes.[50]

Unlike loans of grain, moneylending did not follow any rigid time pattern. Generally, the most common months for transactions were May and October; December and January showed the fewest. The other times of the year statistically do not appear to diverge significantly in the number of Jewish involved loans.[51]

These money transactions were usually disguised, albeit thinly. This was standard procedure in western Christian societies, where moneylending for profit was considered a sinful enterprise. Most of the loans were therefore called obligations: "deuda y obligaçion," "carta de obligaçion," and most frequently, the plain "obligaçion." The phrase "comanda y deposito"—which might refer to capital investment in a commercial enterprise, the original *commenda* contract—was used much less often. In a minority of listed obligations, it is noted that the money was "lent" or that the sum was "received." More rarely still is the word "loan" mentioned, although Pedro Latorre recorded on 28 April 1497, that Duenya Alazar, widow of Ezmel Abnarrabi, "graciously lent" fifty new Navarrese golden ducats to the merchant Pedro de Mongelos by means of a "loan with pleasure."[52]

Aside from the "enjoyment" received by the lender in granting the principal, the profit on the credit extension evidently was gained through penalties on overdue payments or on interest payable on tardily returned principal. Unlike the practice when grain was lent,

monetary debts came due at all months of the year, and the time
allowed for repayment varied widely. Clearly, each case was negotiated individually. When the cart driver Juhan de Leyça, formerly of the village of Azcoytia in Castile and presently of Tudela,
borrowed a sum of money, he was to pay half of the principal of
sixteen florins in eight days and the remainder in the following
week. It is likely that *tragineros* (cart-drivers) were highly mobile
and were therefore considered poor risks. By contrast, in July 1489,
when Sancho Dezacaria of Corella borrowed in *comanda* 145 shillings and six pence from Mastre Mosse, a Tudelan doctor, he did
not have to repay it for two years.[53]

Analyzing the penalties and interest charges listed in the documents leads to the conclusion that these stipulations were solely
pro forma and did not accurately reflect the specifics of each loan
agreement. It is left to us to surmise that the credit charges were
pre-calculated into the principal or simply left unmentioned in the
official loan contract.[54]

It should be kept in mind that penalties were listed as a matter
of course in all contracts, be they for the sale of raw plaster, for
the loan of money, or whatever. Here, as elsewhere, the most common penalty for failing to fulfill the stipulations of a contract—the
most common failure was default—was a fine of half a florin a day.
Generally, two-thirds of the penalty went to the "obedient party,"
(the creditor), and one-third to the *sennoria mayor* (the royal government). The average loan was about nineteen florins, so it would
take only thirty-eight days for one hundred percent interest to ac-
cumulate. Yet the evidence shows tardiness far in excess of five
weeks. According to the records, loans were cancelled as much as
two months before the due date, but this was a rare occurrence.
More often the repayment was belated, as much as twenty-six and
a half months after the due date. This information on loan repayments, gleaned from documents of "quitamiento" and from marginal notes written on the date of repayment alongside the original
entries, indicates that loans were repaid, on average, six months
and three weeks after the loan had been contracted. Clearly, the
penalties would amount to an impossible tariff for the businessman
in debt for these middle-sized sums.[55]

In the four cases where interest rates are openly stated, the rate
is the ubiquitous "cinco por seis" (six for five), or twenty percent

annually. In these contracts, it is difficult to conceive of the lender foregoing interest payments until the due dates, which ran from six months to one year after the day of obligation.[56]

Loans were considered tangible goods and were transferred as such. In the will of Pedro de Berrozpe, dated 12 July 1494, the testator ordered his executors to repay the 150 Navarrese florins together with the *gança* (gain, profit) that he owed to the Jew Jehuda. Fernando de Ciordia in his testament directed his brother-in-law Francisco de Agreda to collect the debt of twenty-one *reales* owed by Jehuda Azamel. In 1495, Aim Alborge made a "donation" of five debts to the Tudelan merchant, Johan de Egues—ranging in amount from a little over two florins to twenty-one *reales*—owed him by various Christians of Valtierra.[57]

As in all contracts, the purchaser obligated his person and his movable and non-movable property. In approximately ten percent of these loan obligations, the debtor identified a specific parcel of land as collateral; so that if he defaulted, the outstanding debt would be collected from it. Further insurances appear in only a few cases, as when Pedro de Roytegui named Pedro de Salbatierra as his guarantor on a loan of twenty-four Navarrese florins from Jehuda Bendebut.[58]

There were other forms of moneylending, whereby the borrower actually transferred the gage to the creditor; such arrangements, however, were rare among Navarrese Jews. In one of the few extant examples, Ximeno de Sant Juhan, a farmer from Verante, pledged to Abraham Chinillo a vineyard he owned in Tudela and received from the Jew thirty florins. The stipulations of this mortgage contract stated that Chinillo would be allowed to sell the property if the farmer did not repay the loan in exactly one year. In another case, from April 1483, complications arose when Salamon Lebi declared in a formal complaint before the lieutenant of the *alcalde* of Tudela that a few weeks earlier he had given some near-black cloth as security, for which he received 4,300 shillings. According to his contract, he was to return the amount in golden florins by Low Sunday. Precisely what went wrong, prompting Lebi's protest, is unclear.[59]

Jews pledged their belongings to raise money for taxes. In 1494 Salamon Bendebut gave some of his personal jewels as security to cover the *pecha* (an annual tax) owed by the native and foreign

Jews. And in 1482, individual Tudelan Jews pledged silver to pay for the salary of the knights (*caballeros*). In all the above cases, the word *empenyada* (pawned) is employed.[60]

The degree to which Jews were integrated into Navarrese society was reflected not only in such daily economic activities as agricultural endeavors, commercial dealings, or grain- and moneylending, by which a few Jews helped grease the wheels of the kingdom's economy. The role of the Jews in Navarrese economic life also encompassed activities in which they worked at the behest of others, positions that reflected the level of confidence and trust that Jews, or at least some of them, enjoyed within Navarrese society, in some cases with the very upper reaches of the political establishments.

Jewish agents were employed by individual Christians and Jews; ecclesiastical institutions such as churches and monasteries; and village, municipal, and royal governments. The biases of the Christian notarial documents reinforce the impression that Jews were often engaged by Christian employers; Jews were not likely to need Christian notaries when appointing agents who were Jewish unless they specifically needed the imprimatur of the Christian courts. At any rate, positions in which Jews served ranged from loan collector to financial steward.

Although the Jewish financial agent has had a long—if overinflated—history in medieval Christian Iberia, it is noteworthy that in the latter years of the fifteenth century, Jews still served in this role. In Navarre, at any rate, they had clearly played this role at least as far back as the second half of the fourteenth century.[61] To begin, Jewish agents (*procuradores*) were appointed by other Jews to aid in collecting debts from Christians. Also, when disputes arose between Jews and Christians or Muslims over important financial transactions, each of the parties appointed an arbiter, generally from his own religious community. The two arbiters, working together, usually had until the end of the month to work out a "sentence of compromise." When their decision was delivered, the arbiters were paid for their efforts. To ensure the impartiality of the arbitration process, each party paid the salary of the opponent's arbiter.[62]

Given the closeness of Jewish–Christian economic relationships and that litigants would only choose an arbiter whom they could trust as representing their best interests, it should not surprise us that Christians designated Jews as their representatives in arbitration. Indeed, in 1483, Gomez de Marquina of Corella and Mayr Bendebut of Tudela were involved in litigation over the ownership of certain houses that had belonged to Mayr's father. Both of them entrusted Abraham Chinillo to render a sole verdict.[63] In one case, when the abbess and nuns of the monastery of Santa María de la Caridat of Tulebras and Johan de Quintana of Cascante differed over the ownership of a textile mill within the convent's boundaries, they agreed to compromise. The monastery chose the Tudelan monk Friar Johan Perez de Tudela as its arbiter, and Quintana picked Levi Benrrabi of Cascante. They had from 7 March 1480 until the end of May to deliver a sentence and had the power to interrogate the parties. The arbiters returned on April 18 with a complicated judgment, and were paid two golden florins each for their efforts.[64]

Christians also appointed Jews as guarantors for their debts, for which the Jews presumably were paid a fee. Abraham Chinillo appeared in this role in 1492, and again in 1497 on some monies owed by Tudelan Christians on which they may have been close to default. In 1492 it appears that city officials forced a debtor to accept a Jew as his *fiador* (guarantor). Another indication that Christians trusted in Jews can be seen on 8 March 1490 in Cascante, when Pedro de Miraglo was attempting to sell a vineyard to Pedro Miguel, a representative of the prior of the see of Pamplona. They could not agree on a price and two people were appointed to settle the issue; Miguel chose as his representative a local Jew named Yento Nazir. Nazir had been involved in many business dealings with Don Miguel Garçeyz, the prior, and clearly was considered to be trustworthy and an ally.[65]

Church officials, like individual Christians showed confidence in the Jews' reliability and business judgment. Salamon Bendebut of Tudela was called upon by officials of a Tudelan church to release them from a bond of guarantee on a royally demanded obligation.[66] More significantly, Jews served churches as collectors of the revenues of ecclesiastically owned land. The role of Jews as tax-farmers has been much discussed in Iberian Jewish historiography, but nearly all the attention has been focused on the Jews who farmed royal imposts. A true appreciation of their role as tax-farmers for the various governments that controlled the peninsula will be achieved only when it is seen as part of their general work as financial agents in the society. So Yento Nazir of Cascante farmed ecclesiastical profits for his business associate Miguel Garçeyz, who was also prior and *maestreescuela* of the collegiate church of Santa María in Tudela. Nazir also performed the same function for Urban de Valladolit, the sacristan of the Santa María church of Cascante. The same Miguel Garçeyz as prior of Pamplona, rented out the 1491 profits of Sant Miguel of Alfaro, Castile, to Juçe Çaraçaniel of Tudela for fifty florins. The collection was to be rendered by mid-September of the same year.[67]

Jews also served as tax-farmers for the Navarrese nobleman, Mossen Pierres de Peralta. On 6 October 1482, Açach Çaraçaniel rented the rights to the Tudelan tannery for one year from Pedro Lopez de Sanguessa, the agent of Pierres de Peralta, for forty-four florins. Thirteen years later on 5 May 1495, Abraham Farach and Johan de Durango leased directly from the nobleman the "casa and renta of the almudi" for one year at 100 florins. That Jews were in the employ of the nobleman Pierres de Peralta prior to our period of study is evidenced in a series of documents from 1477. There Salamon Bendebut sold a vineyard owned jointly by the nobleman and his wife, Ysabel de Fox, countess of St. Esteban de Lerín.[68]

Just as Jews served ecclesiastical and seigneurial authorities, so too did they serve Navarrese municipalities. Tudela, the capital and major city of the district that encompassed southern Navarre, kept many Jews in its employ to perform a variety of functions entailed by both its own internal needs and its district-wide responsibilities. Jews also participated in the policy decisions of Tudela affecting the municipalities under its control. When new irrigation canals that benefited the area surrounding the village of Buñuel were built, a committee of Tudelan citizens, including Mayr Bendebut and Simuel Chinillo, met on 7 September 1496 and appointed representatives to negotiate with the village over the profits arising from the water project.[69]

Jews also served the Tudelan municipality in many *ad hoc* capacities. In 1483, city councillors reimbursed Salamon Lebi for procuring a royal seal and in 1487 paid a Jew named Abençox for securing and transporting a bench for hemp manufacturing from the city's outlying districts. Salamon Bendebut was entrusted with an important and delicate responsibility when he traveled outside the kingdom in 1486 to meet with Juan de Ribera, Ferdinand and Isabella's captain general of the frontier with Navarre. His mission was to convince de Ribera to stop Aragonese depredations of the persons and property of the inhabitants of Navarre.[70]

Jews performed some of the regular municipal functions of Tudela, especially in the farming of a variety of city revenues. The city placed various impositions on merchandise and services within its boundaries and all its inhabitants, including Jews, had opportunities to farm them. Mosse Cardeniel, alias Cahorero, collected the *correduria de oreja*, (the tribute imposed on stock-brokers) in 1482, 1483, 1485, 1487, 1490, and 1491. The granting of these tasks to specific individuals was decided the year before, according to the highest bid submitted. In 1482, Cardeniel placed two bids of fifty and sixty florins and the latter sum was accepted, eclipsing García de Aynar's offer of fifty-five florins. In the years when Cardeniel won the right to collect the tax, his winning bids ranged from fifty-six to sixty-one florins. In 1492, Gento Azamel was appointed *arrendador* of the *correduria de oreja* on a bid of sixty-five florins, and in 1496 Aym Çalama tendered the highest bid, eighty florins.[71]

Jews collected—or at least bid on—eleven of these city taxes in the years starting with 1480, when records of these activities were carefully kept. These imposts included the tax on animal trading; two imposts on fresh fish; one impost on salted fish; levies on candles, fresh bacon, and salted goat meat; penalties assessed when Christians bought meat from the Muslim and Jewish quarters; revenues from bakeries; taxes on foreigners' merchandise; and an impost of one *blanco* on some of its citizens. In some of these collections, such as the tax on bakeries and the animal trade, Jews were almost continuously involved; in others, for example the "tribute of fresh bacon and salted kid," Açach Çaraçaniel once bid seventy-five florins and received one florin for his effort but not the commission to collect the tax. In the duty on salted fish, it appears that Aym Çalama and Mayr Bendebut both bid on the collection rights, and divided the duties for one year.[72]

Rights to collect the imposts were traded among Jews and Christians. On 20 April 1490, a Christian squire of Tudela leased his tax-farming contract on imports and exports to Salamon Bendebut for a period of four years at fifty-five florins annually. Carlos de Cepdevilla, another Tudelan squire, appointed an agent in January 1495 to collect certain fines, a right he had purchased from Açach Çaraçaniel of Cascante.[73]

The city of Tudela issued yearly pensions to doctors, surgeons, teachers, and others who presumably served the municipality professionally. From 1480 through 1487, Mastre Abraham, a Jewish physician, and Mastre Jaco, a Jewish surgeon, received annuities of forty and five florins, respectively. In 1483 and 1484, Mastre Abraham's award was lowered to thirty florins and in 1487, he received a pro-rated sum of fifteen florins for four months' service; Jaco received his full amount in that year, and a marginal note indicates that this was his last payment.[74]

As in Tudela, Jews performed services for the village government of Corella. In 1487, Jaco de Villafranca traveled to Tudela to represent the village in court in a case involving taxes on exported goods. Jews also served as messengers: In 1497, for example, on order of the village council, Benjamin went with the squire Fortunyo to Estella; in 1491, an unnamed Jewish woman carried a document to Alfaro, Castile, at the behest of the village; and in the same year, the village dispatched a Jew named Jaco de la Rabiça to Tudela to negotiate with his coreligionist, Yuçe Orabuena. Orabuena was farming an ecclesiastical tithe and Rabiça was to procure from him a copy of the decree mandating the assessments. Some of these business contracts involved litigation, as when in 1491, a Jew named Symiel and two Christians received settlements from the village.[75]

Probably the most striking indication of Jewish power within the Iberian peninsula, which has garnered considerable attention, is the fact that some Jews attained positions in the highest reaches of the finance and treasury departments of the various Iberian governments. That they were employed as financial advisers, treasurers, and royal tax-farmers has often been adduced to prove Jews' influence in Iberian life and to demonstrate the high degree of Jewish integration within the host Christian society. These indications that Jews possessed some power in the fifteenth century, however, have been obscured by a historiographical debate over the assertion that Jews monopolized these higher financial offices as well as the concomitant claim that Iberian Christians were either socially or characterologically indisposed to such tasks. That Jews wielded such power on the eve of their expulsion had also proved puzzling to some students of the period. Against this background, the efforts of Miguel Angel Ladero Quesada to go beyond the rhetoric on both sides of the argument and attempt to determine the precise number of Jewish financiers in fifteenth-century Castile and identify the exact nature of their work are of great value and significance.[76]

In Navarre in the fourteenth century, as Béatrice Leroy has shown, and throughout the fifteenth century, the Jews not only collected their own taxes but also farmed some of the imposts and fees owed by Christians. Soon they were considered indispensable in the collection and management of royal revenues. Jews also began to supply the royal court with many of its necessities, and before long they were also entrusted with some diplomatic missions.[77]

In the late fifteenth century, royal authorities continued to utilize Jews as tax farmers and collection agents on the many levels of their fiscal administration. After the death of Juan II of Aragon and Navarre, and the eventual accession of Francisco Febo to the Navarrese throne, it appears that many of these contracts were placed under review. On 27 November 1480, Martín de Vaquedano, director of the royal treasury, ordered the *portero real* or other competent officials to sequester the property of five individuals who farmed the *imposiçion* of the city of Pamplona. He claimed that they, including Mosse Oba of Pamplona and Jento Aljamín of Olite, owed the remainder of the first, second, and third installments of this tax. On the same day, Vaquedano ordered the same royal officials to seize the property of the four collectors of the *tablas* in Pamplona, Estella, Sangüesa, and Olite. The outstanding sum was 950 pounds, owed from the second and third payments of the tax. Three of these four tax collectors were Jews: Jento Aljamín and the brothers Simuel and Mosse Oba.[78]

In February 1482, apparently as a result of the Cortes meeting in Tafalla, Don Pedro Cardenal, the infante and viceroy of the kingdom, ordered Martín de Vaquedano and Salamon Beby, the latter identified as the chief tax-farmer of the *tablas, sacas,* and *peajes* of the entire kingdom for 1481, to restore to one Johan Deça of Tudela the right to farm the *tabla* (customs duty) on iron and other imposts that had been granted to him by Juan II in May 1466. They had eleven days to comply with this request or suffer the wrath and indignation of the king. In a related matter, the same Pedro Cardenal, this time in his capacity as *portero*, ordered Mayr Bendebut (who apparently was the *guarda* of the *tabla* on all items in the city of Tudela) to help Johan Deça, presumably by helping to collect the tax.[79]

These problems with tax collection did not hamper Martín de

Vaquedano's farming of royal revenues. On 7 January 1488, as treasurer of Navarre, he contracted out the collection of export, import, and other merchandise duties for the whole kingdom, except the district of Tudela, to three Jews of Pamplona: Sento Mataron, Abram Tellu, and Simuel Oba (who had been accused back in 1480 in the matter of outstanding sums from the Pamplona *tabla*). The contract covered the year 1488, and Vaquedano ordered all officials of cities, villages, and smaller settlements to assist the Jewish tax collectors, who were empowered to sequester the property of recalcitrants, declare fines, and even imprison those who refused to pay.[80]

Of course, tax collection was always prone to disputes and allegations. In October 1487, García Gómez de Peralta, the general collector of all taxes in the district of Tudela, heard legal arguments on the taxes on wool exported from the village of Cascante. The two export and import tariff officers of the district, Mosse Vita and Pedro de Berrozpe, claimed that the wool impost belonged to their collection and was under their jurisdiction. They demanded one thousand *arouas* of wool from the village, due from 1488, and fifty golden florins from 1485 and 1486. A week later, on August 3, the testimony of the treasurer of Navarre and of two Jews, Salamon Bendebut and Yuçe Falaquera, was also heard.[81]

Salamon Bendebut was probably in charge of this collection in Tudela in the early 1490s when he was awarded fifteen thousand pounds for having covered that sum in cash from his own pocket. Bendebut dispatched the governor of the castle of Monreal to collect the money from the treasurer, which the governor did on 23 January 1494.[82]

Agents involved in local tax collection often sought aid from royal authorities. For example, Mayr Bendebut of Tudela farmed the taxes of the small settlement of Buñuel, located near the Ebro in southern Navarre. Dissatisfied with the help of local officials, he complained to the court of the royal chancellery. The leaders of Buñuel did not respond to the charges, so a royal bailiff was ordered on 6 September 1494 to sequester the property of the village's officers. Bendebut's problems with Buñuel did not end with this action. On 26 October 1495, he convinced the town to agree to arbitration about an outstanding sum of 120 florins. A local Christian and a Jew named Rabí Abraham de la Rabiça were chosen as the arbiters, and were to deliver their sentence by the end of November.[83]

A conflict between Salamon Bendebut and the village of Cintruénigo was resolved on 26 January 1498, when Bendebut received the eighty florins ordered by arbitration on an overdue export tax. There was no indication of when this agreement was first ventilated, but another debate over a tax called the *alcabala* of Fustiñana in 1466 was not resolved until twenty years later. The elder Mayr Bendebut of Tudela and the village finally agreed to send the matter to arbitration in October of 1488.[84]

The Jews who farmed the royal taxes in the village of Corella were the same individuals who participated in other official functions of the village. There were three main tributes to be collected: the *alcabala,* the *quarteres,* and the *sacas* (the last applied only to wool).

Açach Çaraçaniel collected the *alcabala* in all of 1480 and for four months of 1481. He first came to collect these sums accompanied by a *portero* but without the official written assessments of the royal treasurer. The Corellans dismissed the *portero* with three groats for his troubles and told Çaraçaniel to bring the papers if he wished to be paid. Açach surely followed this advice, for he was paid twenty-three pounds for his part of the collection of the 1481 taxes. He sold the other two-thirds to Salamon Bendebut.[85]

Salamon also collected the wool export tax in 1481—not, however, without recourse to litigation. Bendebut had the same task and problems in 1482, and in 1487 resistance on the part of taxpayers was again recorded. In that year, village officials paid Jaco de Villafranca to go to a Tudelan court to plead their case in what seems to have been an ongoing controversy.[86]

The village supported the collection of the *quarteres* in 1491, when its councillors paid the *portero* for his trouble in sequestering the property of the recalcitrants and also funded Simuel Bendebut's extra efforts in tax collection. On 3 December 1494, it was again the *portero,* this time Pedro de Falçes, who sequestered the belongings of the tax delinquents. The *quarteres* had been assessed at five hundred pounds by Garci Pérez and Salamon Bendebut, and this figure had been accepted by the village officials.[87]

Benjamin was the collector of the *quarteres* and *alcabala* in 1495, and it appears that the village officials assisted him. On 10

October 1496, the village leaders sent Juhan de Agreda to Tudela with Usua, the "collector of the quarteres and alcavala." De Agreda and Usua stayed there two days, presumably to discuss the assessment for that year.[88]

Complications continued to arise in the 1490s over the earlier collections by Salamon Bendebut. In 1495, Salamon sued the village in the city of Pamplona over its payment of the *alcabala*. On 15 December 1496, the *portero* Pedro de Valejo was seizing property on taxes that were owed Salamon from previous years. On 13 February 1497 Juhan de Agreda traveled to Tudela to speak to Salamon about the foreclosure on property prompted by delinquencies in the payment of the 1489 *quarteres,* which apparently had been collected by a Christian. At the end of September, the village and Salamon came to a compromise about a small sum, but even as late as January 1498, property worth 120 pounds was seized at Salamon's behest.[89]

As in the early 1480s, Salamon farmed the export taxes in 1495 and 1496 with the usual difficulties. On 18 December 1496, the village sent messengers to Tudela to represent it in litigation on these taxes, and on January 3, arbiters were chosen: Fortunyo Escudero, for the village; and Benjamin, for Bendebut.[90]

Jews also worked as agents for royal officials and members of the royal family. In a 1496 property inventory of the city of Olite, it is recorded that a Jew named Jento Cardeniel was the *fazedor* (steward) for Dona Juhana de Navarra. A Jew named Ybray de la Rabiça, according to other sources, controlled certain tax accounts for Johan de Beamont, the prior and chancellor of Navarre. They apparently had a falling-out over business matters, and the issues under contention were put up for arbitration. Açach Çaraçaniel, representing de la Rabiça, and Johan de Quintana, appointed by Beamont, arrived at a compromise, which appears to have been carried out.[91]

Two years earlier, another member of the de la Rabiça family, Abraham, was Beamont's agent in the collection of an ecclesiastical tithe recently granted to the Navarrese king. Because this tithe was to be collected from Corellan parishioners whose village was part of the diocese of Tarazona, Tarazonan officials met to discuss the tax, noting that de la Rabiça had traveled to Corella a week earlier to collect the impost.[92]

In the absence of a quantitative evaluation of the percentages of

Jews involved in these upper reaches of tax collection and money management, and therefore the impossibility of definitive comparisons of their situation with that of Navarrese Jews in the previous century or with that obtaining in the other Iberian kingdoms during the last quarter of the fifteenth century, some general informed observations can and must be made. Jews were a small percentage of those who were engaged in the fiscal management of the Navarrese kingdom, and appear to have been fewer in number than those involved in such endeavors during the period of which Béatrice Leroy has written. As noted in her study, Jews were mainly subcontractors of royal taxes and imposts, and did not enjoy those same high-level positions they had filled in previous centuries.[93]

What has been demonstrated in this chapter is that Jews were important to the financial administration of the cities, towns, and villages in which they lived. And while only a few were integrated into the highest reaches of Navarrese society, the economic activities of many of them continued to be rich and diverse: They owned land; were involved in agriculture; bought and sold a variety of goods; and lent money and grains to their neighbors.

This is not to claim that Navarrese Jewry in the last quarter of the fifteenth century was experiencing the same degree of economic good fortune as had Iberian Jews under Christian rule in the immediate aftermath of the thirteenth-century conquests. Though Jews were clearly not at the pinnacle of their success in late fifteenth-century Navarre, neither they nor the Jews of Castile, Aragon, and Portugal were gasping their last breaths. There was, moreover, another arena in which the Jews played out their daily lives, and here too they appeared vital and creative. That was within their communal life and institutions. Here, although contacts were maintained with Christians and Muslims, the orientation was decidedly internal. For hundreds of years Jews had organized themselves into semi-autonomous communities, and their behavior amongst themselves comprise an equally important aspect of their everyday reality. The communal life of these Pyrenean Jews is the subject of the following chapter.

3. Communities: Structure, Activities, and Taxation

The existence of autonomous Jewish communities, or of some measure of communal self-government at least, was a universal feature of Jewish life in the diaspora in premodern times. These legal communities (*aljamas*) flourished throughout the Iberian peninsula and reached heights of sophistication and power that compare favorably with those of any other period in Jewish history. The political rulers of Navarre, no less than the other Iberian monarchs, encouraged their Jewish subjects to establish autonomous communities wherever they settled. These organized *aljamas* were vitally important in helping the Iberian ruling class extract the greatest economic and political benefit from the Jewish population. Simultaneously, Jews actively sought the creation of the quasi-independent juridical *kahal* (or *aljama*) as an expression of their religio-national ideals and as the vehicle through which they could preserve their laws and traditions and govern themselves accordingly.[1]

By the late fifteenth century, the *aljamas* of Navarre already possessed a long tradition of communal authority. More than three centuries earlier, in the years following the major Christian conquests from the Muslims, the Navarrese sovereigns had recognized the existence of these *aljamas* in the *fueros* (charters of privileges) they had granted their subjects. The rights of Jews were recognized in charters (*privilegia*) by local or kingdom-wide feudal authorities throughout Western Europe from the ninth century on. In Navarre, as in other areas, these communal organizations had preceded the royal license, and the individual *fueros* reflected varying local conditions. To facilitate the collection of certain royal imposts in the fourteenth century, all the Navarrese *aljamas* were considered by the royal authorities to belong to five supercommunities. These groupings included the *aljamas* of Tudela, Pamplona, Estella, and Viana and their respective environs, and the Jewish communities of the Val de Funes. The number of these larger conglomerations rose to six in the fifteenth century, when the *aljama* of Sangüesa was counted as a separate unit.[2]

When King Francisco Febo committed himself to the privileges enjoyed by the distinguished *aljama* of Tudela on 4 February 1482, he recalled many of the rights that had been granted by his predecessors since the early years of the fifteenth century to all the Navarrese *aljamas* as well as to the Jewish community of Tudela. For historians who wish to recreate the structure of Jewish communal organizations in Navarre, the most abundant information is available for the southern Navarrese community of Tudela, and it is for this city that the efforts expended by researchers have yielded the most fruitful results. Not only was the Tudelan privilege of 1482 recently discovered in that city's notarial archives, its fourteenth-century constitution and charters of reorganization have been available to scholars for years.[3]

As Yitzhak Baer noted, the leadership of the community was oligarchic: One representative of each of the eight most prominent Tudelan Jewish families had veto power over regulations and agreements drawn up by the *aljama*'s legislative council. Because the governmental structures of the kingdoms and municipalities in which Jews lived shaped the political constitutions of the many Iberian Jewish communities, it is understandable that the legislative council's structure closely paralleled the municipal *concello* of Tudela. The Jewish body consisted of twenty members, identified as *gedolei ha-kahal* (distinguished men of the community) in a Hebrew source of the period, and identified either as *hombres, mayorales,* or *regidores* in a contemporary Romance translation.[4]

On most issues, the consent of a majority of the council's members was sufficient to enact new legislation or to interpret existing statutes. This majority usually was composed of seven officials (called *mukademin* in Hebrew or *adelantados* in Romance) and four of the other *gedolei ha-kahal*. A smaller committee of two or three officials functioned as the executive branch of the council and its main function was to deliver warnings to those who would violate communal law. An official called a *bedin,* the nature of whose authority is unclear, had a quasi-judicial and police role and may have been mainly concerned with the collection of taxes.[5]

The collection of communal statutes from fourteenth-century Tudela describe a community apparently beset by considerable internal strife. Its ruling oligarchy, at which much anger was expressed, was forced to employ various constitutional measures to preserve its shaky authority. In 1482, during a brief sojourn in Navarre, King Francisco Febo issued a royal privilege that recognized the powers of the existing authorities, both in Tudela and in the other Navarrese *aljamas*. The decree focuses on the relationship of the Jewish corporation to the royal government, yet reflect some of the concerns that were apparent in the earlier Tudelan decrees.[6]

Reassuring Navarrese Jews, who lived, as did native Christians and Muslims, in a strife-torn kingdom, Francisco Febo approved all the privileges that in the past had been bestowed upon the Jewish communities and proceeded to refer specifically to some that had been granted the Jews since the reign of Carlos III. As in the evidence from the fourteenth-century documents, the precise names, numbers, and functions of the Jewish communal officials cannot be adduced. By combining these data with information from sources we have been profitably mining the last two chapters, however, it is possible to offer certain conclusions.

Navarrese Jewish *aljamas* in the late fifteenth century, as in previous years, were apparently governed by a council. Its members were variously termed *jurados, regidores, adelantados, ordenadores,* and *ministros*. These titles apparently did not signify any specialization of function.[7] The number of councillors in the Tudelan *aljama* varied from one to ten or more in contemporaneous sources, there being no indication how many were needed for specific communal transactions. Apparently, the number of these officials in any *aljama* was directly proportional to the density of the population within the specific *judería*. Such had been the case earlier in Navarre, and parallels can be noted in contemporary Jewish communal organization in Portugal.[8]

When a major communal decision was made, whether establishing new communal rules or effecting an economic settlement that would impinge on the well-being of the entire community, it required the presence and approval of the officials and all the Jews of the *aljama*. Accordingly, on 17 May 1490, in Tudela's largest synagogue, three *jurados,* five *regidores,* the charity board minister, thirty-four Jews and "many others [Jews] of the Jewish quarter" met in plenary assembly. There they passed on the sale of communally owned property to the nobleman Mossen Johan de la Carra for the considerable sum of fifteen thousand shillings (*sueldos*).

Such meetings had also been customary in other Iberian Jewish communities in years past. As in those earlier times, the communal decision was arrived at during a previous meeting of *aljama* leaders. The gathering on May 17 for purposes of formal ratification also reflected the officials' responsibility to the community. All the Jews remained in the *sinagoga mayor* to authorize the transaction of another item of communal business, whereby the *aljama* rented at one thousand shillings per year the lands just sold to de la Carra. The community obligated its properties and rents as a surety against the payment of this annual sum.[9]

The Tudelan community clearly had extensive holdings. The *aljama*, for example, collected rents on Jewish and Christian abbatoirs, and on stalls of silversmiths and shoemakers that were located in the *alcaçería* (fortified bazaar) of the Jewish quarter. One of the roles of the communal officials was to administer these financial assets. This was also the burden of the three *adelantados* of the village of Cortes, who in 1497 appointed a local Christian to negotiate an outstanding dispute with Fernando Ezquerro of Mallén. The communal notary testified that the power to compromise was granted to the *adelantados* at a meeting of the community. Mallén was two kilometers from Cortes, across the border with Aragon, where a Jew could not venture, owing to the 1492 expulsion edict. Christian messengers were used by *aljamas*, however, even in the absence of such extraordinary circumstances.[10]

Aljama councillors not only dealt with community property, they also guarded and cared for the life and belongings of individual Jews. When Salamon Arraheni of Tudela died, he left a daughter, Preçiosa, who was legally underage. According to Jewish law, when agents to represent children were not named before the death of their parents, a Jewish court was responsible for appointing a guardian. This was the practice in fourteenth-century Navarre as well as in late fifteenth-century Portugal. Accordingly, the *jurados* of the Tudelan community appointed Jeuda Bennaçan as guardian of Preçiosa and executor of Arraheni's estate. Later, when the girl was of marriageable age and in need of money to conclude her nuptials, Bennaçan decided to sell one of her father's houses to raise the necessary funds. The same officials passed favorably on his decision.[11]

The individual *aljamas* controlled the many organizations that

served the Jewish population. The central institution of each community was the synagogue, and those of Tudela, Pamplona, Corella, and Viana left traces in contemporary documentation. Tudela
possessed at least two houses of worship, and in Pamplona, the
"great synagogue" and two smaller prayer halls serviced the Jewish
parishioners. The "confraria de la teba," a brotherhood that regu-
lated the prayer services and dispensed the honors, helped Pamplona's *sinagoga mayor* function smoothly.[12]

   In Tudela's largest synagogue, there was a *ministro* (administrator) in charge of the properties and rentals owned by the house of
worship, who appears to have been directly responsible to the congregants. For example, when Simuel Vençida, the *ministro* leased
a vineyard in Traslapuente to a Christian couple, the notary recorded that the rental was effected with the knowledge, license, and
express consent "of all the parishioners of the synagogue." Additionally, Abraham Bendebut and Mosse Malach, each a member of
a distinguished Tudelan family, were specifically mentioned as having been among those in attendance. Synagogues also leased lands
from others; Viana's house of worship rented various properties
from the city's Jews.[13]

   At times, synagogues received donations that increased their
holdings. On 18 April 1496, the New Christians Yento and Açeti
Alcalaer donated three parcels of land to the *sinagoga mayor* of
Tudela's Jewish quarter. The properties abutted the houses of worship; two of them had rentals payable to the synagogue. Parcels
owing substantial or minimal rentals to the synagogue were common. The houses of worship probably had owned the property
originally and retained an annual income from the new owner
when it was sold. As could be expected, the synagogues had all the
obligations of other property holders. When improvements were
made in irrigation that benefited a number of parcels, including a
vineyard owned by a Tudelan synagogue, the synagogue bore a
share of the cost.[14]

   The synagogue not only served as a place of prayer but also
as the communal meeting hall. The sale and rental of communal
properties in Tudela on 17 May 1490, which occasioned an official
gathering of all the *aljama*'s Jews, was staged in the city's largest
synagogue. And when the town crier announced economic agreements and legal actions, he did so at the doors of the synagogue,
where the people usually congregated. Often this information was

publicly declared on three consecutive Saturdays, so as to reach the majority of the Jews.[15]

An institution prevalent in most Jewish communities and frequently connected to the synagogue was the *almosna,* or board of charities. In the institutionally complex Tudelan *aljama,* each synagogue had its own *almosna.* The Tudelan eleemosynary boards had extensive landholdings in the city and its environs, which also necessitated the services of an experienced administrator (*ministro*). Indeed, Rabí Mayr Bendebut, "ministro de la almosna de los pobres de la sin[ag]oga mayor," was prominently listed in the documents of sale and rental of May 1490.[16]

The charity board, in continual need of funds to pursue its work, rented out some of its parcels at fixed sums per year. In January 1482, for example, Sento Farach and Yuçe Falaquera, administrators of the *almosna,* rented in perpetuity a plot in the terminus of Callela Açach to Johan Cabello and his wife, Margarita de Murillo. The rentals were generally paid in money, although on 29 April 1490, Sento Benzoar, the minister of the "sin[ag]oga chica," leased a piece of land for a period of six years, during which the yearly sum was to be paid in wheat. An additional source of income to the *almosnas* were fines collected by the local community in its enforcement of law and order.[17]

Given the charity boards' interests, it was inevitable that the *almosnas* were involved in lawsuits. In a dispute during March 1490, the minister Rabí Mayr chose his relative Rabí Abraham de la Rabiça as the Jews' arbiter, and the two Christians appointed Miguel Caritat, the precentor of the church of Santa María of Tudela. The decision is not preserved.[18]

The *aljamas* provided services for Jews of all social and economic strata: The dietary laws required a supply of kosher meat, necessitating the existence of Jewish slaughterhouses. In the 1490s, the Jews of Corella possessed their own abbatoir, whereas those of Pamplona killed their animals in leased stalls ever since the destruction of their slaughterhouse. In Tudela, an *arrendador* was in charge of the business activities of the town's abbatoir. Salamon Bendebut held that position in May 1495, when two Christians, Johan de Jubera and his son, purchased the skins of lamb and sheep killed in the Jewish slaughterhouse, even though Christians buying from Jewish and Muslim *carnicerías* (butcher shops) had to pay penalties. This prohibition was honored widely in the breach, it would seem: The fines were extensive enough to warrant the appointment of a special collector.[19]

The burial of Jews in cemeteries separate from those of the general population was another imperative of Jewish life. The Pamplona Jewish cemetery was located in the king's vineyards, and there are references to a Jewish "fossal" (charnel house) in Corella. In Tudela, an administrator was responsible to oversee the "rents of the bones of the dead." This evidently entailed the management of some financial assets, because in December 1488, Miguel de Landecho and his son promised to repay the official, Sento Benzoar, twelve measures of wheat the following August, a sum calculated at the rate of twenty percent interest annually. The phrase "the bones of the dead" probably is a reference to the charnel house where the bones were kept. Because cemeteries had limited space, bodies would be exhumed and the bones stored.[20]

The Jewish laws of "family purity" required the existence of ritual baths, and the "ospital de los Baynos" of Pamplona's Jewish quarter, besides functioning as a hospital and bathhouse, may well have served as the community's *mikveh* (ritual bath). Medieval Christian law at times forbade Christians to bathe together with Jews; thus these institutions fulfilled another need as well. A brotherhood operated the baths in Tudela, and its officers, called *mayorales* and *regidores,* probably both exercised control over the financial administration of the baths and ensured that the facilities fulfilled ritual requirements.[21]

Communal functionaries also served the legal and economic needs of the Jews, besides providing for their religious and social needs. The *judería*'s notary drew up all requisite business documents and the like, and, as was the case in Christian society, testified to the veracity of alleged arrangements. Indeed, two *ketubbot* (matrimonial contracts) and one document containing appendices to such a contract, all dating from our period of study, were recently found in the notarial archives in Tudela. The *aljama*'s court system operated according to Jewish law and mainly adjudicated civil lawsuits among its own constituents. The *nunçio,* a legal functionary named after his Christian counterpart, summoned people to appear before the community's tribunals. He could also, if needed, appear as a witness to the existence of a contract.[22]

In the *privilegium* issued by Francisco Febo in 1482 to the Navarrese *aljamas,* the king recognized the authority of the Jewish communal organizations and specifically their legal system. By repeating the privileges issued in 1428 by King Johan (later Juan II of Aragon and Navarre) and Queen Blanca in Tafalla, Francisco Febo supported the right of the *jurados* and *regidores* of each *aljama* to fine members of their community "en sostemiento de su ley et de la paz" (to support its system of law and order). He acknowledged the authority of communal officials to solve all conflicts and litigation between Jew and Jew, and declared that if appeal were made to the *alcaldes* (justices) of the royal court, they too would be guided according to the law and counsel of the Jews.

During the Christian Middle Ages, the *malshin* (slanderer) was probably the most frightening enemy to the Iberian Jewish communities and posed the most serious problem dealt with by their legal system. A *malshin* was a Jew accused of informing to non-Jewish governmental officials of activities within the Jewish community that would lead to the harm of the person or property of any Jew. (Technically, even applying for judicial satisfaction to a non-Jewish court might lead to prosecution.) The system was especially sensitive about accusations—for example, non-payment of taxes or non-adherence to a specific law—that would incur the wrath of the Christian establishment. There is much evidence that in the thirteenth and fourteenth centuries Sephardic Jews prosecuted these individuals and, in cases where *aljama* leaders perceived grave danger to the community, sentenced them to death, although this practice conflicted with Jewish law. Those found guilty were delivered to royal or other officials, who often would carry out the Jews' desire to have them killed; after all, once uncovered, these informers were no longer of use anyway.

Although the criminal jurisdiction of Castilian and Aragonese Jews was sharply curtailed toward the end of the fifteenth century, Francisco Febo in 1482 confirmed a 1460 privilege issued by his predecessors Johan and Blanca to the effect that in the event that Jews complained to the royal court and its *alcaldes* about the presence of a *malshin,* and the situation were acknowledged by the *letrados* of each *aljama,* the *alcaldes* of the royal court would investigate the matter according to the guidelines of Jewish law and hang a suspect who was found guilty. After being hanged according to Christian custom—head upward so that no animals would attack the corpse—the body would be returned to his *aljama* for same-day burial, presumably in consideration of the dictates of Jewish custom. The guilty person's property would be confiscated and passed on to the royal coffers, and the *aljama* would pay the Christian authorities twenty-five golden florins for the execution of the sentence.

Although there is no evidence that this privilege was ever exercised during our period, and while there is reason to believe that it never was during this time—no such activity is reported anywhere in the peninsula at this late date in the fifteenth century, the latest reference in Jewish sources being the idealistic *takkanot* (ordinances) promulgated by the Castilian *aljamas* meeting in Valladolid in 1432—one wonders why the Jews were still officially granted this authority. Were the Jewish communities in such turmoil that they felt the need to request this power in 1460 and again in 1482? And even if they were experiencing internal attack were the Navarrese *aljamas* capable of acting with unity on such issues? We do not know.[23]

When Jews sought redress from Christians and Muslims, and *vice versa*, the parties had legal recourse to a royally appointed bailiff. As Francisco Febo acknowledged in the 1482 *privilegium,* quoting the pronouncement of Carlos III in 1413, even in cases between the monarch and the Jews no Christian official could claim any jurisdictional authority save a specially appointed bailiff of this kind. And in 1428, Johan and Blanca ordered that neither the *procurador fiscal* (who was interested mainly in prosecuting antisocial behavior and collecting fines for such activities) nor other royal officials could proceed against a Jew. According to the pronouncement of King Johan in 1460, later reiterated by Francisco, the bailiff was to be especially knowledgeable about the litigation and only he could execute prison sentences. So when Johan de Tuledo and Açach Malach, for example, had a dispute they could not settle, they appeared on 28 February 1492 before the bailiff of the Jews and Muslims of the district of Tudela. There they each appointed an arbiter to negotiate a compromise. If those representatives were not able to decide the issue the bailiff was to designate a third arbiter to deliver a ruling. The same Açach Malach also found himself at odds with Muça Rabaniel, a Tudelan Muslim. On orders from the chancellery, the bailiff of the Jews and Muslims summoned the contending parties to his court.[24]

The induction of the bailiff required the official presence of the

Jewish and Muslim communal leaders of Tudela. At the investiture of Francisco de Agreda as *baile* (bailiff) in January 1494, Abraham Bendebut, *regidor* and lieutenant of the *adelantado*; the *regidores* Rabí Abraham de la Rabíça and Rabí Sento Benjamin; and Rabí Mayr Bendebut, Mastre Mosse Bendebut, Abram Memenir, Sento Farag, Yuçe Albelia, Jaco Lebi, and Simuel Gamiz, *jurados* and *regidores* of the Jewish *aljama*; and the *alcady* and *jurados* of the Muslim community were all in attendance. The monarchs' representative, the *mayordomo* of the infante, officially dispensed the position. Also present at the installation was the previous *baile,* the controversial García Pérez de Verayz.[25]

At the ceremony, Anton de Minylla, a royal *portero,* read the royal grant of possession and the particulars of the office. This was significant because it was the *porteros* who provided the bailiff with the means to enforce his decisions. On the bailiff's order, they could seize the property and belongings of a recalcitrant individual and even imprison him. The *porteros* were also called upon to foreclose on the property of tax delinquents.[26]

Christians were generally reluctant to have the bailiff of the Jews and Muslims adjudicate their litigation with Jews. In November 1487, for example, the church of Santa María of Tudela expressly wrote into a contract with the local *aljama* a stipulation whereby the Jewish community renounced its rights to its own bailiff in the event of a dispute. The Tudelan municipal accounts of 1481 indicate that the city paid that year for the privilege not to have Christians brought before the bailiff of the Jews. Sometimes it was the Jewish community that bypassed its own bailiff and turned to the Christian courts for help, as when the Tudelan *aljama* in 1482 requested the *justiçia* of the city to foreclose on the properties of Johan de Sant Vicent, his wife, and son.[27]

There were instances of cooperation between the Christian legal system and its officials and the Jewish *aljama*. When in 1487 Jeuda Bennaçan was appointed executor of the estate of Salamon Arraheni by the *jurados* of the Tudelan *aljama,* he wished to sell some of the deceased's property to the city's church of Santa María. The document detailing Bennaçan's appointment as executor and guardian of Arraheni's surviving daughter had been registered in the Jewish community and not with the city's notaries before whom the sale was to take place. The Jewish notary who drew up the document, Jaco de la Rabica, petitioned "his friend" (and

Christian counterpart) Juhan Martínez Cabero to accept the Jewish
legal document as a properly executed instrument. De la Rabiça
explained that Preçiosa, the late Salamon's daughter, needed the
proceeds of the sale to be married and that she had neither time
nor money to apply for the relevant document from the Christian
courts. Cabero acceded to the Jew's request and the sale was concluded on the same day. De la Rabiça's petition, written in his own
hand, was bound in Cabero's official notebook.[28]

Tudelan Jewish communal positions were held by men from
varying social and economic strata. Of the twenty-nine Jews who
appear as officials in the late fifteenth century, five—Mayr Bendebut; Sento Beniamil; Jaco, Abraham, and Mayr de la Rabiça—
were rabbis; one, Mastre Mosse Bendebut, was a doctor; and one
each—Yuçe Albelia, Abram Memenir, and Simuel Bendebut—came
from the trades of shoemaking, weaving, and tailoring, respectively. Of the twenty-nine, four—Salamon, Mayr and Simuel Bendebut, and Abraham de la Rabiça—were active businessmen; two
of these same four—Mayr Bendebut and Abraham de la Rabiça—
were rabbis.[29]

The communal leadership was oligarchic; six Tudelan families
provided sixteen of the twenty-nine officials. Five Bendebuts held
communal positions and three of the de la Rabiça clan—all of them
rabbis—were in official posts. The other four leading families were
named Acassar, Falaquera, Farag, and Malach. These powerful
families, however, were relative newcomers to the Tudelan Jewish
power structure. Only three of the fourteenth century's communally active Tudelan clans—Orabuena, Minir, and Falaquera—fur-
nished *aljama* officers during the late 1400s.[30]

While no ordinances that detail the term of communal officials
exist, of the five *regidores* who held the office in 1490, none appears
in a list of nine of these officials made four years later. Only the
Farag family was represented on both lists: Jaco in 1490 and Sento
in 1494. Of those listed in 1494, only Jaco Lebi appeared as a *regidor* again in 1497. The Malach family was represented by Mosse
in 1490 and by Abram in 1497.[31]

It also seems that no person or family appeared more than once
on a charity board. And each time the position of *pregonero pub-
lico* (town crier) was mentioned in the sources, a different person
filled it. This was not true of the post of communal public notary,
which Rabí Jaco de la Rabiça held from at least 1487 to 1496.

Even though officials did not succeed themselves in their jobs, they remained in the public light. Fourteen of the twenty-nine officers held more than one position over the course of their careers; eight held more than one post at the same time. The Bendebut and de la Rabiça clans each had three members who occupied two official positions.

Tax gathering was perhaps the most burdensome task facing the Navarrese Jewish communities and their officials. Imposts were exacted by all levels of government: royal authorities, feudal lords, municipalities, and local churches. Each of these institutions, as was true throughout medieval Iberia, generally had their own patterns of assessment, collection, and rendition. Unfortunately, late fifteenth-century Navarrese documents do not report on the internal taxation system of the *aljamas*.

The Navarrese royal government demanded from its Jews an annual tax known as the *pecha*. This tax—which was not assessed solely of Jews—can be attested to from at least the end of the thirteenth century. The amount that was required of the Jews fluctuated over the course of the fourteenth and fifteenth centuries, and in 1451 the prescribed sum was fixed at two thousand *libras* (pounds). It was apportioned among the six large groupings of *aljamas*. The *pecha* was gathered by the royal collectors (*recibidores*) of the cities and villages, who were assisted by the Jewish communities and the local governments. Indeed, in 1428, the monarchs Johan and Blanca confirmed that each of the Navarrese *aljamas* was to appoint two or three individuals as *regidores* of the *pecha* for the coming year, and evidently the *ordenadores* of the *aljama* were to aid them in the collection. Provision was also made for the notables of the community to meet in council to fashion regulations in support of general *aljama* legislation and specifically of ordinances regarding the *pecha*. Royal officials, too, Johan and Blanca directed, were to execute the sentences of these *jurados* of the *pecha* just as they would carry out similar orders emanating from the *alcaldes* of the royal court. There were limits imposed, however, on the power of royal officials to proceed against *aljamas* or the person or property of individuals in collecting monies owed on *pechas* or other debts without certain specific documentation.[32]

During the 1490s, Mastre Ossua, the *receptor general* of all the Jews, gathered the impost directly from these royal collectors and, bypassing the royal treasury, rendered the monies directly to the monarchs. On arriving in their Navarrese dominions in 1494, Johan and Catalina undertook to overhaul the taxation system of the royal exchequer. Realizing that new tax assessments were bound to elicit resistance, the king and queen decided to negotiate with, among others, the kingdom's Jews. After the talks, the 1495 *pecha* was changed from an annual flat sum to a tax of eight pounds per household of the indigenous Jews; a lump sum of 750 pounds plus other, smaller amounts to be paid by the newly arrived refugees as a group.[33]

The 1495 *pecha* was due before the beginning of that year, and by 6 December 1494, the sums had already been advanced and the monarchs had relieved Mastre Ossua and the other tax gatherers of these specific collection duties. Difficulties remained, however. On the same day, December 6, Salamon Bendebut of Tudela and Rabí Sento Mataron of Pamplona were granted the power to foreclose on the properties of Jews from their respective cities who had failed to remit their assessed share. Bendebut was still unable to raise the needed sums as 1494 drew to a close, so he pawned some of his own personal property, jewels worth two hundred florins, to cover the outstanding amounts.[34]

Discontented with the yield of the 1495 *pecha,* on January 20 of the new year, Johan and Catalina ordered Mastre Ossua to produce a definitive list of the number of Jewish *casas* (households) in the kingdom. Mastre Ossua, too, was dissatisfied with his collection, for some Jews who had converted to Christianity claimed that they were not obligated to pay the Jewish *pecha.* Accordingly, on 21 January 1495, at Ossua's instigation, Tudelan collectors were granted permission to foreclose on the property of New Christians for debts owed on the *pecha* up to the day of their conversion.[35]

The expected arrival of the monarchs in 1494 occasioned new taxes, some of them apparently exacted as a condition of their entrance into Navarre. In an August 1493 meeting in Olite, the Cortes approved the payment of four *quarteres,* of twenty thousand pounds apiece, the first due within four months of the royal arrival. These *quarteres,* unlike many others previously authorized, were also to be paid by the religious orders and the secular clergy, and by the Jews and Muslims of the kingdom.[36]

All these groups resisted the added burden. The Jews and Muslims did not contribute their share to the cities and villages where they lived, and among the clergy, only the Tudelan priests forwarded the assessed sums. The *regidores* of the Tudelan municipality, apparently strapped for funds for the *quarteres*, procured a favorable sentence from the royal court, allowing them to collect a half a gold florin per *casa* from the Jews, native and immigrant, and the same from the Muslims.[37]

The two religious minorities did not avoid other additional taxes levied in the wake of the monarchs' arrival. Both groups remitted a two pounds per hearth impost ordered directly by Johan and Catalina. This kingdom-wide tax, unlike the *pecha*, was transmitted directly to royal treasury agents by Jews of the cities and villages of each *merindad* (district). The sums were not channeled through the six larger *aljama* groupings, nor was Mastre Ossua involved in the collection.[38]

The treasurer identified this two-pound tax as "one of the certain monies" that the king and queen had recently demanded from the Jews. Navarrese *aljama* officials diligently attempted to collect another impost, directed for the "service of the monarchs and their needs," but the local Jews balked at making these payments. The royal chancellery backed the efforts of the *jurados, regidores,* and *ordenadores* of all the *aljamas,* and issued an order on 17 October 1494 directing them to recover the outstanding monies.[39]

Some *aljamas* were more willing than others to raise these extraordinary funds. The Pamplona Jewish community complained to the royal treasury that the other *aljamas* were not aiding them in supplying twenty-three beds for the monarchs. Despite the use of the term "servicio," implying a voluntary contribution, it was expected that the funds would be remitted. Indeed, the monarchs' "financial agents" declared, in turn, that all the *aljamas* had to contribute to this fund and warned, probably at the suggestion of the Pamplonese, that if the tax were not apportioned at "a meeting of the messengers of all the aljamas," the Jews of the capital would have the power to unilaterally decide how much each community would be assessed.[40]

During the last two decades of the fifteenth century, the Navarrese subjects, Jews included, were also liable to special imposts unconnected with the monarchs' arrival. In 1488, the *hermandat* (brotherhood) was revived in order to pacify the kingdom and especially to patrol the frontiers with Castile and Aragon. The taxes levied for the "brotherhood" were heavy and, at the outset, did not exclude any social class. In the years 1488, 1489, and 1490, all

Navarrese (including clergy, secular and religious), Muslims, and Jews remitted two and three *reales* per hearth for the *hermandat*. In later years, the decrees calling for new taxes in support of the *hermandat* did not mention these groups, who probably were no longer liable.[41]

This period witnessed other changes in Navarrese taxation. The sales tax, formerly an occasional grant ceded by the Cortes to the king and called the *imposiçion*, was renamed the *alcabala* and converted into an annual payment. From 1480 through 1483, the city of Tudela remitted two thousand pounds to the royal treasury in order to be exempted from liability for special outright grants, including the *alcabala*. The Tudelan Jews' share of this payment was 150 pounds. The city did not render this tribute during the middle years of the decade but renewed the contribution in 1488, probably because of an increase in the sales tax and the ordering of new *quarteres* for the *hermandat*.[42]

After the inundation of new royal taxes in 1494, the *Libro de cuentas de propios (Book of Receipts and Expenses of the City of Tudela)* reported for that year that the Jews not only paid their portion of the two thousand libras but also advanced their share for the coming years of 1495 and 1496. In 1497, no Jewish payment was recorded, and in 1498 the Jews rendered only a fraction of the original sum.[43]

An indication that Pamplonese Jews were obliged to pay the *alcabala* was reflected in a 1494 sentence handed down by the monarchs' *finanças* (financial agents) in favor of Martin de Vaquedano, the treasurer of the royal household. These *finanças* ordered Vaquedano to collect an *alcabala* on wine that the *jurados, ordenadores,* and *aljama* of the Jews of Pamplona had been remiss in paying for thirteen years. Although Queen Leonor had shown leniency to the Tudelan Jews regarding their *alcabala* payments on wine in 1475 even before the later agreement on outright grants, this time the Pamplonese Jews could not forward the 871 pounds total and a few of their houses in the Jewish quarter were sold to cover the debt.[44]

Other royal imposts fell solely on Pamplonese Jewry. In the capital city, where most of the Jewish quarter was part of the royal patrimony, the Jews remitted a tax called the *fornage* for the use of the royal ovens, and the *vidmage* for the right to cultivate the monarchs' vineyards. They also owed a tax on the purchase of live animals within the city, and one called the *lezta* on the meat slaughtered by Jews in the abattoirs. Some royal taxes were paid only by Tudelan Jews and included an annual sum for the use of the tanners' stalls; a percentage of the fines levied by the community on antisocial behavior; and taxes called *sisas* on meat and wine, for which Açach Orabuena was the "resçeptor y cogedor."[45]

In 1492, the governor general of the kingdom was dissatisfied with the degree to which Tudelan Jews fulfilled their tax obligations and ordered them to pay the taxes owed in money, grains, and other foodstuffs. Similar examples can be readily adduced. Despite this and other such professions of annoyance at the Jews, royal officials in 1499 wistfully remarked of New Christians, that as Jews they had paid "above and beyond the pechas and the obligatory and voluntary imposts. . . ."[46]

The civil war that raged in Navarre during the late fifteenth century affected the taxes owed by the kingdom's Jews. Some communities fell under the control of anti-royal feudal lords, whose leader, the conde de Lerín, required an annual *pecha* of two florins from each of his Jewish subjects. The civil strife increased the tax burden of the Jews in loyalist areas: Tudelan Jews, for example, frequently had to contribute to their city's military security, although in 1472 Queen Leonor relieved them of certain payments in support of recent royal victories.[47]

In 1484, the Tudelan Jewish community remitted twenty-one pounds in payment of a "half-knight" war tax that the municipality calculated according to the number of Jewish *casas*. The sum was far less than that owed by their fellow minority group, the Muslims, who were liable for underwriting the support of one knight. The same one-to-two ratio obtained between the two religious groups in 1486 when the *jurados* of the city decreed a tax to pay for the lances of twelve knights. The Jews were assessed one florin for each *caballero* (knight), whereas the Muslims were to pay two florins toward the support of each of these soldiers.[48]

As the civil war continued into the 1490s, the Jews were again called upon to assume part of Tudela's responsibilities in supporting the loyalist cause. In 1494, the Jewish community forwarded sixty florins toward the expenses the city incurred during the siege of Larraga. The Jews' obligation grew steeper in 1497 when a special tax for the knights had native Jews collectively contributing 187 florins and the immigrant Jews, 162. In the same year, both groups also paid fifty florins because of the city's efforts in Melida, a village approximately thirty kilometers northeast of the city.[49]

The Jewish community likewise aided Tudela's peaceful attempts to settle conflicts and consolidate its position within the kingdom. The *jurados* of the *aljama* gave forty-five pounds in 1487 toward the sending of "certain embassies," and often assisted in outright grants the city delivered to its political overlords. The community contributed twelve pounds in 1491 to a sum presented to the "senyor inffante" and an identical sum in the following year for the "senyora reina gobernador." In anticipation of the expected arrival of the Navarrese monarchs, the community forwarded seventy-five florins in 1493, and when Princess Magdalena died in 1494, native Jews donated thirty pounds and the immigrant Jews twenty-two to aid in her burial.[50]

Many of the taxes levied by the Tudelan municipality, including those payable by the city's Jews, were in some way connected to the Ebro river and its traffic. In 1486, the *aljama* contributed toward the building of a structure designed presumably to prevent the river from overflowing its banks. In 1493, the Jews remitted fifteen florins for waterworks and irrigation canals leading from the Ebro. The bridge over the river led to fertile farmlands and the cost of its repairs in 1489 was shouldered in part by the Jewish community.[51]

Tudela was the major Navarrese port on the Ebro and the city played a large role in the transportation of goods within and without the kingdom. The Jews shared in an expedition of city-registered ships to the cove of Alfaro, Castile, in 1491, and in two domestic journeys down the Ebro in 1494. After an agreement with the city's *jurados* in 1496, the native and foreign Jews remitted their part of the export fees on wheat transported in ships sailing under the city's flag.[52]

When grains and other items were imported into Navarre, the goods first had to be measured in a special royally owned building, called the *almudi* in Tudela. From 1490 to 1494, Jews and Muslims paid for the privilege to be free from the *almudi*'s measurements. This sum, called the *franqueza*, was originally assessed according to the number of Jewish houses and amounted to just over twenty-seven pounds. The payment apparently became a fixed sum after the arrival of Castilian and Aragonese Jews in 1492: The native

Jews remitted thirteen pounds and the immigrants fifteen, approximating what the Jewish community had rendered in total before the newcomers' arrival.[53]

In addition to paying royal and municipal imposts, Tudelan Jews also remitted taxes to ecclesiastical authorities. Those who worked the vineyards and other lands belonging to the *capitol* of the church of Santa María owed a tenth of the harvested produce (the *deçimas*) to the church. The efforts expended in collecting these tithes were considerable, so the church regularly engaged tax farmers. Viticulture was an important activity of the Jewish community and the tithes on the grapes they harvested were customarily farmed by a prominent Jew in name of the entire *aljama*. From 1485 to 1488, the grape tithes were assessed at forty-seven pounds per yearly harvest and in 1488 the sum was renegotiated for a ten-year period at sixty pounds a year. The tithes of the green barley appear to have been paid directly, and the collection of the tenth of lambs and kids, raised on church lands by Jewish and Muslim graziers of Ablitas in the district of Tudela, was farmed out to Christians.[54]

Considerable friction arose between the church of Santa María and the Jews when the church claimed rights to the first fruits grown on property that Jews had recently acquired from Christians. Tension between the Jewish community and Church authorities over taxes payable to the Church was a permanent feature of the medieval landscape. As recently as 1459 in Tudela, inventories of property owned by Jews were drawn in both Hebrew and Romance, in order to indicate property subject to ecclesiastical tithes and property exempt from them. Additionally, the church traditionally collected *primiçias* (first fruits) from Christian farmers but the new Jewish landowners in our period, not surprisingly, refused to render payment. On 11 March 1490, in the choir-loft of the Tudelan church, the treasurer, *maestreescuela,* and canons of the *yglesia* (church) met with the Jewish community to arrange a compromise. The church officials appointed as their arbiter their vicar general, Miguel Caritat, and the Jews selected Rabí Abraham de la Rabiça.[55]

Eight days later, Caritat and de la Rabiça arrived at an agreement. In the document of compromise, they explained the parties' positions. The *aljama* had argued that it "never ever" paid the first fruits and that it had displayed its "privilegio," which proved its exemption from this tax. The church had pointed out that the Jews not only owned properties acquired through inheritance, but had recently purchased land from Christians. It saw no reason to lose income from the acquired properties, and had all along been protesting that each year when the taxes were collected there was great confusion as to which properties were liable.

The arbiters' "definitive sentence" stated that, starting December 1, the Jews were to pay six pounds per year to cover the first fruits the church lost on the formerly Christian-owned property. With this annual payment, the Jews were free of the obligation of surrendering the first fruits on these lands. The payment would continue to be required and would remain fixed at six pounds no matter how many parcels of land were to change hands later. The Jews did not compromise on their principle of refusing the obligation to pay the *primiçias*; the agreement to forward an annual remittance was to assuage the church for its losses.[56]

Salo Baron has suggested that Navarrese Jewry "was . . . dying . . . even before it was struck down by the formal decree of expulsion in 1498."[57] But what our study of the everyday life of its last generation has taught is that these Jews, though not scaling the political or economic heights attained by their predecessors, were demographically vital, economically vibrant, and communally capable of providing for the needs of their fellow Jews even as they maintained the welter of financial obligations to the Navarrese political entities to whom they were subject. The famed *convivencia* of medieval Iberian society which allowed the Jews not only daily contact with their Muslim and Christian neighbors but also afforded them positions of trust, including administrative and financial posts in the various levels of government, remained largely intact. Although the sources we analyzed so far reflect the Jews' economic well-being (and the same, it can be argued, was the lot of other Iberian Jews at this time), these documents also indicate— as the concluding section of the book will chronicle—that events beyond the borders of this smallest of Christian Iberian kingdoms would dramatically affect the fortunes of what was to be the last Jewry on Iberian soil.

2. The Crisis in Iberian Society

Map 2. Navarre and Its Iberian Neighbors

4. New Christians and the Struggle Over the Inquisition

As a result of the massacres of 1391, which decimated many of the Jewish communities in Castile and Aragon, a new group emerged within Iberian society comprising a variety of types of erstwhile Jews, ranging from those who converted to Christianity to avoid certain death at the hands of the mob to those who apostasized out of sincere belief in their adopted religion. The numbers of these *conversos* continued to swell even after the killings had stopped, as the Jewish communities became progressively demoralized by Christianity triumphant and as their social, economic, and political status gradually eroded. The crisis of faith that beleaguered Iberian Jewry was further heightened during the early fifteenth century by the twenty-one-month-long disputation at Tortosa. Although the Jewish position was valiantly defended there by representatives of the Aragonese *aljamas,* the relentless prosecution of the debate by the Christian disputants had a devastating effect on the stability of the Jewish communities. About as many Jews, scholars suggest, flocked to the baptismal font at the beginning of the fifteenth century as had come to Christianity during the pogroms of 1391.[1]

All the *conversos,* sincere and opportunistic converts alike, however, found that although their immersion in the baptismal waters damaged their ties with their former coreligionists, the act was not sufficient to carry them through the portals of Christian society. Conversion did not magically open doors for the Jews; the millenium-old promises proved of ephemeral value. The Iberian *conversos* continued in the main to live in their old quarters, to work at their traditional occupations, and to possess a shadowy status compared to the older recognized religious communities.[2]

Some of these Castilian and Aragonese *conversos* found their way to the kingdom of Navarre during the course of the 1400s. Many immigrated during the last quarter of the fifteenth century, when the first major attempt to solve the *converso* problem in Castile and Aragon was realized in the establishment of the "Spanish" Inquisition. Their numbers increased again when all professing

Jews were expelled from Castile-Aragon in 1492 in order, as Ferdinand and Isabella's edict explained, to prevent the Jews from subverting the faith of these *cristianos nuevos* (New Christians).[3]

At this point in our discussion, certain methodological and procedural matters need intrude. Documents about Navarrese *conversos* are hard to locate, because scribes and notaries did not always append the description *cristiano nuevo* to a *converso*'s name. Furthermore, a person with a Jewish name who possessed a Christian alias cannot necessarily be said to have been a New Christian. The difficulties in amassing evidence having been acknowledged, it remains to be indicated that in this chapter the term *converso*s will generally be used to designate the body of Jewish converts, whereas the term "New Christian" will be utilized when dealing with individual cases, as this is how they are described in the archival sources.

Although for many *conversos* the adoption of a new religion did little immediately to change their occupational profile, for a few it eventually afforded entry into public positions, both ecclesiastic and governmental, previously off-limits to them. The Daybar clan, for example, was able to achieve high municipal and church positions in the city of Tudela. Johan Daybar, who, like Alonso and his uncle Miguel, originally came to Navarre from the village of Huesa in Aragon, was in 1497 the *procurador* of the city in charge of the receipts and expenses of the municipality. His son-in-law, Johan Miguel de Munarriz, who may or may not have been a New Christian, was also *procurador* of Tudela. The merchant García Daybar was a *jurado* of the city and also its agent.[4]

The Caritat family included Miguel, who was the precentor and vicar general of the collegiate church of St. Mary, and Pedro, who was a local *escudero* (squire). Johan de Miranda was also a squire, a canon of the church of St. Mary, a magistrate (*justiçia*) of the city, and a member of its council. Matheo de Miranda was a *jurado* of Tudela, serving on its *plega* (council). Other New Christians held public positions in Navarre but lived outside the kingdom. Ferdinand of Aragon was able to name Mosen Luis Santángel as *alcalde* of Pamplona, and Luis Sánchez as *prior* of Arguedas.[5]

Other New Christians simply continued to conduct the same trade that had occupied them before they converted, as their documented involvement in the trade of hides and furs, and in viticulture, is testimony. The convert García de Falces struck a deal with his former coreligionist Abraham Farag, whereby Falces was to deliver three dozen sheepskins in exchange for each measure of cleaned hemp. Falces "swore on the cross" to abide by the agreement, which would be in effect from Easter until 15 June 1496.[6] In January 1498, Gregorio Derquenigo, a New Christian, purchased a substantial vineyard in the Beaxon terminal of Tudela for thirty-two florins from a Christian, a skinner named Johan de Mendigorria.[7]

Simuel Çadoque continued his financial pursuits unchanged after his conversion. In November of 1493 Simuel Paçagon lent four thousand Aragonese shillings to Çadoque, and when Çadoque returned the money in cash on 11 April 1494, he had converted and his name was now Alonso Daybar.[8] This action by the neophyte Alonso was not an indication of a sudden loss of interest in moneylending and speculation, because on the same day (August 11), Miguel Daybar, Alonso's uncle, admitted having received three thousand Aragonese shillings in *comanda* from his nephew. The sum was to be repaid in five years' time.[9] The former Simuel Çadoque's business agreements that were negotiated prior to his conversion were still awaiting resolution in 1497. A moneylending contract of January 4 of that year indicated that Sancho de Legasa and Sancho de Mauleon owed almost twenty-six golden Aragonese florins to "Simuel Çadoch of the Tudelan *judería*," and that they promised to pay within one month.[10] Similarly, on 14 March 1497, Mastre Andreo declared that he owed "Simuel Çadoch, Jew of Tudela" sixty-seven golden Aragonese florins, which he promised to pay by the end of March. And on 15 May 1497, "Simuel Çadoque, Jew, received the sixty-seven golden florins from Mastre Andrea." In both cases, because the obligations were incurred when Çadoch was a Jew, he is designated as such in the documents.[11]

Navarrese New Christians were greatly concerned with settling the business affairs of their families. The neophyte Francisco Navarro and his brother Salamon Baço (who remained Jewish) represented other New Christian and Jewish members of their family in disposing of the estate of their father Ussua Baço. They also released Pedro del Polo and his son from debts owed to their father Ussua, and each son swore according "to his Law."[12]

Brothers who came to hold different faiths sometimes had to resort to arbitration to settle their differences. On 1 May 1493, the New Christian Johan Royz sued his brother Aym Çalama both on his own behalf and as guardian of his nephews Migalico and Johana Royz. Before young Migalico and Johana's father died, he had entrusted some of his estate to Çalama, probably to avoid the transfer of property to the members of his family who had converted. Because of the large sums involved and the theological overtones of the ensuing debate, the local church became involved in the case. Miguel Caritat, the vicar, decreed that Pedro Caritat and Pacual de Ayenssa would serve as arbiters and deliver their opinion by the coming Saturday.[13] Clearly in deference to Çalama the Jew, the decision was not announced until Sunday—that is, after the Jewish sabbath. Under penalty of one thousand golden florins in case of noncompliance, Çalama was to pay Royz forty-six hundred shillings over the space of three years. As demanded by Royz, Çalama had to present guarantors for the sum by Monday and at the same time deliver two strings of pearls to the arbiters who were to hold them for Royz's wife.[14]

In a similar case, the Jews' notary Jaco de la Rabiça was requested by Abram Gamiz to draw up a document assigning all his property to his son Gento. After Abram's death, his other son, Johan de Miranda, formerly Simuel, sought to recover his share of the estate. The two brothers themselves arrived at a satisfactory accord.[15]

Adjustments in business matters, as in the disposition of inheritances, were sometimes needed when one of the parties converted to Christianity. Jehuda Bendebut of Tudela had sold some houses in the heart of the city's Jewish quarter to another Jew, who then converted and assumed the name Pedro Pasquier. Pasquier was not satisfied with the contractual arrangement, and the case was sent to arbitration. According to the sentence, the sale was cancelled and Bendebut was ordered to pay eight florins to Pasquier within two weeks. At that point Pasquier could exercise the option to repurchase the houses for forty-seven florins, which in fact he did.[16]

Converts could also provide legal support to their former coreligionists. For example, Simuel and Abram Chinillo had been the arbiters of a family dispute between Jeuda Chinillo and the widow of his brother Mastre Vidal. Simuel and Abram arrived at a decision, but in time its exact stipulations were forgotten. At Simuel's suggestion, Gracian de Vasquin, the former Abram Mangan, was called to give a deposition before the *justiçia* of the city. Gracian lived in "foreign kingdoms" and thus had to be subpoenaed immediately, as soon as it became known that he was visiting Tudela. He testified that he and Mastre Vidal's son Crescas were witnesses to the arbiters' sentence, and then described the contents of the decision as fully as he could recall.[17]

While some New Christians encountered difficulties in maintaining their business interests and inheritance rights once they converted, others may have realized financial gain on separating from their former coreligionists. It was in response to the latter possibility that the royal chancellery ordered on 21 January 1495 that the collectors of the Jews' taxes—Mastre Ossua at their head—had a right to sequester the property of neophytes, as a result of taxes owed up to the day of their conversion.[18]

Current Iberian and Jewish historical literature expends great energy debating the "Jewishness" or sincere Christianity of the majority of the *converso* population. This is not the appropriate forum for an analysis of the competing views on this point, for the scant evidence from the Navarrese archives is not likely to sway any of the parties to the conflict from their positions. In presenting the data from Navarre that we do possess, I do so in the hope that others will follow suit and publish additional information about localized areas as it comes to light. Present-day religious and political opinions have had their chance to influence the debate; the presentation of new material might elevate the argument beyond the mere grinding of ideological axes.

The New Christians Johan Munyoz and his wife María displayed continued concern for their former community after their conversion. The former Yento and Açeti Alcalaer had held two properties located in Tudela's Jewish quarter and disposed of them after they became Christians. They sold and relinquished the rights to one of them to the Jewish *confraría* (brotherhood) for seven golden florins. This *cambra* (chamber) carried a *cens* payable to the brotherhood and was located between its offices and the home of Sento Falaquera. It appears likely that the "chamber" in question was the *mikveh* (ritual bath) and that the *confraría* was in charge of it.

The other property consisted of three conjoined parcels of land, which the Munyozes gave as an irrevocable donation to the small synagogue of the Jewish quarter. These lands were located below the synagogue, abutted on the walls of the castle, and carried *censes* owed to the house of worship and the communal charity board.

The parcels were to be transferred immediately and were to be legally attached to the synagogue.[19]

The two transfers were part of a business deal. On the sale of the chamber, the Munyozes granted the land to the synagogue. This transaction not only illustrates the kinds of relations that existed between the *conversos* and the Jewish community, it also shows that public donations by New Christians to Jewish institutions were not considered foolhardy acts in Tudelan society.[20]

Although the behavior of Johan and María Munyoz may depict the sensitivity of neophyte converts to their former coreligionists, the actions of Mastre Mosse, a Jewish doctor from Tudela, show one Jew's distress at his son's conversion. Mosse's son had converted and taken the name of Alonso Caritat. Alonso's mother (Mosse's wife) had died, and the convert sued his father for his portion of the estate. The Tudelan church of St. Mary considered the case to be under its jurisdiction and appointed Miguel Caritat and Pascual de Magallon, respectively its precentor and presbyter, to arbitrate the case. Their decision was intended to cause embarrassment to the Jewish father.

The arbiters ordered Mastre Mosse to surrender to Alonso the inheritance due him, one hundred florins, which were to be remitted in five yearly installments of twenty florins each. These funds were to enable Alonso to take instruction in Christianity. On the same day, Alonso and Miguel de Caritat (who probably was a neophyte) appointed Miguel Caritat and Pascal de Magallon as agents to collect whatever sums were owed them by the city, the cathedral chapter, and others. It may well be that these two New Christians had been offered money to convert.[21]

Alonso's "scholarship" in Christianity was to begin on Christmas 1492 and continue through *Navidad* 1497. On 5 November 1495, however, Alonso recognized that he had already received his father's last two installments, amounting to forty florins total, and released his father from the five-year "contract." Mastre Mosse may have been relieved to dispense with this burden ahead of its appointed time.[22]

The *conversos* of Navarre, unlike those in the neighboring kingdoms of Castile and Aragon, were not subject to the jurisdiction of the "Spanish" Inquisition until 1513, after Ferdinand of Aragon conquered Navarre and attempted to merge its political organization with that of the kingdom of Castile. In those early years, though, it was the officials of the Aragonese Inquisition who were nominated to important posts within the newly created tribunals and charged with investigating heresy within the dominions of the Pyrenean kingdom.[23] Hence Navarre did not officially possess its own tribunals until the second decade of the sixteenth century, yet, as we shall see, the establishment of the Inquisition in Castile and Aragon in the 1480s already had an immediate and profound effect on Navarrese New Christians and, indeed, on the kingdom itself.

Two years after the papal bull of Sixtus IV of November 1478, which authorized the establishment of a national Inquisition in the dominions of Ferdinand and Isabella, the Catholic Monarchs appointed inquisitors to head the Inquisition's first functioning tribunal, which was held in Seville. Three more tribunals were created in the kingdom of Castile by 1484, at Córdoba, Ciudad Real, and Jaén. In the same year, and after much negotiation with the Cortes of Aragon, Ferdinand established an Inquisition in his kingdom under the jurisdiction of the Castilian Inquisitor, Fray Tomás de Torquemada.[24]

One of Torquemada's first steps in the kingdom of Aragon was to organize a tribunal in Saragossa, and on 10 May 1484, an *auto-de-fe* was held in the city's cathedral. After this event, *conversos* and others rose in opposition to the Inquisition and no *autos-de-fe* were scheduled there during the next eighteen months. A tribunal was also established at Teruel and it encountered even greater hostility. The Aragonese Inquisition then determined to overcome the resistance both there and in Saragossa.[25]

Some *conversos* in Saragossa concluded that the protests at Teruel were ineffective and that only the murder of the inquisitor, Pedro de Arbués, would put an end to the Saragossan Inquisition. In the spring of 1485, an unsuccessful attempt was made on the inquisitor's life. On September 15, several men fatally stabbed de Arbués in the cathedral of Saragossa and on September 17, the inquisitor died.[26]

The conspirators had miscalculated. The assassination did not put an end to the Inquisition; rather, the populace, previously hostile to the institution, was by now inflamed with a virulent hatred against the *conversos*. Ferdinand could not be appeased by the offers of money, and he—together with the city's officials, including

its judges—made a concerted attempt to apprehend the perpetra-
tors. Those captured were brought to trial immediately.[27]

The kingdom of Navarre thus became involved in a murder that
had taken place outside its boundaries when some of the accomplices to the assassination of Arbués fled across the Aragonese border and settled in the city of Tudela.[28] Concerned that a neighboring
kingdom was harboring fugitives from his Inquisition, and probably more important, to ensure that Navarre not pursue any foreign or domestic policy that ran contrary to the political designs
of Castile-Aragon, Ferdinand wrote to Tudela's magistrates on 27
January 1486, instructing them to attend to all the requests of the
Aragonese inquisitors, a practice he claimed was being followed in
his own kingdom.[29] To the consternation of both Ferdinand and
Isabella, the Tudelans responded by prohibiting the promulgation
of any inquisitorial edicts in the city and preventing the ministers
of the Aragonese Inquisition from gathering any information about
the Arbués murder.[30]

Moreover, the Tudelans also put teeth in their declaration
against the Inquisition: One official of the Aragonese Inquisition—
who, Ferdinand and Isabella later claimed, was unaware of the
Tudelan resolution—was almost captured when horsemen chased
him more than four leagues out of the city.[31] In another instance,
an *aguazil* (constable) of the Inquisition of Barbastro was taking
some Saragossan refugees from Tudela when he was overtaken by
thirty Tudelan horsemen in Aragon and his prisoners returned to
Tudela.[32]

Ferdinand and Isabella complained of Tudela's actions in a
signed letter of May 4 addressed to all the city's municipal officials.
They also charged that the guilty Saragossan heretics (Ferdinand
and Isabella had labeled them such) who had taken refuge in
Tudela were using the city as the headquarters for their attacks on
the Inquisition. The heretics, according to the Catholic Monarchs,
had sent messengers to Rome to spread false information and to
carry documents that they employed to disrupt the workings of the
Inquisition. The guilty ones were also sending envoys to Saragossa
and Barbastro, where they presented "bulls and rescripts" in favor
of the heretics.[33]

The guilty Saragossans had no respect for the inquisitors, who,
proclaimed Ferdinand and Isabella, were "judges and ministers of
our very Holy Father." And the Tudelan municipality, they added,

was acting "in great disservice to God and in opprobrium to the Holy Catholic Faith." As to the city officials' argument that their *fueros* and liberties instructed them to defend the refugees, the Castilian and Aragonese monarchs countered that their own kingdoms also possessed such laws but that no government of Catholic Christians could use such rules to protect heretics. The Tudelans, they warned darkly, were jeopardizing the health of their souls.

Ferdinand and Isabella demanded that the city officials deliver the refugees to inquisitors or their officers who would be arriving in Tudela. If that were not possible, they insisted that the Tudelans expel the heretics from the city and promise not to receive them again within their jurisdiction. Ferdinand argued that the Inquisition was empowered to pursue transgressors wherever found and to proceed against their supporters.

On the latter point, Ferdinand clearly misrepresented the powers of the Inquisition, as the tribunals did not acquire these rights until April 1487. But the Catholic Monarchs knew that neither the threat of a nonexistent law nor prayers for the Tudelans' salvation would influence those Navarrese city officials to deliver the heretics. Ferdinand and Isabella therefore ended their missive explaining that they themselves could not be excused from their obligation to God's service, and that this service would entail a declaration of war ("mandar facer guerra") and grave damage to Tudela. They closed by noting that it would hurt them greatly to destroy the city's peace, for they bore great love toward it and indeed toward the entire Navarrese kingdom.[34]

It was therefore not only the *souls* of the Navarrese that were in danger. While Ferdinand and Isabella's attempt to force an Aragonese institution on another Iberian kingdom was a measure of their increased political power and a possible reflection of their future political designs,[35] this attempt surely was a reflection of Tudela's considerable involvement in activities against the Inquisition, an enterprise aided by local New Christians and Jews as well as those implicated in the Arbués murder.[36]

Following the lead of Ferdinand and Isabella, the Aragonese Inquisition, probably on its own initiative, instructed Juan de Ribera, the captain general of the frontier, to move against Tudela. He refused, and on June 30 of 1486, the inquisitors complained to Ferdinand. They then asked Ribera to proceed against the southern Navarrese city simply to capture the suspect Martín de Santángel, and again he demurred. This time Ribera asked for a formal request from Torquemada himself, which apparently was not forthcoming.[37]

After the failure of the inquisitors to move Juan de Ribera to a military solution, they turned to religious measures to force the Tudelans' hand. The bishop of Tarazona, whose ecclesiastical jurisdiction included Tudela and the southernmost area of Navarre, issued a writ of excommunication against the churchmen and inhabitants of Tudela. One interdict included the prohibition of reciting the Divine Office (that is, the daily services), in any of the churches of the city.

The bishop's action so disturbed the Tudelan city councillors that they sent Don Miguel de Eguaras, a fellow *jurado,* and Don Pascual de Magallon to speak to the bishop about the cessation of public prayers.[38] The mission proved unsuccessful, and so a few days later, in October of 1486, the *jurado* had Xymeno de Villafranca and Johan de Miranda travel to a meeting of the Navarrese Cortes being held in Pamplona. There they would also meet with Alaín, Señor de Labrit, the governor general of the kingdom. Villafranca stayed twelve days, and Miranda, who was a New Christian, remained one day more.[39]

Miranda had an additional mission in Pamplona. He was to secure documents relating to the actions of the "confessos," those who had taken refuge in Tudela.[40] The Tudelan officials would be using these papers in their fight against the Aragonese Inquisition.

Those New Christians involved in ecclesiastical and municipal governmental circles in Tudela were probably influential in their city's welcome of the refugees and in its activities against the Inquisition. The New Christian Johan de Miranda was a messenger of the city council, sent to deal with the problems caused by the harboring of suspects in the Arbués murder. And some of the officials of the major church in Tudela, the collegiate church of St. Mary, were New Christians. Another factor in Tudela's struggle with the Inquisition was the municipality's determination to avoid the preemption of its own judicial system, notwithstanding its fear of the wrath of Ferdinand and Isabella.[41]

While the Tudelan city council was active in rebuffing the Inquisition, Juan de Pero Sánchez—he was the prime mover behind the Arbués assassination plot and was burned in effigy at an *auto-de-fe* on June 3 of 1486—turned to more mundane matters. Sánchez, described in a document of 28 October 1486, as a "merchant of the city of Saragossa presently residing in Tudela," leased, in his role of business agent for the priory of Arguedas (a village in Navarre), all Arguedas' benefits, rents, and other incomes to García Pérez de Verayz. The lessee was the *alcayde* of the castle of Tudela, who later became the bailiff of the Jews and Muslims of the city. The two witnesses were Charles de Yraycoz and Martin de Berrozpe, both canons of the local church of St. Mary.[42]

Although Tudelan municipal officials and some canons of the collegiate church were defending the interests of the Saragossan "fugitive heretics" and of the New Christian community in general,[43] not all the church officials were pleased with the turn of events that had brought the ecclesiastical censures upon them and their flock. Mossen Gonçalez de Ogea and Marco Miguel, respectively the treasurer and canon of Tudela's St. Mary, officially protested the recent actions by the Tudelans. In their petition, they told how the inquisitors and vicar general of the Saragossan tribunal had proceeded with the admonitions and excommunications against the lay people and churchmen of Tudela. According to the Saragossans' warnings, the Tudelans were to deliver the accomplices and their properties to the Inquisition. The Tudelan churchmen argued that they ought to follow these orders because of the danger to their "benefices and consciences." Their concerns about matters material and spiritual prompted them to go on record as being willing to obey the inquisitors.[44]

From November 1486 until the end of the year, matters between the Tudelans and the Catholic Monarchs appeared to be at a standstill, and on 23 January 1487, Ferdinand made it clear to the deputies of the Aragonese parliament that they should preserve peaceful relations with Navarre.[45] The king of Aragon explained that the visit to Navarre of Juan de Ribera, the captain general of the Aragon-Navarre frontier, should not be construed as a preliminary step towards war with their northern neighbor.[46]

The Catholic Monarchs decided now to intervene directly again in bringing those culpable in the Arbués murder to justice and turned to the church at Rome for help. In April 1487, they were able to procure a papal letter from Innocent VIII, which proclaimed that no Christian ruler of any land, under penalty of excommunication, could admit refugees fleeing from the authority of the Castilian and Aragonese Inquisition. If any such refugees did enter a kingdom, they were to be returned to the Castilian-Aragonese frontier within thirty days of a simple request by the Inquisition. This power, previously claimed by Ferdinand in his letter to the Tudelan leaders, was now given legal justification by the Holy See.[47]

The papal letter occasioned in mid-May of 1487 a flurry of diplomatic activity in Tudela by both civil and ecclesiastical authorities in order to protect the "refugees." The city council sent Mossen Calçena to speak with the Bishop of Tarazona, whose diocese, as mentioned, included Tudela. There, Calçena also copied a summons that was on file in the offices of the Tarazonan see.[48] The citation, executed in light of the new papal directive and which probably demanded the return of the heretics, required careful study by the Tudelans.

On May 16, García Pérez de Verayz, the *alcayde* of Tudela's fortress and an ally of the New Christians, sent a messenger to Miraglo to collect its vicar for a trip to Saragossa. The next day, the two—together with the New Christian Johan de Miranda and Don Juan, the cleric of the vicar general of the collegiate church of St. Mary—set out for Saragossa to consult with the inquisitors. While in Aragon, the Tudelans also procured a transcription of the charges leveled against them by the Inquisition. The notary, Juhan Martínez Cabero, who also functioned in this capacity for the collegiate church, was to use these papers in the preparation of an appeal to Rome.[49]

During the preparation of the appeal, the Aragonese Inquisition was able to establish an inquiry in the village of Fitero, a village located in the southeast corner of Navarre. In response to this action, the Tudelan city councillors on May 25 asked Juhan Martínez Cabero to draw up papers, presumably a petition, to counter the inquest. The next day, Mossen Calçena again traveled to the Bishop of Tarazona to present him with this remonstrance. He told the bishop that the appeal had been presented to the inquisitors and that they had refused to accept it.[50]

Tudelan officials were fighting the Inquisition on the local front, preventing it from gaining a foothold in Navarrese territory, while defending Tudela's rights against it before officials of the church in Rome. During this time, the "fugitive heretics" themselves were not idle: In June of 1487, Pedro de Almazán the younger, accused of complicity in the Arbués murder, appointed two agents to prepare his appeal for presentation to the Inquisition.[51]

Other inhabitants of Navarre became involved in the continuing conflict between the Inquisition and Tudela over the individuals the city refused to surrender. On 8 November 1487, Johan de Berrozpe, Beltran de Sarria, and Felipe de Baygorri, all of them inhabitants of Navarre, appeared before various church officers in Tudela and related that they had been held captive for nine months by inquisitors at the village of Monzón in Aragon. They confessed that in Monzón they had committed acts against their conscience (informing against certain Tudelans, probably) which they wished to rescind, and asked clemency in light of extenuating circumstances. The judges' response to the testimony about the unidentified acts was reported to be favorable though qualified.[52]

During 1487, not only Tudela but also the southern village of Corella defended itself against the Inquisition. The Corellans prohibited the Holy Office from engaging in activities within the village, "because we have no business (*cargo*) with said inquest." As in Fitero, the Inquisition had been attempting to gain a foothold in Navarre. When the inquisitors attempted to override the Corellans' decision, village officials on 15 October 1487, sent a local vicar (as in Tudela, village and church officials apparently acted in tandem) to Tarazona to meet with the bishop. The Corellans asked the bishop to travel to Saragossa and straighten out matters with the inquisitors. The vicar also carried "cartas" to the bishop, which he was to take with him to Saragossa. These documents presumably were the village's royal privileges (those granted by past Navarrese monarchs), which, they claimed, exempted it from the Inquisition's jurisdiction.[53]

By the end of 1487, Corella's defense against the Inquisition was being coordinated with that of Tudela. At this time, Ferdinand and Isabella displayed a change in policy toward Navarre, menacing it militarily and disrupting commerce across the frontiers. Yet discussions were underway as well. On December 28, Corellan village officials sent Pedro Pradilla to Tudela to ascertain the status of its negotiations with "the Castilian monarchs." Pradilla also sought advice about the Corellan interdict launched against the Inquisition, which apparently was postponed until the middle of January. He carried documents that the village had presented to the inquisitors and asked the Tudelans how to deal with two cases (not described) that the inquisitors had refused to hear.[54]

The cooperation between Tudela and Corella continued into the following year. Pedro Pradilla and Ferrando de Mayanas traveled

from Corella to Tudela to discuss the details of a combined delegation to be sent to the inquisitors in Saragossa.[55] Not only was Tudela then negotiating with Ferdinand and Isabella but it was also,
together with Corella, attempting to deal directly with the Inquisition itself. The suspension of the Corellan prohibition of the Inquisition was probably issued to soften the inquisitors' hard-line
stance.

The Navarrese and Ferdinand and Isabella finally achieved a
"compromise," which was reflected in a declaration made by two
Tudelan deputies before the *Reyes Católicos* on 21 February 1488.
Pedro Gómez and Guillen de las Cortes, on behalf of the Tudelan
city council and all the city's inhabitants, declared submission to
the inquisitors in exchange for the lifting of the censures proclaimed
against the city in 1486 for harboring the "fugitive heretics." According to the Tudelan messengers, the censures were proclaimed
after sentences had been issued at inquisitorial trials. Gómez and
de las Cortes claimed themselves to be "faithful and Catholic Christians" and asked for absolution and penance from the *padres
inquisidores.*[56]

The messengers' protest was that the submission was limited to
the fugitives' persons, and not their property, as the sentence had
it. This interpretation was contrary to the specific requests of Ferdinand and Isabella's financial agents.[57] The messengers declared
that their sentence should in no way be construed as acknowledging
any other rights over the heretics' property. Ferdinand and Isabella
accepted the protests without prejudice to their own claims against
the guilty ones and their property. Such was the compromise between Tudela and Ferdinand and Isabella.

Tudela's responsibility for aiding the heretics also was acknowledged before inquisitorial tribunals at Saragossa. At an *auto-de-fe*
on 10 February 1488, Jayme Díez de Almendaraz, the Señor de
Cadreyta, was penanced for having sheltered Martín de Santángel,
García de Moros, and Gaspar de Santa Cruz and his wife. His penalty was sixty golden florins.[58] On 2 March 1488, Pedro Gómez
(Tudela's *alcalde*) and eight of its *jurados* were penanced for having
harbored some of the fugitives. By this time the heretics had already
left Navarre.[59]

As a result of these proceedings, Tudela allowed the Inquisition
to investigate and proceed against individuals having any connection with cases pending before its tribunals. Tudela insisted, how-

ever, that the Inquisition had no jurisdiction over the property of any of the accused, a point contested by Ferdinand and Isabella. The prevailing view of historians that the Inquisition was not established in Navarre until the conquest of the kingdom in 1512, albeit technically true, is misleading. The Inquisition was, in fact, able to pursue suspects and carry out investigations in Navarre from its headquarters outside the kingdom.[60]

This rapprochement of Tudela with Ferdinand and Isabella should probably be understood in light of the Treaty of Valencia of 21 March 1488, which the Catholic Monarchs negotiated with Alaín de Albret, governor of Navarre since 1486 and father of young Johan (husband of Catalina), the heir apparent, and destined to be king of Navarre. Whether this treaty, which allowed for the pacification of the kingdom—Navarre's civil war was always cleverly manipulated by Castile-Aragon and France—should be understood as the finalization of a Castilian protectorate over Navarre or simply as an outgrowth of previous understandings between the kingdoms, the resolution of the issues regarding the Inquisition was surely part of the negotiations. By the close of 1488, Navarre was also cooperating with Ferdinand and Isabella in their request for funds to help finance the "crusade" against Granada. The Catholic Monarchs were thankful and for this directed Juan de Ribera to aid the Navarrese in their pacification efforts. At the time, the war against Granada was uppermost in the minds of Ferdinand and Isabella.[61]

Meanwhile the activities of the Inquisition were still producing ripples in Tudela. Johana Manyos, a Tudelan, had been arrested by the inquisitors and a dispute arose over the disposition of her property. A cleric named Johanes de Soria testified on 29 January 1489, that he was with Johana on the day of the "abduction," and that she had ordered him to go to her house and collect a trunk containing clothing. There he met Sancho de Paluet, who now was in court demanding the trunk's contents. Johanes related that he had told Sancho of Johana's wishes. The court entrusted the property to Johan de Roncal, who would have to return it when so requested.[62]

Although Tudela had concluded an understanding with the Inquisition and Ferdinand and Isabella, it was at best an uneasy truce. On 14 March 1489, the city officials sent a courier to Saragossa to speak with the inquisitors regarding "exchanges" that had been stipulated, and to bring back their response.[63] The inquisitors' reply was not recorded, but on March 28, the city council paid the expenses of two men who had traveled to the governor of Navarre in Olite. The men had taken with them a prisoner who was identified as a *nunçio* of the inquisitors.[64]

Tudela clearly perceived that the tribunal was not carrying out its side of the bargain in a possible exchange of Tudelan citizens such as Johana Manyos for the imprisoned official. The *nunçio* may have been sent to Olite for safekeeping, and also in order to involve the royal government of Navarre in the negotiations. While the Inquisition in Aragon had by 1489 "overcome all resistance and the kingdom lay at its mercy," the same could not confidently be said about its influence in Navarre.[65]

The Inquisition next appears in Navarrese records in the year 1495, when the city of Tudela was evidently using its own judicial and investigative powers to conduct an inquiry into the affairs of the friar Miguel de Baquedano, a master of theology and lector and superior of the convent of Sant Francisco in Tudela. The inquest was executed in the style of the Inquisition and was surely undertaken with its support. Tudela's action may have been an attempt to curry favor with Ferdinand and Isabella in a year of great political turmoil and simultaneously to curtail *converso* power within the city.[66]

When the investigation began on 13 February 1495, Fray Miguel had already been accused, probably of judaizing. In his defense, he had persuaded the *justiçia* Johan de la Cambra to ask the court's *nunçio* to call three Christians to testify. On February 13, Pedro de Basquin, Pedro de Quintanilla, and Johan de Linyan appeared before the *justiçia*. They were asked three questions: first, whether they knew the Tudelan New Christian Pedro de Quintanilla; second, whether they knew that Miguel de Baquedano had directly or indirectly advised Pedro de Quintanilla to act against the Holy Inquisition and its officials especially its *acesor,* and if Fray Miguel advised Quintanilla to draw up writings against anyone; and third, if Miguel de Baquedano supported Quintanilla and his children for other than charitable reasons.[67]

Quintanilla, the first deponent, answered the second question by claiming that Baquedano never advised him to proceed against the Inquisition or its officials, including the *acesor,* nor did he encourage him to attack it in writing. In fact, Fray Miguel advised him to "hold his tongue" lest his body suffer. As for the charity, it was done for the service of God and not because of any interest in judaizing.[68]

The testimony of Pedro de Basquin followed. He admitted that he knew Quintanilla and was often in the presence of Quintanilla and Mastre Miguel, and that they talked frequently of the Inquisition. He testified that Baquedano counseled Quintanilla to "tape up his mouth" and not speak ill of the Inquisition. He never heard Baquedano advise Quintanilla about any writings and that as far as he knew, the donations were given solely for the love of God— that Quintanilla was so poor, he often went without eating.

Johan de Linyan, a painter, added in his testimony that he had heard Mastre Miguel advise Quintanilla to buy two sewing needles, one for his clothing and the other for his mouth. The latter would cure him of speaking ill of the Inquisition and its officials.

Another witness, Yento Salton, was called by Fray Miguel. Because he was a Jew, his testimony had to be recorded before García Pérez de Verayz, the bailiff of the Jews and Muslims of the city and district of Tudela. There Salton, an inhabitant of Cortes, could be sworn according to his law.[69]

Salton was first asked if he knew Baquedano, and he replied that he had not met him until that very day. He was then questioned about a matter that had not been raised earlier in the investigation: Did Salton know that when Fray Miguel traveled to Castile to the royal court, it was on behalf of certain New Christians? Salton replied that Quintanilla had simply informed him that Baquedano went to Castile on some *converso* business and that he had also traveled to Aragon for the same reason. Salton claimed further that he knew nothing of *conversos* giving money to Baquedano generally or for the specific purpose of supporting Quintanilla. Salton did say that Quintanilla told him that he received "raçiones" from Baquedano but Salton was not apprised of the motive.[70]

In response to other questions, Salton testified that he did not hear directly from Quintanilla that he was bribed to leave the city but did learn of it from others with whom Quintanilla had relations. The last question Salton was requested to answer was had he written a letter against Baquedano, to which he replied in the negative.[71]

These testimonies contain all the extant information about the case. They clearly show how the Inquisition gained influence in

Navarre by implanting fear among the Tudelans, especially the
New Christians, and through its capacity to pressure Tudelan officials to investigate any actions against it. Although this inquest was
not an official inquisitorial inquiry, it may have been prompted and
guided by the Inquisition. According to the agreement of 1488 between Tudela and Ferdinand and Isabella, the Inquisition had the
power to investigate matters pertaining to its own cases beyond its
territorial jurisdiction in Castile and Aragon.

From the depositions, it appears that Baquedano, a prominent
churchman who may or may not have been a New Christian, was
accused of judaizing, a charge that probably had already been leveled against him by the Castilian and Aragonese Inquisition. Such
activities by a Tudelan churchman are not surprising, given the
number of New Christians occupying high ecclesiastical positions
in Tudela.

The testimonies also afford a glimpse into the ways some Navarrese tried to influence the Inquisition, for example, by traveling to
the royal court in Castile. They also illumine the division among
Tudelans about how to handle the Inquisition and its officials.
Jews and *conversos* also consulted together about the threat of
the Castilian-Aragonese tribunals.

Even though the Inquisition was not officially established in
Navarre until the next century, when openly professing Jews no
longer resided in the kingdom, the effects of the tribunals were already felt by the Navarrese people during the 1480s. The citizens
of Tudela, at first resistant, finally had to bend the knee to an
increasingly stronger Inquisition. The influence of the neighboring
Iberian kingdoms once again would affect the policies of Tudela
and all of Navarre as the exiled Jews of 1492 sought to find a haven
for themselves and their families.

5. Castilian and Aragonese Jewish Exiles in Navarre

On 31 March 1492 in the city of Granada, Ferdinand and Isabella signed the edict that expelled all professing Jews from the kingdoms of Aragon and Castile. These Jews, most Jewish observers who were their contemporaries noted, traveled mainly to Portugal and the various countries bordering the Mediterranean. Only two of them, however, recorded that the Jewish émigrés also sought refuge in the kingdom of Navarre. Don Isaac Abravanel, the illustrious rabbi and statesman, who was one of the many exiles, tersely noted that some Jews fled to nearby Navarre.[1] The sixteenth-century chronicler Yosef ha-Kohen explained more fully that because "the king of Navarre did not expel them from his country . . . many of the Jews that were in Aragon went there to settle."[2] Among Christian contemporaries of Ferdinand and Isabella, the country priest Andres Bernáldez was alone in remarking that Jews living in Castile-Aragon near the Navarrese frontier crossed into the Pyrenean kingdom.[3] Fortunately, Hebrew and Spanish literary works are not the only sources for this chapter in Navarrese Jewish history.

A document drawn from the municipal archives of Tudela first brought to light a century ago the existence of native opposition to the immigration of these Castilian and Aragonese Jewish refugees. It tells us that on 8 June 1492, the village council officials (*alcalde, justiçia,* and *jurados*) of Tafalla wrote to their counterparts in the city of Tudela. The Tafallans were responding to a previous missive sent by the Tudelans that apparently had warned of the expected arrival of Castilian Jews in Navarre and suggested that a deputation be sent to the Navarrese monarchs. The leaders of Tafalla expressed their gratitude for the information and agreed to the call for a delegation to the sovereigns, arguing that the royal action to admit the Jews was contrary both to religious principles and to the well-being of the kingdom. They affirmed that they would not allow any Jews to enter their village until negotiations with the royal couple were completed. On that very morning (8

June 1492) they wrote, they had expelled to beyond the Tafalla
town limits Jews who had entered secretly during the night. The
Tafallans closed by asking the officials of Tudela to keep them
apprised of all developments so that a uniform opposition could
be maintained.[4]

Historians of medieval Iberian Jewry pondered this letter and
speculated on the events that may have led to its composition.
Meyer Kayserling, without citing any sources, claimed that Jews
from Saragossa, Burgos, and other cities and towns close to the
Navarrese frontier had petitioned the Tudelan city council for permission to enter the city.[5] There is, however, no indication in
Tafalla's response that the Tudelan officials had been acting on a
specific request by Castilian or Aragonese Jews. More likely, Jews
had been arriving in Navarre since their receipt of the edict of
Ferdinand and Isabella, as evidenced by the Tafallans' remark that
some Jews surreptitiously had entered their villa the night of June
7–8.[6] The Jews obviously had known that their entrance was either
against the law or that they would not be received positively, and
hence had chosen to infiltrate Tafalla under the cover of darkness.

Although it appears from the letter that the policy of the
monarchs was to allow the Jews to cross the frontier, there is no
evidence that the Navarrese royal couple had issued a formal decree.[7] E. H. Lindo, however, in his *History of the Jews of Spain and
Portugal*,[8] cited a "Ms. Hist. de Estella," which related that the
king, (Juan de) Labrit, and his queen, Leonora, had addressed a
letter on June 8 to the magistrate, judge, and commander of Estella
ordering "that if any Jews of those expelled from Castile and Aragon, by order of Ferdinand and Isabella, should come to that city,
they should afford them a safe transit and every possible accommo-
dation because they are a docile people, that can easily be brought
to reason." Lindo added that since the sovereigns were afraid that
the Jews of Estella might be ill treated as they had been "exactly a
century before," they warned the officials of punitive measures if
the Jews were not protected.

Kayserling doubted a century ago that the Navarrese rulers
would write a letter of this kind to Estella and questioned the existence of the "Ms. Hist. de Estella." He argued that the dating of
the letter to Estella on June 8, the same day as the Tafalla–Tudela
communication, was suspect. He also noted parenthetically that
Catalina, not Leonora, was the wife of Juan de Labrit.[9] Besides the

points raised by Kayserling, it should be noted that none of the Navarrese chroniclers or historians quoted this source in their writings, casting a dark shadow on the validity of Lindo's reference.

Kayserling assumed that although the Tafallan letter expressed the opinions of Tudela and Tafalla, all the Navarrese cities were in accordance with their wishes. It was therefore unlikely that the royal government would have granted permission for Jews to cross the border. Amador de los Ríos contended that with the opposition of all the cities and villages, the Jews surely were not able to enter the kingdom without difficulty. Quoting the Hebrew chroniclers, the two authors concurred that Jews did arrive in Navarre.[10]

A most unlikely source sheds a fascinating light on the attempt of Jews of Castile and Aragon to seek refuge in Navarre and on the methods employed to either facilitate or prevent their entry. The first volume of the *Libro de cuentas de propios* spans the years 1480 to 1521 and briefly reports the annual receipts and expenses of the city of Tudela. Like the letter of Tafalla to Tudela, it can be found in the Tudelan municipal archives.

Turning to the report of the year 1492 and to the section on expenses, we find an expenditure of one pound fourteen shillings noted in the entry of May 25. This money had been authorized by the Tudelan *jurados* to be remitted to a courier who was on his way to Estella to meet with the governor of the kingdom and to certain messengers who departed earlier and had already arrived there. The keeper of the records added to the report of this expenditure the reason for the missions: "a causa de la venida de los Judios," because of the arrival of the Jews.[11]

The decree of expulsion was not made public until May 1;[12] evidently Tudela was reacting swiftly to prevent an influx of Jewish refugees. Although Tudelan officials ordered this payment on May 25, it is also noted that when the Tudelan courier arrived in Estella, the other messengers from Tudela were already there, presumably to influence the governor to forbid the Jews' entry.[13] By mid-May, it is certain, Tudela was attempting to deal with the arrival of the immigrants.

It can well be assumed that Tudela's strategy was to appeal first to the royal authorities. Because the monarchs were absent from the kingdom (they were staying in their French dominions), the Tudelans appealed to the governor, Gabriel de Avenas, the royal representative in Navarre. The messengers sent earlier obviously had not been entirely successful, necessitating this new effort. It is not known, though, whether the courier was carrying relevant documents, a bribe, or only a letter.

The failure of these attempts is evidenced by the next relevant entry in the expense sheets. A week later (on June 2), there was a payment of four pounds ten shillings ordered by the *jurados* to yet another courier, who carried letters to Sangüesa, Estella, Pamplona, Olite, and Tafalla. Again, the reason was stated simply: "because of the Jews."[14] Having been rebuffed by Gabriel, as its next step, Tudela contacted the five major population centers of the kingdom to convince them not to let the Jews enter their jurisdictions.

It is safe to assert that this was the letter that Tafalla acknowledged having received from Tudela in the reply we have just analyzed. The Tafallan officials were concerned with the same problem that occupied their correspondents from Tudela, and so they answered the Tudelan letter promptly (on June 8). It is not certain if the other four recipients answered, but their attitude can be inferred from the next entry in the Tudelan account books. On June 9, Tudela dispatched another courier to carry letters to Estella, Sangüesa, and Pamplona, asking that their representatives come to Olite to consider whether "to send certain messengers to the monarchs on account of the Jews."[15] It is immediately worth noting that Tafalla was not sent this message.[16] This makes sense inasmuch as the Tafallan officials were in accordance with Tudela's position on the refugees and had concurred with the strategy of sending a delegation to the Navarrese monarchs. That, obviously, was not the case with Pamplona, Estella, or Sangüesa.

Tudela could not afford to waste any time. Jews had already begun entering Navarre, and it was less than two months before they would be barred from residing in Castile and Aragon. Something had to be done before the July 31 deadline. City officials immediately sent two representatives to the proposed Olite meeting: Payments were made on June 16 to Pedro Gómez and Martín de Mezquita, who had gone to Olite "because of the messengers that were to travel to the monarchs because of the arrival of the Jews." Pedro Gómez returned after four days, which means that he arrived in Olite no later than June 12, three days after the call for the assembly had been issued.[17]

Gómez and de Mezquita were not mere couriers[18] but deputies of the Tudelan officials entrusted with the task of securing the acceptance of Tudela's decision to send a delegation to the monarchs and were presumably meant to influence the composition of the group and, of course, its aims. While there is no hard evidence that indicates which, if any, of the invited cities sent delegates to Olite and no evidence that the meeting took place, it is known that Pedro Gómez stayed in Olite for four days and that Mezquita remained even later "until he would receive an answer from the city."[19] This cryptic remark is problematic, to which particular city does this reference pertain? Did Pedro Gómez return with questions directed to the Tudelan officials, for whose answer Mezquita was waiting? Or was Mezquita expecting a decision from the city of Olite? A later entry informs the reader that de Mezquita stayed through July 24. Apparently, enough was happening to keep him from returning to his native city, which was only a few hours away.

In the meantime, Tudela was not idle. On June 23, two pounds was remitted to someone referred to as Mastre Jayme for "having brought articles of the sentence that the Castilian monarchs and the Prior de Santa Cruz had given in reference to the Jews." Mastre Jayme had been sent by the Tudelan *jurados,* presumably to Castile or Aragon, to procure a copy of the expulsion decree.[20] What Tudela planned to do with this document is evident from the very next entry in the *Libro de cuentas de propios,* which states that "on account of the arrival of the Jews," Martín de Mezquita and Pascual de Magallon were sent on June 24 as messengers to the Navarrese royal couple in Pau, their seat in their French dominion of Bearne.[21] There is no doubt that these two distinguished messengers[22] traveled to Johan and Catalina in Pau with the copy of the expulsion order in hand.

No evidence exists that the delegation to Bearne received the blessing of a consensus reached in Olite. What is known is that Mezquita waited in the former Navarrese capital for Magallon to arrive, and then traveled with him to see the Navarrese monarchs. Did Magallon bring a message from Tudela, and did that cause a last-minute breakthrough? Or did Mezquita stay in Olite until the last moment, hoping for a positive response from the gathered envoys?[23]

The ambassadors to Pau returned to Tudela on July 14, twenty-one days after they had set forth.[24] If it took a week for travel to and from Bearne (a conservative estimate), they spent fourteen days at the royal court. Nothing is known about the visit. We do not know whether they spent two weeks in constant discussions with the monarchs or if they had to wait long for an audience. Nor is there any information as to what Magallon and Mezquita, representing the Tudelan officials, planned to do with the Castilian-Aragonese expulsion decree. They may have wanted to inform Johan and Catalina about the root cause of the influx of refugees, but had the monarchs not been aware of this notoriously bold action, which had been public since the end of April? Could the ambassadors have sought to impress upon the young rulers that these Castilian and Aragonese Jews, unwanted by their own rulers, Ferdinand and Isabella, should perforce be denied admission to Navarre? Or, the most intriguing conjecture, were they attempting to convince the royal authorities to expel all the Jews from Navarre as was done in Castile and Aragon, using the expulsion decree as legal precedent?[25]

Later evidence makes it clear that Jews did enter Navarre and thus that the Tudelan embassy to Bearne was unsuccessful in keeping out the refugees. However, in the Tafalla–Tudela communication of June 8, the Tafallans had agreed not to let in any Jews until the negotiations with the monarchs were completed. This may indicate that the municipal officials were ultimately willing to admit the exiles in return for some recompense from the royal authorities. If so, the discussions on recompense may have succeeded. Surely, however, this was not the primary objective of the delegation. Tudela had expended much effort and expense on the refugee issue. The mission to Bearne alone cost seventy-five pounds—including thirty florins to Mezquita, and twenty to Magallon—at the rate of about one florin a day per messenger. Additionally, had Tudela only wished to receive compensation from the monarchs, all the Navarrese cities might have joined them in this enterprise.

Although the embassy had returned to Tudela from Bearne on July 14, the news that the Jews would be allowed to continue crossing the border and to settle in Navarre was not yet common knowledge. In a document preserved in the notarial archives of Tudela, the sense of insecurity experienced by a newly arrived Jewish refugee is conveyed, along with an idea of how he dealt with the apparent fragility of his situation: On July 15, in the southern Na-

varrese town of Cascante near the Castilian border, Bonafox Co-
stantos, formerly of Soria, rented some houses in the village from
a local inhabitant, Johan Enrríquez de la Carra. The rental for one
year was seventeen florins, of which Constantos paid one-third immediately. The agreement contained this remarkable clause: ". . . if
the Jews leave, what is paid should remain paid. And if the Jews
do not leave until the one-third term had passed and then leave before the completion of said year, they should be charged according
to a prorated schedule for the time they were there."[26]

Both the immigrant Jew (Constantos) and the Christian (de la
Carra) were clearly unaware of the outcome of the Tudelan mission
to Pau. Because neither could be sure whether the exiles would
be allowed to stay in Navarre, they struck a deal that accommodated both parties. Constantos was to pay immediately one-third
of the yearly rental and receive no refund if he were to have to leave
Navarre before four months had elapsed. If he remained longer
than that, for a period of up to one year, he would only pay for
the precise amount of time that he occupied de la Carra's houses.
No details about what would obtain after the year was over were
specified; at the time no one, Jew or Christian, could hazard a
guess.

The Tudelan officials, who by July 15 had failed to convince the
governor, their counterparts in other major cities, and the monarchs to stem the entry of Jewish refugees into Navarre, must have
resigned themselves to let the Jews stream across the borders. The
August 10 entry of the *Libro de cuentas de propios* contains the
first reference in that source to the refugee issue since the failed
Bearne embassy. Ten days after all professing Jews had left Aragon and Castile, the *jurados* of Tudela sent Pedro Gómez to Olite
"on account of the Jews."[27] By this time, the messengers to Bearne
surely had reported to any and all of the interested parties on the
events at Pau. There may, however, have been necessary need to
consult on what should be the policy on the official treatment of
the newcomers. It is not known who attended this meeting.

The final chapter on Tudela's efforts during those fateful months
of 1492 was written in the receipts section of the *Libro de cuentas
de propios*: "Received from the foreign Jews because they have
arrived, two hundred pounds."[28] Not only had Tudela's officials
stopped opposing the Jews' entry into the kingdom, they acknowl-

edged the refugees' presence in their city and imposed on them a
fee of two hundred pounds, which was twice the amount the officials had spent in attempting to keep them out.

José Yanguas y Miranda, the nineteenth-century Navarrese archivist and historian, interpreted Tudela's activity in attempting to
prevent the refugees from crossing the borders of Navarre as an indication of the great rise of religious intolerance in the Pyrenean
kingdom.[29] Amador de los Ríos explained Tudela's actions differently, hypothesizing that this southern Navarrese city was fearful
of the reaction of Ferdinand of Aragon should the Jews he had expelled have come to live in its country. Tudela therefore turned
to Tafalla and to the other cities for help.[30] Kayserling, for his
part did not speculate on the motives of Tudela, and instead
dwelled on the response of Tafalla. He described the Tafallans as
being particularly noted for their intense hatred of the Jews, citing
as proof the resolution of the Cortes held in Tafalla in 1482, which
had ordered that Jews not leave the *juderías* on Christian holidays
nor stroll through the streets among Christians until the mass had
been said.[31]

Although the *Libro de cuentas de propios* clarified both Tudela's
activities and the responses of the cities and authorities of the kingdom, it does not explain the motives of any of the participants in
the drama. These documents show only that for a few months, Tudela actively sought to achieve its goal through many diplomatic
maneuvers, that it was taken as a serious issue, and that a sense of
urgency characterized the Tudelans' response.

The one source that explains why the Jewish refugees should be
kept out of Navarre is the letter of June 8 from Tafalla to Tudela.
The Tafallan officials, when they agreed to Tudela's suggestion to
send an embassy to the monarchs, stated to the royal couple the
reasons for excluding the Jews as formulated by Tudela: That to
let in the expelled Jews was contrary to the service of God and of
the monarchs and that it would lead to the ruin of the polities (*republiquas*) of the kingdom. The leaders of Tafalla wrote that they
were in accord with the arguments (unfortunately not listed) that
were advanced as proof of these contentions. They added that other
reasons could have been added; that it was "without doubt a mys-
tery of God and a curse" that the refugees should be welcomed.

Had the original Tudelan letter survived to our time, we could read the "proofs" it adduced that the refugees would be a harmful influence. Nevertheless, the overall argument is clear: The Jews' entry would be sacrilegious and cause political damage. Tafalla, for its part, ratified these arguments by reiterating the religious issue and asserting that the admission of the Jews would cause damnation.

The religious arguments raised by Tudela and Tafalla jibe very well with the degree of anti-Judaism that existed in the kingdom of Navarre and, especially, in Castile and Aragon. Yanguas was correct: The spirit of religious intolerance and hatred of the Jews had become part of the fabric of Navarrese society. It is mistaken to argue, as Kayserling did, that the decision of the Cortes of Tafalla reflected anti-Jewish attitudes uniquely belonging to the Tafallans. At meetings of the Cortes in the 1480s and 1490s, statutes of anti-Jewish content were issued frequently. Other extant documents from this period also point up similar tendencies.[32]

What of the reasons given by Tudela, namely, that the Jews' entry would be contrary to the service of the monarchs and would cause the ruin of the *republiquas* of the kingdom? The admission of the exiles was clearly not solely a religious issue. As Amador de los Ríos suggested, Tudela may well have feared the response of the Catholic Monarchs (of Ferdinand, especially) as well as the possible adverse effect on itself and the kingdom. Although the Tudelans had resisted strenuously Ferdinand's efforts in the 1480s to force the Inquisition on the citizens of Navarre, by 1488, owing to the capitulations of the Tudelans and other Navarrese, the Inquisition—although never accepted formally—no longer encountered any obstacles in pursuing its operations in the Pyrenean kingdom. For Tudela, admitting the Inquisition meant forfeiting a large measure of internal jurisdiction over its citizens, yet it surely would lose even more of its authority if Ferdinand were to enact any reprisals because of the refugees.[33]

Indeed, in May 1492, Navarre was slowly gravitating into the orbit of Castile-Aragon; it was becoming, in fact, the quasi protectorate of these powerful kingdoms. Although the precise state of affairs between Navarre and its Iberian neighbors in the subsequent months of June and July cannot be pinpointed, it is not surprising that Tudela and Tafalla were concerned to avoid giving offense to the Catholic Monarchs.[34]

Why, then, did the other cities not display the same religio-political concerns as those expressed by Tudela and Tafalla? Only conjectures can be offered, inasmuch as the extant documentation sheds no light on the question.

Perhaps the controversy over the entry of the immigrants was an extension of the ongoing battle between the Beaumonteses and the Agramonteses, the two parties in the Navarrese civil war. Tudela and Tafalla were associated with the Agramontes side, and it is likely that the leader of the Beaumonteses, Luis, conde de Lerín, did let some Jewish refugees settle on his lands. The validity of this theory is difficult to determine, owing to the constantly shifting political alignments of the time. How Estella and other of the Navarrese polities were aligned at this time is difficult to establish. Further confounding this hypothesis is that Ferdinand and Isabella—who were surely no lovers of Jewish immigration into Navarre—backed the Beaumonteses in the civil war, whereas Tudela and its party generally favored the Navarrese rulers.[35]

The reluctance of the other cities to join Tudela in its campaign to bar Jews from entering may have resulted in part from disagreements with Tudela's strategy or from resistance to Tudela's leading role in the diplomacy. Or perhaps Tudela was more urgently concerned about the prospective flood of Jewish immigrants because it already was a major center for Jews, and, situated as it was on the main land and water routes into Navarre, it faced the largest influx of immigrants. It is also possible that the economies of the other cities could support the new arrivals more easily than could Tudela and Tafalla.[36]

Problems also arise in attempting to explain the apparent willingness of the Navarrese royal couple to allow the entrance of Jews into Navarre. That they were aware of their political dependence on the Catholic Monarchs and the risk entailed in admitting the Jews was clear; could they have been seeking a bargaining chip in future negotiations with Ferdinand and Isabella? Although it is true that Johan and Catalina had enacted anti-Jewish legislation, they may have reasoned that the economic benefit to the kingdom, especially in increased tax revenues, would be very advantageous. Historical precedent was on their side. Jews had been crossing the frontiers of Navarre in both directions since the thirteenth century. In the mid-fourteenth century, for example, Queen Juana had offered many economic and political benefits to the Jews who fled from Castile during the civil war. In 1391 and at other times during persecutions in Castile and Aragon, Jews had been welcomed in Navarre. The same benefits the refugees had brought to the kingdom in times past may have helped to secure their entry in the summer of 1492.[37]

One final question remains—how to assess the role of the silent figures in this historical drama, whose position is undocumented yet whose wishes must have been carefully considered? It is hard to imagine that Ferdinand and Isabella, who expelled their kingdom's Jews, would have been pleased to see them accepted in a neighboring kingdom. They could have exerted pressure on the Navarrese monarchs, whose political dependence they manipulated for their own ends. Their troops were often poised at the Navarrese borders during this period to aid their interests in the ongoing civil war. Ferdinand and Isabella had received concessions from the queen mother Magdalena, both in Granada in May and in Saragossa in August; they could have easily advanced their position. They seemingly did not force the issue; we remember that Tudela had to send for a copy of the expulsion decree.

Ferdinand's drive to extend inquisitorial control into Navarre reflected his preoccupation with "religious" matters beyond his actual frontiers. He would have preferred that the Jews converted instead of leaving the kingdom: On 30 July 1493, Ferdinand and Isabella issued a call for Jews who had gone to Portugal and Navarre to convert to Christianity, assuring those who did that they could return. They may, however, have been content for the time being to have the expelled Jews close by in case any business transactions had to be completed.[38]

It is difficult to determine from where in the Spanish dominions of Ferdinand and Isabella most of the refugees emigrated. Yosef ha-Kohen, alone among the sixteenth-century Hebrew authors in providing such information, wrote that "many Jews of Aragon came to settle" in Navarre.[39] The Spanish chronicler Bernáldez, treating only the Jews of Castile, mentioned that the Jews who had entered Navarre were those who had lived near its frontier.[40] The published letter of Tafalla to Tudela, we recall, warned that the Jews who were expected were emigrating from Castile.

When Yosef ha-Kohen in his *Emek ha-Bakha* cited Aragon as the source for the Jews who entered Navarre, was he simply reflecting the experience of his own family, who had traveled from Ara-

gon to Navarre and later on to Provence? The Tafallan leaders who
mentioned the Castilian refugees, could have been simply using a
shorthand term for all the Jews affected by the edict of expulsion.
Bernáldez in his chronicle wrote at length about how the Jews of
Castile entered Portugal through various border towns and may
have assumed that those areas of Aragon and Castile that served
as the conduits for the expelled Jews entering Navarre were also
their places of origin.

Although the accuracy of Bernáldez on this point may be
doubted, his surmise was what the logic of the situation demanded.
Just as the Jews near the Portuguese border surely availed themselves of the opportunity of crossing that frontier, so too must
have many of the Jews of both Castile and Aragon who lived near
Navarre. Indeed, the few documents involving the émigrés that
mention their place of origin support this contention. All of these
immigrants, who came to reside in the district of Tudela, had lived
less than 150 kilometers away in Castile and Aragon. The majority
came from frontier villages in both kingdoms and from the city of
Saragossa.[41] The land routes that existed during this period provided relatively easy access into Navarre from both its Iberian
neighbors, and the major water route, the Ebro river, wound its
way from Castile along the border with Navarre through Tudela
into Aragon.

Whatever the origins of these refugees, Lindo, Kayserling,
Graetz, and, finally, Baron, maintained that twelve thousand Jews
entered the Pyrenean kingdom.[42] Unfortunately, these writers did
not cite sources. Of the chroniclers, only Bernáldez dealt with the
number of émigrés, and he had written that "two thousand souls"
fled to Navarre.[43] The more recent historians may have considered
this number to represent heads of families and multiplied by six to
arrive at the figure of twelve thousand individuals. They also may
have confused *dos mil* (2,000) with *doce mil* (12,000). It is difficult
to imagine, however, that once that mistake was made, the others
would have accepted this figure uncritically.[44]

Kayserling, Graetz, and Baron further contended that a propor-
tionally large percentage of the immigrants settled in the county
(*condado*) of Lerín. These writers cited as proof the 1495 population statistics for various towns within this county, quoted by
Yanguas. Amador de los Ríos, although somewhat skeptical of the

figure of twelve thousand, admitted that the Navarrese archives from which Yanguas drew his information tended to support this contention.[45]

The document that was said to reflect the settling of large numbers of Jewish refugees within the *condado* de Lerín is extant in a copy made on 18 November 1591 from the original, then located in the royal archives in Simancas. It was a 1495 report detailing the villages and other lands owned by the conde of Lerín, as well as the rents and taxes he collected in his own territory and in which the Navarrese monarchs had rights of ownership. This account had been ordered by Ferdinand and Isabella in order to give him equivalent properties in the newly conquered kingdom of Granada and elsewhere and thereby to remove him from Navarrese politics.[46]

The report mentioned five places in the county where the Jews were listed as inhabitants. The population of these were as follows: The village of Lerín had 61 Jews and 137 Christian *vecinos* (inhabitants); Larraga contained one Jew and 62 Christians; Mendabia, 3 Jews and 82 Christians; Andosilla, 11 Jews and 66 Christians; and the village of Sant Adrian registered one Jew and 28 Christians. Although these numbers were said to describe the total population of these villas, most probably they took into account only the tax- or rent-paying members. Nevertheless, the total number of Jews was seventy-seven, hardly a large figure. It was not indicated anywhere that these seventy-seven Jews arrived after 1492. Indeed, the majority of villages mentioned contained no Jewish taxpayers. The statements of Jewish and Spanish historians that there were twelve thousand émigrés and that most of them settled in and around Lerín both appear to have no support.[47]

There are other documents that yield some clues to the number of Jewish refugees elsewhere in the kingdom. In the *Libro de cuentas de propios* of Tudela of the year 1484, both the *aljama* of the Jews and the *aljama* of the Muslims paid a tax that was calculated according to the number of *casas* (houses) contained within their respective communities. The Jews registered ninety houses, and the Muslims ninety-five.[48] In 1490, the Jews and Muslims are listed as paying another tax that was assessed per *casa*. The tax collector listed 101 taxpayers for the *aljama* of the Jews and 112 for that of the Muslims.[49] If it is safe to assume that the same methods were used to count the houses, between the years 1484 and 1490, both communities registered increases in the number of dwellings liable to taxation.

In 1494, the treasurer of Navarre, Johan de Bosquet, was charged by the Navarrese monarchs to collect from all the Jews of the kingdom a tax of two pounds per hearth (*fuego*). In his accounts, he listed the considerable figure of one hundred and sixty Jewish *fuegos* in the city of Tudela. Charged to collect the tax from the Muslims as well, Bosquet recorded ninety-five hearths in Tudela for the year 1495.[50]

Before arriving at any conclusions on the change in population,[51] the term *casa*, as used in the *Libro de cuentas de propios*, and the term *fuego*, as used in the account of the Navarrese royal treasurer, must be examined. Whether the two terms can be considered equivalent is problematic.[52] It is clear, however, that in 1484 the number of Muslim *fuegos* equalled the number of *casas*. Arguing that there are therefore marked similarities between the two terms in this time period, a remarkable seventy-eight percent increase of the Jewish population liable to taxation can be noted in the city of Tudela from 1484 to 1494, and a sixty-six percent increase during the four years between 1490 and 1494.

Although only for Tudela do we have figures for the years approaching and following 1492, there are other number in Bosquet's account that must be examined. There was an incomplete "census" in 1353 and 1366 but no population statistics for Jews for most cities and villages are available for subsequent years.[53] That there was an increase in population because of the arrival of the refugees can therefore be advanced only with caution.

The number of *fuegos* in the Jewish *aljamas* of both Pamplona and Estella was similar in the 1366 tabulation and again in 1494. In 1366, Estella and Pamplona both had eighty-five hearths, and in 1494 Pamplona registered fifty-three and Estella fifty-two. A different picture emerges when one looks at cities and villas close to the borders of Castile and Aragon. Twenty-five Jewish *fuegos* are registered for Sangüesa in 1366, whereas fifty-seven are recorded in 1494. More striking are the figures for three southern border towns in the district of Tudela. There were three *fuegos* of Jews in Cortes in 1353, twenty-four in Cascante, and nineteen in Corella, and by 1494 the numbers had risen appreciably—to forty, fifty, and sixty hearths, respectively. While changes in population—especially over a period of a hundred years—are the result of myriad factors, the probability is that the 1492 influx of émigrés contributed to swelling these figures.[54]

The argument is strengthened if the figures in these years for the *aljamas* of the Muslims are examined. In the areas of Tudela where the Muslims resided, only six localities are mentioned in the 1494 listing. Comparing the figures given in the 1494 list with those for 1353 and 1366 (even using the 1366 cipher for Ablitas, which was lower than in 1353), the population evidently declined from 162 hearths to 143. Two of the six areas of Muslim residence increased in population: Tudela from 79 to 95; and Murchante, from 10 to 20. It is not clear why the other localities listed in 1355 and 1366 as areas of Muslim habitation were not recorded in 1494. Nor are any data available relating to Corella, Cascante, and Cortes for 1494. Still, given the data we have, we have to suppose that the Muslim population decreased, whereas the population of Jews rose over the same period.[55]

Other tax records in the *Libro de cuentas de propios* provide information on how much native Jews, émigrés, and Muslims paid for the same taxes during the years 1492 to 1498 in Tudela. No pattern emerges that would seem to reflect the proportion of the immigrant Jews to the natives or to the Muslims. In 1493, for example, the Muslims rendered ten pounds, the native Jews thirteen, and the émigrés fifteen pounds for the *franqueza del almody*.[56] Yet in the same year, whereas the Muslims paid three hundred pounds of the two-thousand pound tax levied on the city of Tudela, both the immigrant Jews collectively and the native Jews collectively remitted only one hundred and fifty apiece.[57] When money was being raised in 1495 for the burial of Princess Magdalena, the émigrés paid twenty-two pounds ten shillings; their indigenous co-religionists, twenty pounds; and the Muslims, thirty-seven pounds ten shillings.[58] Because it is not known how these taxes were assessed, however, we cannot make any inferences as to the population of the immigrants.

Another illustration of the difficulties of extracting population information from tax-related documentation can be found in an entry dated 6 December 1494 in the register of the royal chancellery. Here is to be found a record of an order to either the royal treasurer or to Mastre Ossua (the *receptor* of the Jews) to collect the tax called the *pecha* owed by both the native and immigrant

Jewish populations. The indigenous Jews had been assessed eight
pounds per *casa,* whereas the émigrés were to pay collectively the
sum of 750 pounds and "otras tantas" (other such amounts).[59] If
the immigrants and the natives were assessed at an equal per-*casa*
rate for this tax, it could be determined by simple calculation that
there were approximately ninety-four *casas* of immigrants in the
areas under royal control. If that were so, however, why would not
the same assessment be clearly stated for both groups? Could the
intention have been to assess the émigrés as the natives, except that
the immigrant *casas* were hard to tally? However, in the above-
cited tax of 1494 of two pounds per hearth, it appeared that the
refugees' hearths were included in the tabulations.

The population of the Jews, both immigrants and natives, in fact
was not known to the satisfaction of the royal treasury. In another
entry in the register of the royal chancellery on 28 January 1495,
not long after the order of 6 December 1494, the monarchs again
issued a directive to Mastre Ossua, demanding an account of the
casas of the "naturales y estrangeros de todo el Regno," presumably so that the tax revenues would reflect the correct number
of Jews.[60] Mastre Ossua's report unfortunately, is nowhere to be
found.

Apart from scattered references in other sources to individual
émigrés, this seems to be all the evidence we can find on the size
of the immigrant population.[61] To calculate medieval population
figures is a difficult enough task; to uncover the number of refugees,
whose existence as a group lasted only six years, borders on the
impossible. The documentation adduced so far is of course biased
by the provenance of the sources. What has remained in archival
collections are mainly royal materials or those of municipalities under the rule of the Navarrese monarchs. There are indications that
the Jewish émigrés settled in other places in Navarre besides the
royal domains. No sources are extant from these places, however.[62]

Before closing this discussion, it must be determined whether the
number of Jews who immigrated into Navarre can be deduced from
what is known about the total number of Castilian and Aragonese
refugees and the numbers of the Jewish émigrés that entered other
countries.

The prevailing opinion of historians is that it is impossible, based
on current available evidence, to determine the number of Jews
who chose to emigrate from the Spanish dominions of Ferdinand

and Isabella. The fifteenth-century chronicler Bernáldez did not employ precise terminology; and extrapolations of population from tax levies generally entail too many problems to be very useful.[63] Baer's estimate of between 150,000 and 175,000 émigrés followed the assertion by Bernáldez; and Suárez Fernández' suggestion that there were approximately fifteen thousand Jewish families (with an average of six members per family) employed the latter method utilizing tax levies as a source.[64]

In fact, however, there is reason to compare the number of Jews who entered Portugal with the number of Jews who crossed into Navarre. These countries were undoubtedly attractive to Jewish émigrés because they were not far from their former residences and the promise they offered of a relatively safe journey; their inhabitants were socially and linguistically similar to the inhabitants of Castile and Aragon; there was the possibility of there being family connections; and they were close enough to enable the emigrants to keep up with business interests left behind. Yet there were differences between these two kingdoms, ranging from intangibles, such as which of them was perceived as a more attractive place to live and which was perceived as more hospitable to Jews, to the concrete realities of the nature of the roads into Portugal and Navarre, the size of the tax burden entrants would encounter on entering one country or the other and then on taking up residence; and last but surely not least, the ease with which they expected they could leave their new home if they so wished.

Although Portuguese and Jewish writers have declared that 120,000 Jews (the majority of them refugees) crossed the Castilian border into Portugal, this figure is problematical in ways similar to those described above. Recently, however, a study by Maria José Pimenta Ferro Tavares based on research in the Portuguese archives was published, and it helps shed light on the actual number of immigrants. Pimenta Ferro argues that approximately 23,320 refugees entered Portugal.[65]

If figures for general population and land area at the beginning of the sixteenth century as well are consulted, it can be estimated that Navarre had twelve and a half percent of the population of Portugal and thirteen and a half percent of its area. Accepting the figure of twenty-three thousand–plus Jewish émigrés in Portugal, then, gives us a figure of about seventeen hundred to eighteen hundred for Navarre, which accords with the figure of two thousand mentioned earlier. Yet it must be admitted that these estimates are based on the most tenuous of assumptions, namely, that relative land mass and population density were good gauges of the migration pattern of the refugees. Instead, the relative merits of settling in Navarre and Portugal as perceived by the refugees, which cannot be quantified, were surely the major considerations in their choice of refuge.[66]

In the foregoing discussion it has been shown that the number of Jews who crossed the frontiers of Navarre during the summer of 1492 cannot be truly determined. Kayserling, while contending that twelve thousand Jews entered the Pyrenean kingdom, declared that only a few of them settled there.[67] Yosef ha-Kohen, in describing his family's wanderings from Aragon through Navarre, wrote that they left the next year (1493) for Provence. According to Yosef, Ferdinand allowed erstwhile Aragonese Jews to travel through their former homeland by ships, presumably down the Ebro river to the Mediterranean, where they would embark for their new homes.[68]

A document in the Archivo de la Corona de Aragón in Barcelona bears out Yosef's report. On 9 March 1493, almost one year after the probable entry of Yosef's family into Navarre, Ferdinand granted safe passage to the expelled Aragonese Jews who had gained refuge there to pass through his kingdom and embark from its ports. Consistent with Yosef's report, this document states that the Jews had first asked Ferdinand's permission.[69]

Although Suárez Fernández argued on the basis of this source that all the Aragonese Jews who fled to Navarre then left the country,[70] this in fact is nowhere implied in the document. There is no indication how many Jews were expected to take—or actually took—advantage of this offer. Although Ferdinand's edict referred directly only to Jews who left Aragon, it is not conclusive that this was to the exclusion of those from Castile or even of those who were Navarrese natives.

The exit procedures were precisely detailed. The Jews were to leave Navarre for Mallén, a village just beyond the border with Aragon on the Tudela–Saragossa road. They could remain there for thirty days in preparation for the journey down the Ebro to the Mediterranean ports. In Mallén, they were to arrange transportation and purchase provisions; local Christian merchants were warned against price gouging. While in the village, each Jew, except very young children, had to pay two *ducados* to the treasurer of Aragon or to his agent, Vicente de Bordalba. In return, the Jews received a license to travel down the Ebro River.

Luis Díez and Miguel de Gotor were placed in charge of the flotilla of ships carrying the émigrés and were ordered to help and protect them. In payment, Díez and Gotor had the right to use the Jews' property for their own needs and purposes during the trip. The Jews were expressly permitted to take all their possessions, including gold, silver, animals, and clothing, and were guaranteed that their property could not be appropriated for reasons of debt and the like. The émigrés were not to be harmed or even inconvenienced during the journey; tolls were to be charged them at the same rate as that exacted from others using the river. If the Jews' ships were to run aground, or were the travelers to encounter other problems, they were to be helped by the local inhabitants and billed according to accepted prices for labor and provisions. The Jews had twenty days to complete the actual journey and leave the kingdom. During that time, they were allowed to stay overnight on the banks of the Ebro, so long as they did not camp near populated areas.

This scenario took much planning and was probably the result of negotiations between the Jews and Ferdinand. The king was aware that the expulsion edict had to be temporarily suspended, but there was much to be gained. In addition to the bribe the Jews surely had given him, he received an exit fee of two *ducados* per capita. Although the émigrés were allowed to transport all their goods, including gold and silver, they would have to spend some of this money traveling through the kingdom and expend even larger sums when trying to embark from the Mediterranean ports. Much of the precious metals would therefore be left within the kingdom.

The Jews would be in Aragon for at most fifty days and would remain mainly within the guarded atmosphere of Mallén. During their journey, the travelers were expressly forbidden to lodge near populated areas; this would not only minimize escapes but also severely curtail the possibility of the religious contamination of the local inhabitants. By allowing this exodus, Ferdinand and Isabella would reduce the number of Jews within Navarre, a situation surely agreeable with their ultimate religio-political designs on the entire Iberian peninsula.[71]

Some Aragonese and Castilian immigrants who left Navarre were not professing Jews. On 30 July 1493, Ferdinand and Isabella acknowledged having received the information that some Jews who had fled to Portugal and Navarre because of the expulsion edict had petitioned for safe reentry into their native lands. A few had already converted to Christianity, and others had conceived such intentions on entering Castile-Aragon. They claimed they feared harm to their persons and property because of insults they had suffered previously as Jews and because of false accusations that had been leveled against them. They requested a letter of assurance that they not be attacked in any way and instead that they be guarded and helped by the royal authorities. The Catholic Monarchs acceded to their demands and promised safe passage where relevant and secure residence to all of them. Those who would return as Jews were to convert in the first place where it was possible to do so within Ferdinand and Isabella's dominions.[72]

There are earlier documents that—although they deal only with those Jews who emigrated to Portugal—can be assumed to reflect a similar policy covering the Jews who had crossed into Navarre. On 10 November 1492, Ferdinand and Isabella declared that Jews who converted in Portugal or who wished to enter Castile to do so, be welcomed back into Castile and assured of safety for themselves and their belongings. They added that the former houses and property of these New Christians should be restored to them; if they had sold these parcels before emigrating, they would be allowed to repurchase them at the original price. Debts owed them prior to the expulsion would also be collectable.[73]

A careful combing of the Spanish archives would help us ascertain how many people took advantage of these royal assurances.[74] There was clearly considerable incentive for all the refugees to return. The economic hardships they encountered in the new countries could be exchanged for the standard of living they had enjoyed prior to the expulsion. A letter of the *jurados* of Saragossa to their counterparts in Tudela in August 1497 highlights some of the issues encountered by a returning convert.

Pedro de Torellas and the other Saragossan municipal officials explained that when the Jews were expelled, many of them—especially those from their city—took refuge in Tudela. Among them was Mosse de Leon, who, "cognizant of his great error," returned to Saragossa; professed Christianity; received baptism together with his wife, children, and "companya"; and took the name Joan Ferriz.[75] Here the now-common story takes an interesting turn. The Saragossan leaders, on behalf of their newly converted coreligionists, claimed that the Jews of Tudela had placed a lien on properties that Joan Ferriz owned in that city and throughout the Navarrese kingdom. They argued that the Tudelan Jews wished to punish the former Mosse de Leon for his faithlessness in converting to Christianity.[76] The Saragossans asked that the properties be freed from any restraints and returned to Joan Ferriz, labeling the Jews' action as contrary to the service of God. Remedying the situation, they suggested, would be looked on favorably by the Redeemer and the Holy Trinity, in that it would afford the new convert the ability to enjoy his temporal belongings just as he could now enjoy his spiritual life.[77]

It might appear from the previous discussion that most of the refugees of 1492 saw the kingdom of Navarre mainly as a temporary way station from whence to proceed as Jews to other countries. Some may have viewed Navarre as a place where the decision was finally made to return to their native lands as Christians, a step that had already been taken by many of their coreligionists during those fateful months of 1492. Thus, the very brief references by Yosef ha-Kohen to his family's sojourn in Navarre seem to describe the attitudes of most of the émigrés. When he wrote of the Aragonese Jews who requested permission to leave Navarre, he portrayed them as "touched by God in their hearts to leave the iron cauldron because they were afraid for their lives." This description of how the refugees felt about their new home may have led Kayserling to conclude that very few of them settled in Navarre, and Amador de los Ríos to surmise that those who remained hardly prospered in the six years from 1492 to 1498.[78]

Whether or not those Aragonese Jews who left were more prescient about the prospects of Jewish survival in the small Pyrenean kingdom, or indeed in the entire Iberian peninsula, heretofore undiscovered documents from the Navarrese archives paint a different picture. Not only did Jews come to Navarre in 1492, they stayed and settled. They developed their own institutions and in some instances became integrated into general Navarrese society.

Tudela in southern Navarre was presumably the major center for the refugees. Yet although precise population statistics are unob-

tainable, it is possible to identify other locales that attracted Jewish
émigrés in significant numbers. Towns such as Cortes, Cascante,
and Corella in the district of Tudela all witnessed an influx of Jews.
The county of Lerín welcomed the refugees; however, the numbers
of Jews who settled there cannot be calculated easily.

Baron, citing the case of the conde de Lerín, assumed that the
Jews were "well protected in territories under control of feudal
lords."[79] There is evidence to support his conjecture. The royal
tax records of 1495, for example, point to the existence of a sizeable Jewish population in Uxanavilla and Viana, both technically
located within the district of Estella. Although Viana was not included in the 1495 evaluation of his property, it is noted there to
have been in the power of the "Senyor Condestable de Lerín."
Uxanavilla (also known as Xenevilla and Genevilla) was under the
control of the duque de Nágera.[80] It is a town on the western border of Navarre, approximately twenty-five kilometers from Laguardia (then in Castile), a distance that a Laguardian Jew named Osua
traveled in July 1492.[81]

The migrant Jews also settled in Sangüesa and Pamplona,[82] indicating that the immigrants settled in the western, southern, and
eastern sections of the kingdom. Most likely, the immigrants established themselves throughout the kingdom in the same areas as
the existing, native Jewish community. This may account for there
being no mention of émigrés settling in the northernmost part of
Navarre, where Jews were rarely to be found at any time in the
past.[83]

That the Jews from the other Spanish kingdoms not only remained a distinct group but eventually formed their own community within Navarre was an unprecedented development in
medieval Navarrese history[84] and indeed in all medieval Iberian history.[85] The immigrants' particular status was first observable in
1493 and 1494, when they remitted various municipal taxes separately from the indigenous Tudelan community. Another indication
can be seen in the tax accounts of those years. In them, the émigrés
were labeled as *foranos* (foreigners) or *nuevamente venidos* (newcomers), whereas the native Jewish community was called by its
legal corporate status, the "aljama de los judios de Tudela."[86]

Toward the end of 1494, a striking innovation was instituted in
the nomenclature of these two groups, reflecting the clear bifurca-

tion of the Navarrese Jewish community. On October 25, in the register of the royal chancellery, the indigenous Jews were designated for the first time as the "aljama de los judios nativos."[87] Prior to this, the adjective *nativos* had not been part of the phrase. On December 6, references were made to taxes owed by both *judíos nativos* and *nuevamente venidos* of the kingdom. Here the scribe added "to each aljama according to its obligation."[88] Not only were the émigrés set apart for taxation purposes, they were now accorded the legal status of constituting an *aljama*.[89]

Little, however, about the structure of the *forano* communities can be gleaned from the extant documentation.[90] Communal officials are mentioned but twice; one reference is to the *regidores* of the *judíos foranos* of Sangüesa,[91] the other to their counterparts in Tudela.[92] Salamon Anbron, Rabí Çarça,[93] and Jaco Ayeno held the position of *regidor* in Sangüesa, and Juçe Atortox,[94] and Simuel Feci were *regidores* in Tudela. These sources do not explain whether the establishment of the immigrant community was formalized at the instigation of the Jews, themselves, native or foreign, or at the behest of the municipal and royal governments.[95] The documents are concerned solely with the assessment and collection of tax revenues and shed no light on this question.

Despite these references to the immigrants' responsibilities in administering tax collections, a comprehensive account of the tax burden on the *foranos* cannot be compiled.[96] What can be done here is to outline some of the taxes paid by the immigrants and to compare these with the payments by the indigenous Jews.[97] The immigrants' tax burden, it will be observed, changed with their new institutional status, and this shift affected their relationships with the native Jewish communities.

The *Libro de cuentas de propios* indicates that in the first year of the émigrés' residence in Navarre, they remitted two hundred pounds to the city of Tudela.[98] From 1493 through 1498, this source yields additional information on the taxes paid to the municipal government by the immigrants. According to the reports of 1493 and 1494, for example, the *judíos foranos* paid fifteen pounds per year for the privilege of exemption from the payments to the *almudi*.[99] The *aljama* of the Jews (i.e., of the native Navarrese Jewry) and that of the Muslims also enjoyed this exemption and annually remitted thirteen and twenty pounds, respectively.[100]

Because the *Libro de cuentas de propios* is a record of all receipts taken in and expenses discharged by the *procuradores* of Tudela, it tells us not only which groups rendered certain imposts but allows us to derive *ex silencio* who was not obligated (or did not pay for whatever reason). So we note that the *aljamas* of the Jews and the Muslims each contributed seventy-five florins in 1493 toward the four hundred florins to be raised for the arrival of the monarchs in Navarre from their French dominions.[101] The immigrants were not mentioned in regard to this impost, and it is fair to assume that they did not have to shoulder any part of the burden. Indeed, when there was a remission of some of these funds in 1494 to native Jews and Muslims, the *foranos* were not included among the recipients.[102] Four other imposts that were paid by the official *aljama* of the Jews and not by the immigrants were listed in 1493 and 1494.[103]

More complicated is the question of the two thousand pounds that the city of Tudela raised each year, apparently as an *alcabala* payable to the monarchs. The share of the official Jewish community both in 1493 and 1494 was 150 pounds, which was rendered in one annual sum.[104] The *judíos foranos* remitted half-yearly payments in 1493; the first contribution was for seventy-five pounds and the second evidently was for the same amount.[105] Yet in 1494 the Tudelan receipts record only one payment by the immigrants for the months of July through December.[106] Interestingly, the native *aljama* not only paid their full obligation that year but advanced three hundred pounds to cover their bill for 1495 and 1496.[107]

A document from the notarial registers of Pedro Latorre helps us understand why the émigrés, who did not pay the *alcabala* for the first months of 1494, remitted the second semiannual payment. On 12 June 1494, the *alcalde, jurados,* and other members of the entire *plega* (council) of Tudela met in session and granted legal authority to the *jurados* to assess how much the *judíos foranos* were to pay for the "via del alcabala."[108] Although the immigrants had paid 150 pounds in 1493, they surely now claimed either that the assessed sum was unfair or that they were unable to raise this amount. Remarkably, the only apparent results of the effort by the *jurados* was the immigrants' rendition of the seventy-five pounds for July to December 1494. There is no record of their payment in 1495, and only in 1496 did they remit the 150 pounds, acknowledging the "composycion" (arrangement) that they had negotiated with the city.[109]

These negotiations over the *alcabala* should be viewed within the larger framework of the emerging decision at this time to alter the legal standing of the immigrant community. The record of native and immigrant taxes from 1492 to 1494 clearly showed that the tax burden fell unequally on the two groups; the *nativos* of Tudela had far more obligations than their *forano* coreligionists. The fact that the entire *plega* met to discuss the issue reflected its seriousness. The Tudelan officials had to introduce a tax structure for the immigrant Jews, and they may have offered, or the immigrants may have demanded, an upgrading of their communal status. The meeting of June 12 could have been a step toward negotiating such an arrangement.[110]

There is more concrete evidence that the increase of the émigrés' taxation burden closely paralleled their new institutional footing.[111] The register of the royal chancellery of 6 December 1494 reveals that the native and newly arrived Jews of the entire kingdom reached an agreement with the monarchs on the *pechas* they were obligated to pay for the coming year. This was the first time that both groups were labeled *aljamas* and were treated together in the same document. While it is clear that the two groups were not assessed equally, the taxes were to be administered in an identical fashion. Mastre Ossua was charged on the same day to collect these imposts from both communities,[112] and Salamon Bendebut of Tudela and Rabí Sento Mataron of Pamplona were ordered to foreclose on the property of any "debtors" (those who would be remiss in their payments).[113]

The collection of the *pechas* of 1495 was of concern to both Tudelan Jewish communities and they joined together to meet this challenge. These taxes, or at least part of them, apparently had to be paid in advance, and the money was not available. Salamon Bendebut therefore pledged small jewels and certain valuable trinkets to raise money owed by both the immigrants and natives of the entire *merindad*.[114]

No spirit of cooperation animated the two Jewish groups in Sangüesa. In an entry of December 10 in the register of the chancellery, the *jurados* of the native *aljama* joined with the *fiscal* of the kingdom in issuing a summons to the leaders of the immigrant community to appear in the royal court on December 18.[115] The émigrés may have been reluctant to accept their new tax obligations and, unlike the Jews of Tudela, the Sangüesans were unable to resolve amicably their differences.

The gathering of the *pechas* of the Jews of all Navarre was indeed a formidable task. To that end, Mastre Ossua, the *receptor* of the Jews, was ordered on 20 January 1495 to "know the number of *casas* of the *judíos naturales y estrangeros* of the whole kingdom." The monarchs added, with respect to the *estrangeros* alone, that Ossua was granted the authority to act in any way to assure their payment, whether through the taking of collateral or by statements of guaranty.[116] This was another indication of a lack of trust in the immigrants' reliability in forwarding their taxes. Measures had to be taken to insure that the foreigners shouldered their burden.

After the immigrants became a separate *aljama* sometime in 1494, the *Libro de cuentas de propios* of Tudela shows that they were obliged to pay nearly every tax imposed upon the native community. In 1495, when Tudela was raising two hundred florins for the burial of Magdalena, princess of Viana, three successive entries record the payment of the share of the three *aljamas*: the *moros* (Muslims), the *judíos nativos,* and the *judíos foranos.*[117] In 1496, both Jewish communities paid the identical sum for the *alcabala,* and, again, unlike in previous years, the two groups rendered taxes on the export of wheat.[118] This may reflect further integration of the immigrant Jews into the business activities of the indigenous Tudelan group.

The municipal receipts during the last two years of official Jewish life in Navarre serve to confirm this trend. The *aljamas* of the *nativos* and *nuevamente venidos* contributed toward a special impost to support cavalry stationed in Tudela.[119] Both Jewish groups also paid for unspecified "great expenses" that the city had incurred.[120] Notarial documents of May 1497 show that the Jewish communities were delinquent in other payments. The *portero real* threatened to place a lien on "cloth of diverse colors" if the *regidores* of the *foranos* and the *naturales* did not deliver certain sums of money. The immigrant and native officials had to present, separately, two Jews as guarantors and "depositarios de cort." No details on the reason for these debts are given.[121]

Not only is there no record that the *forano* community paid the *alcabala* in 1497,[122] in the following year the immigrants remitted the *forania*[123] (the *alcabala* owed by persons not having official residence within the municipality).[124] This most probably represented not a downgrading of the immigrants' status but rather an indication that the *foranos,* unhappy with their 1496 agreement, renegotiated their *alcabala* as a *forania,* which resulted in a slight reduction in their payment.[125]

Turning now to documents concerning individual immigrants, we discover that the immigrants not only involved themselves in Navarrese society,[126] but expended much energy in settling their Castilian and Aragonese affairs. According to Ferdinand and Isabella's edict of expulsion, the Jews who chose exile had until the end of July 1492 to liquidate or otherwise dispose of the properties they held in Castile and Aragon. They could take with them all their possessions except "gold or silver or coins or other items prohibited by the laws of our kingdoms." Permissible merchandise and bills of exchange were expressly sanctioned.[127]

There was a very short period of time between the publication of the decree and the last day of legal Jewish residence, which made it very difficult for Jews who owned land and merchandise to sell their property. Recognizing the pressures the Jews were under, the Castilian and Aragonese Christians offered the soon-to-be exiles extremely low prices for their possessions.[128] Jews who were creditors to public institutions could not in most cases demand restitution in advance of the payment date stipulated in the loan agreements. They therefore either transferred their rights to these transactions to people to whom they owed money or gave powers of attorney to *procuradores* to collect these loans when they came due. These *procuradores* could also sell the Jews' property at a later, more profitable, moment.[129]

Some Jews were not able to sell or transfer their credits or designate *procuradores* before they left Castile-Aragon. They did do so on their arrival in their new homeland, and there are records of this activity in Navarre. During the last week of July 1492, Juhan Martínez Cabero, a Tudelan notary, appears to have accommodated the needs of some of the new immigrants. On July 26, Ezmel Abnarrabi, formerly of Saragossa, sold all debts of merchandise and other items that were owed him in the kingdom of Aragon to Pascual de Ayenssa, a prominent Tudelan Christian, who purchased them for ten thousand shillings.[130]

During the last two days of July, Cabero registered three acts involving the appointment of *procuradores* by immigrant Jews. Two of them were former residents of the village of Almazan in Castile, and one was from Calatayud, in the kingdom of Aragon.

All three of them empowered citizens of their former lands to collect their loans, settle any lawsuits, and free those who had fulfilled
their obligations. Mayr Abenrrodya of Almazan also wished his ap-
pointees to gather all the movable and immovable property that he
owned in both kingdoms. In one of the three cases, the *procurador*
was an *alcayde* of a local fortress; in another, a canon of a church
in Calatayud. These documents mention, not only the usual Christian and Jewish witnesses but also an "extra" Christian, who hailed
from the Jew's place of origin; he was included presumably to verify the identity of the appointee.[131]

The immigrants, after settling in Navarre, continued to appoint
procuradores to gather any and all property that they had left behind. On 12 September 1492, Bonafox Constantos directed his
procurador, who lived in Soria in Castile, to collect any sums of
money owed him,[132] and on June 2 of the following year, Çulema
Arruesi, formerly of Mores in Aragon, commissioned Pedro Pascual
to retrieve a dark-skinned ass with its pack saddle and riding ac-
coutrements from someone who lived in Arnedo in Castile.[133]

Jewish creditors feared that once they had left their native lands,
there would be little chance that their loans would be repaid. There
remains extant a reply by Ferdinand and Isabella to a complaint of
this kind addressed to them by a Jew, formerly of Castile, who now
resided in Navarre: Osua had lived in the *villa* of Laguardia until
1492, when he left for Uxanavilla in Navarre. He wrote the Catholic Monarchs that many citizens of his hometown owed him money
through contracts, obligations, and other agreements and that owing to the shortness of time, he could not collect on many of them.
This caused him great personal harm, and so he requested a royal
directive assuring him of his due. The monarchs addressed their
reply on 6 August 1492, to the *alcaldes* and *justiçias* of Laguardia
and to all other locales to process Osua's claims post haste to the
benefit of Osua and to whomever he gave authority to represent
him in these matters.[134] Clearly not all the immigrants were able to
elicit action by Ferdinand and Isabella, but Osua's predicament was
not unique.

Obstacles had arisen in the repayment of Jewish creditors, which
also might have provoked Osua's concern. Debtors claimed they
were not liable because the terms of the loans were usurious. Although this was not a new issue in Iberian Jewish life, the accusations had become almost commonplace in the wake of the

expulsion decree, and royal commissions were ordered to determine the veracity of the charges of usurious practices. On 6 October 1492, Juan de Ribera, the *capitán general de la frontera de Navarra,* was directed by Ferdinand and Isabella to investigate, within his jurisdiction, the legality of debts originally owed to Jews.[135] These debts, as mentioned, were now being collected by those who had bought them from the exiles or who were *procuradores* of the creditors. This order surely affected the émigrés in Navarre, many whom, like Osua, emigrated from the immediately surrounding area.

It was not only the immigrants who felt that they were cheated out of what was rightfully theirs owing to the expulsion. Clearly, some Christians of Castile-Aragon were unable to settle all their accounts with the exiled Jews. As late as February 1494, a citizen of Borja, Aragon, was in Tudela to demand certain property from Abram Orabuena "who used to be from Tarazona."[136]

Moreover, it was often impossible for Jews to dispose of their landed property before leaving, and so they sold properties after the expulsion, when they were already settled in Navarre. In Cascante, close to or on 5 November 1492, Astruc, originally from Agreda in Castile, sold houses that he owned in his hometown to Johan Gonçalez de Jate, an Agredan *clerico* who was *beneffciado* of the local church of Sant Johan. Gonçalez did not have the asking price of 13,824 *maravedís,* and so he had to borrow the sum from Ximen Cunchillos of Cascante. Because Gonçalez was not able to carefully appraise the property while in Cascante, Astruc promised that if the houses were not worth the price, he would release Gonçalez from his debt to Cunchillos.[137]

The options offered by Ferdinand and Isabella in the expulsion edict, namely, to convert or leave the kingdoms, often caused families to split up. One of the many secondary effects of this phenomenon—litigation over the disposition of inheritances of Jews who chose to emigrate—is documented in Navarrese sources. In Tarazona, a father and daughter had chosen to convert and had taken the names of Miguel Barçeloni and Gracia(?)a Degues, respectively. The mother and Çaçon Franquiel (the mother's brother? father?) had fled to Navarre and had taken up residence in Tudela. The mother died and Franquiel apparently inherited her property. Miguel Barçeloni brought suit against him on behalf of his daughter to recover her inheritance. On 22 August 1494, Barçeloni absolved

Franquiel from any and all legal action, claiming that he had received in his daughter's name all that she could have inherited from her mother. Clearly a settlement had been reached that left both parties satisfied.[138]

More information exists on another case of this kind, which ended in compromise through the acceptance of binding arbitration. Rabí Abram Benamias and his wife Vida had left Cornago, a small town near Alfaro in Castile and had established a new residence in Tudela. Soon after their arrival, Rabí Abram died and Vida inherited his estate. A *clerigo* named Andrei Martínez, and Ferran Sánchez de Alfaro, both of Arnedo, protested at this. Aym Rogat, the father-in-law of Sánchez and probably a Jew of Tudela, also appears to have registered disapproval of the disposition of the inheritance and cast his lot with his Christian son-in-law.

On 28 January 1495, two Christians and one Jew were chosen to adjudicate the case. The Jew was the experienced arbiter and noted communal leader, Rabí Abraham de la Rabiça. One of the Christians was Fray Miguel de Baquedano, *maestro en santa teologia* and *lector* and *guardiano* of the church of Sant Francisco of Tudela. They promised to decide by the end of February; owing to the press of other unrelated business, however, they did not deliver their ruling until March 19.

Because the total value of Rabí Abraham's estate cannot be determined, there is no way to judge if the ruling was more favorable to either of the parties. Vida was ordered to transfer to the plaintiffs two private notes (*albaranes*), one in the amount of three thousand *maravedís,* and one for one thousand *maravedís,* respectively. Other items to be turned over by Vida were a gold ring and a parchment belt that at present were pawned. A cloak of Rabí Abraham also had to be delivered to Ferran Sánchez because of his "need."[139]

The expulsion from Castile-Aragon often caused other, unexpected problems for Jews who chose exile in Navarre. Salamon and Soli Gotina had been married in Aragon prior to 1492, when they moved to Cortes in southern Navarre. Soli then converted to Christianity, took the name of María de Lerín, and moved to Ablitas (in Navarre). She sued her husband for the rights stipulated in her marriage contract. The contract itself she offered as evidence for her position. The *duquesa* of Villa Fermosa heard the petition and called in "loyal Jews" to examine the document and verify its validity. They reported that the contract was signed neither by witnesses nor by a notary, and that it was not accompanied by "other of the matrimonial stipulations that are done among Jews." What is more, they added, as a result "of the expulsion and the destruction of the *aljama* of the Jews of Borja" (the town where the marriage had taken place), there was no way to determine whether the contract was legal. The *duquesa* ordered the case to be put to arbitration, with each side choosing its own representatives. The outcome is unknown.[140]

That there were restrictions on what could have been taken across the borders by the exiles has been noted. There are many indications, however, that these rules were honored more in the breach that in the observance. In September 1492, Ferdinand and Isabella ordered an investigation of citizens of Castile-Aragon who had helped Jews remove gold, silver, and other forbidden goods from the kingdoms. One of the many areas investigated was the group of cities and towns that bordered Navarre. Although we can assume smuggling did take place, there is no way to determine how many people and what quantities were involved.[141]

The immigrants, using whatever they had been able to salvage, began to establish themselves in their new country. As early as 15 July 1492, Bonafox Constantos, rented houses in Cascante from Johan Enrriquez de la Carra, which reflected his desire to settle within the kingdom.[142] Most of the other extant documents bearing on the activities of the émigrés within Navarre are concerned mainly with money loans of moderate sums, and most of them reflect the business of only a couple of individuals. In only one instance was the *borrower* clearly Jewish: Ezmel Abnarrabi, a Jew, borrowed twenty-one florins from his grandchild, who evidently was a New Christian.[143]

In tracing the heretofore unknown story of these immigrants in their struggle to enter the kingdom of Navarre and sketching the formation of their new community, we find a different picture than that drawn by Yosef ha-Kohen. The *foranos,* in fact, did see Navarre as their new home and sought to put down roots there. Navarre was not quite perceived as an "iron cauldron," where the Jews feared for their lives. Those who left, as did Yosef's family in 1493, may have concluded that Jews could not survive as Jews anywhere in the Iberian peninsula, or may have had private reasons for moving on. Patently, however, others were prepared to stay.

6. The Road to Expulsion

In 1498, King Johan and Queen Catalina, as had their royal Iberian counterparts Ferdinand and Isabella six years earlier in Castile and Aragon, ordered the expulsion of all professing Jews from the kingdom of Navarre and instructed them, native and immigrant alike, to either convert to Christianity or leave the kingdom. Whether Castilian and Aragonese Jews were taken unawares by the expulsion decree in 1492, as Don Isaac Abravanel had reported, or were given ample forewarning of the impending dissolution of their communities, by the end of the 1490s the possibility of another such edict should not have seemed remote to Navarrese Jewry. After all, these last remaining Jews on Iberian soil not only had witnessed the traumatic events (or, at least, the effects) of the Castilian-Aragonese edict of expulsion, they surely had heard of the similar decree issued by King Manuel of Portugal in December of 1496. Unless they were totally misled by the security of their own lives in the northern Pyrenean kingdom, such an eventuality was definitely conceivable. And if Johan and Catalina were moving inexorably toward such a decision during the last decade of the fifteenth century, the Jews should have been quite prepared when the final decree came.[1]

But *was* the situation of Navarrese Jews as vulnerable as it might now appear in retrospect? Was expulsion from the kingdom all but inevitable for the Jewish population? By returning our attention to 1479, the chronological starting point of our study, we will be able to decide whether the political status of the Jews did deteriorate over the course of the next twenty years, and thereby determine how and when Johan and Catalina finally arrived at the decision to expel the Jews. We might then be able to understand the political response of the Navarrese Jewish communities in (what we now know were) the waning years of their existence in the Pyrenean kingdom.

Twenty years prior to the expulsion decree, tranquility was not the lot of Navarre, which had been troubled for a generation by internecine civil war. Although Juan II of Aragon died in January of 1479 and Navarre was able to wrest itself from the direct control of its more powerful neighbor to the east, the political machinations continued apace. Leonor, the daughter of Juan II and sister of Ferdinand of Aragon, died only twenty-four days after being named queen, and her eleven-year-old grandson Francisco of Foix legally inherited the throne. Neither Ferdinand nor his Navarrese clients, the Beaumonteses, were pleased that a vassal of the king of France—whose French dominions of Bearne, Bigorre, and Foix far outstripped the small Pyrenean kingdom in wealth and would therefore be more significant to him—would now be crowned King Francisco Febo of Navarre. Even Luis XI of France, brother of Magdalena, who was Francisco's mother and regent of the kingdom, was unwilling to support the coronation of Francisco Febo until he received assurances of greater influence in Francisco's French dominions.

During 1480, the civil war erupted once again, but because both Luis and Ferdinand were at that moment interested in preserving the peace, the Navarrese Cortes was able to meet in Pamplona late in the year to make the necessary arrangements for Francisco's coronation. In 1481, it passed on the expenditures for the royal trip to Navarre, and Ferdinand and Luis offered their troops to safeguard the public order. Francisco Febo entered Pamplona on 21 November 1481 and was finally crowned on December 8. He traveled to Tudela on December 24 and swore to uphold the *fueros,* and presided over a meeting of the Cortes in Olite on January 31 of the following year. Probably because of the reemerging civil war, Francisco and Magdalena immediately crossed the Pyrenees and left the kingdom. Francisco never returned, and died—most likely of tuberculosis—on 29 January 1483.[2]

Whereas these bare facts about Francisco's short reign are generally known to students of this period, the recent discovery of Francisco Febo's acknowledgement of the privileges of the Jews of Tudela and of Navarre in general illumines a little-known facet of his brief tenure and also reveals the important place of the Jews within Navarrese society during these years.[3] On 4 February 1482, Francisco, barely two months into his reign, reassured the Jewish communities by recalling many of the privileges that they enjoyed in Navarre, some dating from the early years of the fifteenth century and the reign of Carlos III. This was surely a sign to the Jews that, in the midst of all the domestic and foreign disturbances, their situation was secure in the eyes of the Navarrese monarchy. It also indicated to the other players in the Navarrese civil war, in case any had thought otherwise, that the Jews were to be protected by the monarchs. Most striking of all, this *privilegium* reflected the importance of the Jews in that they had, it seems likely, succeeded in securing an audience—and a successful one at that—with the young king so soon after he had acceded to the throne.

But just as the political and military influence of Castile-Aragon (and of France, as well) necessarily influenced the fortunes of the Navarrese kingdom, the strengthening of anti-Jewish attitudes in Castile and Aragon perforce had a major impact on Navarrese Jewish society. The fortunes of the Jews and *conversos* in the entire peninsula would be affected by the unification of the monarchies of Ferdinand and Isabella in 1479. Within the first few years of the next decade, sweeping anti-Jewish measures were passed by the Cortes of Toledo; the Jews of Andalusia were expelled; and the Castilian and Aragonese Inquisitions were established on a sure footing.[4] Although Navarrese royal and municipal authorities did not promulgate any anti-Jewish or anti-*converso* decrees during the same period, by 1488, after a two-year resistance to Ferdinand and Isabella's Inquisition, Navarre effectively allowed the Holy Office to conduct investigations within its borders. The influence of the Catholic Monarchs continued unabated with the issuance of the Corellan edict on May 6 of the same year.[5]

Corella had been active with Tudela in resisting the Inquisition, and as late as January 1488 was considering an interdiction against the actions of the Holy Office. But on May 6 in their castle at Pau in southern France—ten weeks after Navarre's capitulation to the Inquisition—the Navarrese monarchs ordered that all Jews presently and in the future living in Corella must reside in the district of Parte Casa, where the synagogue was located. Corellan Jews who lived among Christians had until the end of December to leave these neighborhoods.[6] Johan and Catalina claimed that the ordinance was executed according to the wishes of the Corellan municipality, relayed by the Corellan representatives Juhan de Gurpide and Pero Pradilla (the latter had been a courier in the actions against the Inquisition).

The segregation of the Jews, Johan and Catalina argued, served to avoid scandals caused by Jews living among Christians, scandals offensive to God. This was not a new argument in medieval Christian Iberia, and as recently as 1480 it had been used by the Cortes of Toledo to separate the Jews (and Muslims) from Christians, in order to prevent Jewish influence on the *converso* population.[7] The separation of Jewish and Christian residential quarters was an important item on Ferdinand and Isabella's religio-political agenda, and the monarchs were surely behind the promulgation of this decree. Just as they had recently forced their Inquisition into Navarre, they also were able to impose another of their religious policies upon their smaller northern neighbor.

The segregation of Jews from Christians in Corella must have proved especially rewarding to the Catholic Monarchs inasmuch as the village had resisted the entry of the Holy Office. The Corellan municipality, probably on receiving notice of the impending Navarrese royal edict, was determined to exact as many concessions from Johan and Catalina in exchange for its compliance. Their representatives succeeded not only in receiving a standard endorsement of the village's privileges, which had new importance in light of the entry of the Inquisition and the decree of segregation, but also in gaining greater powers of taxation, an important victory for the financially strapped village.[8]

The Corellan edict opened with a confirmation of the privileges, freedoms, and liberties that Navarrese monarchs had bestowed upon the municipality over time. After the injunction regarding the Jews, Johan and Catalina permitted an annual property tax of five groats per *cafizada* (a unit of measure of land) to be assessed on foreigners and other noncitizens who held land in the village. The Corellan officials also were allowed to collect from noncitizens certain taxes (*quarteres*) owed royal authorities if Corellans could not pay the entire amount themselves. If these imposts were eventually received by the municipality, Johan and Catalina maintained they were to be used to rebuild village walls and fences. The Navarrese monarchs concluded their edict by exempting Corella from the payment of certain outstanding fines and taxes.

These activities of Ferdinand and Isabella emboldened other elements in Navarrese society to become outspokenly anti-Jewish. The Cortes convened in 1488, 1490, and 1493, and each session registered bitter complaints about the "briberies of the Jewish tax and rent collectors." Requests for a royal promise to prevent the machinations of these Jews were routinely attached to grants of various *alcabalas* and *imposiçiones* to the Navarrese monarchy.[9]

Once again, however, it was an action of Ferdinand and Isabella that dealt the next major blow to the Navarrese Jews: When the Catholic Monarchs expelled their Jews in 1492, the municipalities split on whether to accept the refugees. Tudela and Tafalla were opposed to their entry, whereas Estella, Pamplona, and Sangüesa appeared to favor it. Indeed, Tudela may have gone so far as to use this opportunity to try to convince the Navarrese monarchs to expel from the kingdom all Jews, native Navarrese included. Although Tudela in southern Navarre may have been the most affected by the influx of the immigrants, its attempt to keep out the refugees and possibly expel the natives may also have stemmed from a desire to protect its own *conversos* from the Inquisition and to allay the wrath of the increasingly powerful Ferdinand and Isabella. The Navarrese monarchs, by contrast, probably viewed the immigration as advantageous to their kingdom and its treasury, and as a possible bargaining chip in the ongoing negotiations with the Castilian-Aragonese rulers.[10]

The rise of anti-Jewish feeling in 1492 coupled, however, with the determination to protect the Jews, motivated the decree suggested to the Navarrese Crown by the three estates meeting that year in Estella. At the request of the Cortes, and after meeting with the royal council, Gabriel, señor of Avenas and the royal representative in the kingdom, forbade native and foreign Jews to walk in the streets or leave their *juderías* or houses until midday on Sundays and church festivals. By that hour, the mass would have been celebrated. Exceptions were made for doctors and surgeons visiting the sick and performing other necessary activities.

The reasons given for this edict, a type that had a long history in medieval Christian Iberia, were that the representatives at the Cortes had complained that the first people they met when going to mass in their cities and villages were Jews, who, on "those days more than others," were involved in business. This they claimed set a "bad example for all catholic Christians," meaning both *conversos* and Old Christians who might be affected by such behavior. The royal representative further explained that the law would help "prevent the inconveniences . . . that might follow in many places," that is that it would protect the Jews from possible harm. To enforce the edict, Gabriel ordered a fine of ten pounds for each transgression, half to go to a representative of the Crown (*procurador fiscal*) and half to the accuser. To insure widespread compliance, the ordinance was sent to all the royal officials.[11]

Earlier in that eventful year, charges of usury and speculation had been leveled against Jews, accusations that had been raised with increasing frequency in Castile and Aragon following the accession of Ferdinand and Isabella. Gabriel, Navarre's lieutenant general, reported on his inquiry into the subject of usurious practices and accused Muslims and Christians as well as Jews, offering economic reasons for the many incidences of usury. Navarre, Gabriel argued, was suffering adversity because of crop failures and the resultant scarcity of bread. This hardship caused people to lose their fear of God, conscience, and their appreciation of justice, and to act against natural and divine law.[12]

He then singled out the Jews, who, he claimed, through speculation and fraudulent contracts bought grain in advance of the harvest and then resold the produce for two to three times the purchase price. Jews were also prone, he said, to lend money at twenty percent interest through usurious contracts and *comandas,* with the result that many Christians found themselves needing to pawn their lands to the Jews.[13] His report then focused on the district of Olite and its village of Açagra, where an investigation was to be launched into the actions of Christians, Muslims, and Jews, and where it was hoped to imprison violators, absolve those falsely accused, and fix the damages caused by such practices. The guilty parties would have to pay a fine of one thousand florins to the royal coffers and could have their property sequestered.[14]

Whatever fears for their well-being and safety the enlarged Jewish community of natives and foreigners may have harbored in 1492, by two years later they had good reason to believe that the worst had passed and the storm had already been weathered. After many years of negotiations with all the rival political parties, Johan and Catalina entered the kingdom in 1494 and proceeded to implement strong centralizing policies. New coinage was minted, new imposts were decreed, and old taxes were reassessed and collected. The Jews were subject to these imposts and the Jewish refugees from Castile and Aragon were constituted as a separate *aljama.*[15]

These were sure signs of stability. It appeared, moreover, that spurious anti-Jewish accusations would be dismissed by the royal authorities. For example, Mossen Farach had been arrested in Olite charged with having "been found in a house with a Christian woman, Maria Destoriaga." Royal investigators were unable to find any evidence for this "suspicion," and the monarchs pardoned Farach on 12 October 1494, and returned all the fines he had paid.[16]

An investigation that was publicly launched in 1495, however, may have tempered the high hopes of the previous year and pointed up the underlying tenuousness of the position of the Jews and *conversos*. In February, at the instigation of Ferdinand and Isabella's Inquisition, a probe of possible judaizing by the Tudelan Franciscan Fray Miguel de Baquedano was launched, an inquiry that surely had been in preparation for many months. This inquest, which called both Jews and Christians to testify, served as a potent reminder of Castile-Aragon's power within Navarre, especially at a time of tensions following a brief period of rapprochement that had made the coronation of Johan and Catalina possible. Tensions between Castile-Aragon and Navarre had erupted anew, only to be resolved temporarily by the treaty of Madrid signed in March.[17]

In the following year, some of the familiar anti-Jewish accusations were leveled again by the Cortes.[18] On 1 June 1496, the monarchs acknowledged the complaints presented to them by the Cortes meeting in Pamplona. The three estates submitted that because of the "wickedness (*maliçia*) of the times," many Christians, in dire necessity, borrowed from Jews. The Cortes portrayed the debtors as unsuspecting Christians who trusted the Jews when they told them they they did not expect profit from the transactions. The parliament further said that the Jews tricked the Christians by attaching large penalties for noncompliance with these contracts (*cartas de comanda*). When the debts were not paid, the deputies of the Cortes tried to have the monarchs believe, the Jews "destroyed" the debtors and their properties, behaving as if the Christians had borrowed the money at interest.[19]

The absence of anti-Jewish decrees in 1497 meant that Navarrese Jewry could feel relatively secure, yet events unfolding on the western coast of the Iberian peninsula might have given them some concern. The forced conversion of Portuguese Jewry during that year provided a clear example of how Ferdinand and Isabella could use their political leverage to affect the policies of a neighboring kingdom toward its Jews. Although, as everyone knew, Navarre lacked the political or military strength of Portugal, during 1497 Navarrese Jews nevertheless engaged in their customary commercial activities with the same vigor as in the past. The possibility of an expulsion from Navarre was not allowed to have any practical effect on their daily pursuits. Indeed, Jews entered into long-term contracts during this period. Yuçe Falaquera, for example, had two years from 8 August 1497 to clear his debt with the merchant Pedro de Magallon, and Simuel Benaçan had until October 1498 to pay Diego Ortelano for a horse. Then there was Jehuda Bendebut, who gave a Muslim couple until August 1498 to repay a grain loan, and Habran Aboçach, who allowed Juhan Perez Dannyorue until Shrove Tuesday of 1498 to complete installment payments on a shipment of animal hides.[20]

As the fateful year of 1498 began, the expulsion edict was published and the Jews realized that their days in Navarre were numbered. Even if the sale[21] of a *majuelo* by a Jew named Yuçe Auena to the Tudelan merchant Juhan de Carriazo on January 8 did not necessarily indicate that Auena foresaw the need to prepare to move on, other transactions clearly show such preparations, as when two prominent Jews severed their long-standing business connections: On January 26 Salamon Bendebut settled his account with the councillors of the village of Cintruénigo. An arbiters' sentence pronounced by a Christian and a Jew proclaimed that Bendebut was to receive eighty florins from the village; in return, Salamon was relieved by the councillors of any future obligations.[22]

On March 6, the elder Rabí Abraham de la Rabiça confirmed an *albaran* (note) dated October 1496, whereby he had released the *jurados* (officials) of the Muslim *aljama* of Ablitas from all debts owed to him, his father, and his brother-in-law. It was apparently in view of his possible departure from the kingdom that Rabí Abraham was requested to reaffirm that the Ablitas Muslims had paid all "fines, wheat, merchandise, and other items" that they "individually or generally" had owed his family.[23]

When the expulsion decree was published, some Jews sought refuge on church lands, believing that in that way they could remain Jews yet avoid being exiled from the kingdom. Don Açac Çaroniel, a *vezino* (inhabitant) of Cascante, took up *vecindad* (residence) in Fitero and promised to pay a golden florin annually for the privilege. Fitero was the site of a Cistercian monastery and the arrangement was done according to the abbot's wishes.

Three witnesses—Simuel Moneque, Fray Miguel de los Arcos, and Guillemos—declared that the abbot had received Çaroniel as a *vezino*.[24]

Açac Çaroniel and the witness Simuel Moneque were not the only Jews to take up residence in Fitero. On 1 March 1498, Fray Miguel de Peralta, the abbot of the local monastery of Santa María, sentenced a Jew named Jaco to exile from the village of Fitero: According to the decision read in the main square of the village, Jaco, a newcomer to Fitero, had libeled another newcomer (a man named Rui Díaz), declaring that he had overheard that Díaz "observed the Sabbath as a Jew." Asked by the abbot the reasons for his actions, Jaco answered that he had bad words with Díaz, who in turn bore him ill will. Jaco pleaded that his repentance be accepted and that he had only said such words because the devil had overtaken him. The abbot, in order to set an example, ordered Jaco to leave Fitero within three hours, and ruled that he never be allowed to return, even if he were to convert.[25]

Such were the kinds of tensions between Jews and New Christians just prior to the expulsion. Fitero had probably been chosen as a refuge because of the monastery's anomalous political allegiance and its claim to a measure of autonomy: Located in the southwest corner of Navarre near both Cascante and Corella, it had been claimed during the Middle Ages by both Castile and Navarre. Why the monastery welcomed the refugees is not clear, but money may have been the deciding factor. At any rate, given the large number of Jews and New Christians who took up residence there, the abbot understood that such strife, as between Jaco and Díaz, was intolerable. He was also aware that when Jaco was expelled from Fitero, he might, instead of choosing exile as a Jew from Navarre, decide to convert and attempt to return as a Christian to the monastery's lands.[26]

Although the expulsion decree has not survived, documents composed in 1498 after the edict went into effect clearly refer to it. It appears that the last day Jews were allowed to live in Navarre was between 7 March and 28 March 1498. The decree had been published at the beginning of the year, or at least was public knowledge by then.[27]

The expulsion edict afforded the Jews the choice of leaving Navarre, or staying and converting to Christianity. According to the seventeenth-century author Francisco de Alesón, the decree "order(ed) that without delay, those who do not become Christians must leave the kingdom." The sixteenth-century Hebrew chronicler Yosef ha-Kohen also mentioned that "the king expelled the Jews that remained in Navarre"; the phrasing was meant to exclude Yosef's own family, who had already left in 1493.[28]

The edict was signed by Johan and Catalina, and they took pains to ensure that it was executed faithfully. Although the decree was issued by the Navarrese monarchy, the major impetus for it was the influence of Ferdinand and Isabella. From 1494 on, Castilian and Aragonese influence in Navarre had been growing, and there were any number of projects devised by Ferdinand to annex or at least carve up the Pyrenean kingdom into Castilian-Aragonese and French spheres. Rumors abounded in the wake of the treaty of Lyons between France and Castile-Aragon in February 1497, for example, that Johan and Catalina would surrender their rights to Navarre and would be granted adequate compensation in Normandy. Ferdinand and Isabella would then become Navarrese monarchs in exchange for allowing France to pursue its designs in Naples.[29]

In late 1497, Ferdinand increased his pressure on the Navarrese monarchs and demanded guarantees of their loyalty so as to ward off French pretensions to the kingdom. Johan and Catalina, although they had welcomed Jewish refugees in 1492 and favored the Jews again in 1494, realized that the presence of Jews in their kingdom was an impediment to Ferdinand's vision of uniting the peninsula under his control, a dream strengthened since 1497, when Jews no longer officially resided in Portugal. Navarrese Jewry was expendable at this juncture, not because of the native hatred of the Jews on the part of other Navarrese, but if only to demonstrate to Ferdinand and Isabella that they need not invade the kingdom. Throughout 1497 and 1498 Johan and Catalina attempted the difficult task of wresting themselves from the tutelage of the Catholic Monarchs, while simultaneously resisting French expansionist designs.[30]

The expulsion edict—while not totally unexpected by this last group of Iberian Jews, who had watched the growing political strength of Ferdinand and Isabella over the last two decades and, as recently as 1496, had observed the long arm of the Catho-

lic monarchs intervene in Portuguese internal affairs—was surely
the cause of much dread. Unlike Castile, Aragon, and Portugal,
Navarre was landlocked and offered the Jews no easy route for departure from the peninsula. The Jews were apparently aware of the
bleakness of their situation, especially after the forced conversion
of Portuguese Jewry in 1497, but there was no easy remedy. The
Catholic Monarchs did not permit them to pass through their kingdoms as Ferdinand had allowed the refugees to five years earlier,
and there was no way for the Jews to reach Provence, their nearest
haven to the east, without traveling through territories closed to
them for more than a century. The Jews presumably recognized the
lack of easy egress; there are no documents of sales involving Jews
and their property during February and March 1498. Most of the
Jews of Navarre were planning to remain there.[31]

Some Jews—they were few—did manage to escape. The perils
of one successful journey were described in Shemtov ben Shmuel
Gamil's harrowing account of how he finally arrived in Fez, many
months after leaving Tudela. Y. M. Toledano brought this account
to light in 1928 and dated the reported events to 1493, to explain
why Shemtov encountered such difficulties in exiting the peninsula.
He did not realize that because Tudela was in Navarre, and because
Navarrese Jews were expelled in 1498, anyone who attempted to
leave the peninsula through Castile-Aragon without permission
from Ferdinand and Isabella was courting extreme danger. Placing the start of Shemtov's travels in 1498 would also have helped
Toledano understand why other Iberian exiles were already flour-
ishing in Fez (Morocco) when Shemtov arrived.

Toledano claimed in 1928 that this was the only extant reference
to Shemtov. But recently in the notarial archives of Tudela a number of *ketubbot* (Jewish matrimonial contracts) were found, and
one of the signatories on a 1480 *ketubbah* executed in Tudela is
Shem Tov, son of Shmuel ben Gamil. There is no doubt that he is
the author of our account.

According to Gamil, he crossed the border into Aragon and attempted to contact his children, who lived in a town in Valencia
where Gamil possessed a business. There he discovered that although his children had safely fled the town (he did not specify the
reasons for their flight, but it appears to have been owing to their
Jewishness), his business had been plundered. Gamil reports that
he was then imprisoned for three weeks in Valencia and escaped

with the help of a young Muslim. He thereupon successfully contacted his scattered children and attempted to leave the peninsula by sailing from Tortosa. It appears that members of the Gamil family were recognized as Jews and so, fearful of the Inquisition, they decided to travel to Almería and thence to Oran (Morocco). (It should be remembered that up through the final years of the century, Muslims were able to leave the former Muslim emirate of Granada for North Africa with relative ease.)

The Gamil family traveled south, passing through Valencia without incident (Gamil says the Inquisition was looking for them there) and arrived in Almería, only to be recognized as Jews once again, and on that account imprisoned. Once more, it was a Muslim who helped them escape (and as before, Gamil expressed his gratitude with profuse praise). The helpful Muslim convinced the authorities that Gamil and his entourage were Muslims by having them pray according to Muslim custom (passing for Muslims afforded probably the easiest way to leave).

The group then retreated to Granada for four months and paid a large sum of money to join a group of a hundred people headed for Fez. They were imprisoned yet again, this time for a couple of days in Vélez Málaga, where their Muslim friends were treated worse than they themselves for having had falsely presented the Jewish family as Muslims. From Vélez Málaga they were taken to Carmona, near Seville, and held there for four months before being returned to Vélez Málaga for another two-and-a-half months of imprisonment.

Gamil then relates how the "king" sent for them; had them taken back to Granada, where items of value such as silk and gold were returned to them; and then had them put in prison for another month. Gamil's two "small children," Yehoshua and Ya'akov, were taken away from him and placed in separate custody; but, he proudly reported, none of them forgot his God. Finally his custodian put him on a ship traveling to Safi (Morocco), and on the fourth attempt they successfully set sail.[32]

Those Navarrese Jews who, like Gamil, succeeded in departing the peninsula may have settled, as did their Castilian and Aragonese coreligionists, throughout the Mediterranean littoral. According to some traditions, they were able to establish their own community in Salonica. Over the course of decades, erstwhile Navarrese Jews and their descendants may have wended their way to southern

France and eventually England, the Netherlands, and other European countries, as the presence of the family name Nabarro among Jews in those countries may suggest.[33]

Most Jews, however, were trapped in Navarre and converted to Christianity. Yosef ha-Kohen explained that "the road was closed upon them and they turned from God, the Lord of Israel." The Navarrese chronicler Francisco Alesón reported that "not many left since almost all converted to our Holy Faith."[34]

The Navarrese monarchs appreciated the value of their Jewish population, as did their Portuguese counterparts, who engineered the forced conversions of 1497, and they were aware that most Jews would have to remain and convert. And so it happened: On the day of the expulsion of the Jews, Ybraym Paçagon and his daughter were baptized by Pedro de Murillo, the subvicar (*sozvicario*) of Tudela's church of Santa María. The father took the name Enrriq de Berrozpe. In late October and early November in Cortes, Mosen Diego García, the lieutenant of the village's vicar, reported on the recent baptisms that had taken place. He stated that on October 26, Abram Abenabez, his four sons, and daughter-in-law converted, taking the names Pablo, Martín, Migel, Pedro, Juan, and Leonor de Olguerin, respectively. On November 4, Simuel Gotina and his wife Luna became Felipe and Graçia de Logran; another Jewish woman named Luna took the new name María Nabarra; the Byenbenis family converted and adopted the surname Cortyllos; Abram Çarça and his wife were baptized Mernant and María Gorita de Aybar; and Solibença Adios became Ana Royz. Witnesses to some of these baptisms included other Jews who had just converted.[35]

Almost all Tudelan Jews, including those who arrived in 1492, converted. Among those new Christians was Mastre Ossua, physician and chief tax collector of all Jewish imposts in the kingdom, who took the name Mastre Gabriel when he converted. Members of his family and some other Tudelan Jews, however, attempted to contravene the expulsion edict by hiding from the royal authorities in a small Navarrese village. The monarchs received word of these attempts and on 15 July 1498 ordered the Tudelan *alcalde* Jayme Diaz Darmendariz and the *justiçia* Miguel de Eguaras to confiscate the property of the *converso* brothers Tomas and Jayme Benedit and impose a fine on them. Jayme, who originally was named Jaco Almarcabi, fled at the time of the expulsion to the village of Uxanavilla, near the western border of Navarre. There he was hidden by his brother Tomas, who had already converted. In their order respecting this matter, Johan and Catalina made reference to other Jews who had traveled to Uxanavilla, naming the widow of Abraham Chinillo and the mother-in-law and sister-in-law of "Mastre Gabriel our physician."[36]

After their conversion, the Tudelan Jews did not immediately disappear as a community. The *aljama,* the erstwhile Jewish corporation, still had to settle outstanding financial indebtedness. Just after the Jews' change of faith, on 29 March 1498 a sentence was passed condemning the New Christians Frances de la Sala, Pedro de Vega, Miguel del Espirtal, Pedro de França, Jayme Savastian, and all others who "formerly represented the *aljama* of the Tudela's *judería*" and ordering them to pay thirty-four florins to Martín Partinus and sixty-six florins to Pedro de Falces. On August 23 of that year, Mossen Johan de la Carra renounced all rights he had in certain orchards stemming from obligations owed him by Jews of the Tudelan *judería.* The property was now owned by García de Aybar and Miguel de Eguaras.[37]

The newly baptized Christians, as a group, also had to pay the taxes they had owed when still Jews. The native and foreign communities paid one-sixth of the annual two-thousand-pound impost to the Tudela municipality in 1498, presumably for the months of January and February. In the village of Corella, taxes were newly assessed for the neophytes, who had to pay their entire 1498 tax debt as New Christians.[38]

Much of the former Jewish communal property was confiscated by the royal patrimony and some of the parcels were given as gifts to groups and individuals. The synagogue in Viana was kept by the royal authorities. Pamplona's *sinagoga mayor* was given to the municipality to be used as a school for the study of grammar and other subjects, and that of Cascante was granted by Johan and Catalina to its Christian residents for the establishment of a church. The Jewish cemetery in the city was acquired by the friars of St. Augustine, who were expressly exempted from taxes on the property.[39]

Thus ended the almost six-hundred-year-long existence of the Jewish community of Navarre and, with it, the distinguished history of the Jews in the Iberian peninsula. Jews had lived in the small Pyrenean kingdom from its very birth and continued to do so almost until the date of its formal annexation by Castile in 1515. The everyday lives of Navarrese Jews, the last remaining professing Jewish community on Iberian soil, during their last two decades in Navarre resembled those of other Iberian Jews during the era of the Iberian expulsions. Well integrated into the society, they felt secure in their religio-political status. Even after 1496, and the intervention of the Catholic Monarchs in the internal affairs of Portugal, the volume of property sales and debt liquidations did not rise, suggesting that the Jews felt no sense of alarm.

The Jews knew Navarre was landlocked, and their only response was to trust in their local community's continued existence. The events of the 1490s seemed to indicate that their choice was a good and reasonable one.[40] The pressures of international politics, specifically the machinations of Castile-Aragon, did not have any discernible effect on the pattern of their lives. The Navarrese Christians, amongst whom they lived, for their part, did not display any greater degree of anti-Judaism than they had at any point in the recent past. The Jews could not foresee that Navarre, which by 1498 had gradually become a vassal of Castile-Aragon, would not be able to retain its Jewish inhabitants (nor could anyone else foresee it). Nor did the Jews of Navarre divine that less than twenty years later, Ferdinand would no longer tolerate an independent Navarre, and would instead incorporate the Pyrenean kingdom into the Crown of Castile. In that new country, religious differences and regional characteristics were less tolerated, as the Spanish Crown slowly attempted to fashion a unified religious and political identity that it had never possessed before.

Notes

Introduction

1. Regarding this harsh attack on the Jews' "weakened political sensitivity," see Benzion Netanyahu, *Don Isaac Abravanel, Statesman and Philosopher,* 2d ed. (Philadelphia, 1968), p. 45. A refreshing general corrective is Ismar Schorsch, "On the Political Judgment of the Jew," *Leo Baeck Memorial Lecture* 20 (1976).

2. See Abravanel's introduction to his commentary on the Book of Kings in *Perush al Nevi'im Rishonim* (Jaffa and Jerusalem, 1955), p. 422 and his preface to the commentary on the Book of Daniel in *Ma'ayenei ha-Yeshu'ah,* published in *Perush al Nevi'im u-Ketubim* (Jerusalem, 1959), pp. 222–223. The biblical passage quoted by Abravanel is from the Book of Obadiah, verse 20.

3. Symptomatic of this attitude is the statement by the great Jewish historian Yitzhak (Fritz) Baer, who in *A History of the Jews in Christian Spain* (Philadelphia, 1961) 1:187 explained that Navarrese Jews "will be treated in our subsequent discussions only to the extent to which it helps clarify the development of Spanish Jewry as a whole." Still it must be noted that Meyer Kayserling in the last century wrote *Die Juden in Navarra, den Baskenlaendern und auf den Balearen* (Berlin, 1861) wherein he collected information about Navarrese Jews, mainly from the older standard histories of the kingdom. Indeed Baer himself devoted a separate section to Navarre in his monumental documentary compilation *Die Juden im Christlichen Spanien* (Berlin, 1929) Part 1.

From Iberian historians of a previous generation, the only full treatment of Navarrese Jewry was Mariano Arigita y Lasa's essay *Los judíos en el país vasco* (Pamplona, 1908). It covered, in a shorter form, the same material as Kayserling. Arigita y Lasa feverishly emphasizes that Navarrese Jews had no social or religious influence on the Christians. Their only contributions, according to Arigita y Lasa, were in the political, administrative, and economic spheres.

Recently the situation has changed, thanks mainly to the efforts of Béatrice Leroy, who has written *The Jews of Navarre* (Jerusalem, 1985); "Le royaume de Navarre et les juifs aux XIVe–XVe siècles: entre l'accueil et la tolérance," *Sefarad* 38 (1978):263–92; and "Recherches sur les juifs de Navarre á la fin du moyen age," *Revue des études juives* 140 (1981):319–

432. These works mainly cover the fourteenth century. See also the efforts of Juan Carrasco Pérez: Among them are "Prestamistas judíos de Tudela a fines del siglo xiv (1382–1383)," in *Miscelánea de estudios árabes y hebraicos* 29 (1980):87–141; "Acerca del préstamo judío en Tudela a fines del siglo xiv," *Príncipe de Viana* 166–167 (1982):909–948; "Los judíos de Viana y Laguardia (1350–1408): aspectos sociales y económicos," in *Vitoria en la edad media* (Vitoria, 1982), pp. 419–447; and "La actividad crediticia de los judíos en Pamplona" in *Minorités et marginaux en France meridionale et dans la peninsule ibérique (VIIe–XVIIIe siècles)* (Paris, 1986), pp. 221–263.

As far as Portugal is concerned, it is of course the work of Maria José Pimenta Ferro Tavares that has ended the drought in Portuguese Jewish studies. See her *Os judeus em Portugal no século xiv* (Lisbon, 1979) and *Os judeus em Portugal no século xv* (Lisbon, 1982) 2 volumes.

4. Of all the Iberian kingdoms, Navarre probably has been the most neglected. Its small size, a result of its having been effectively blocked in its territorial ambitions during the thirteenth-century Christian conquests, has confined it to relative historiographical oblivion. There have been important works written on Navarre in the last twenty years. Among them are Javier Zabalo Zabalegui's *La administración del reino de Navarra en el siglo xiv* (Pamplona, 1973) and the aforementioned Juan Carrasco Pérez's *La población de Navarra en el siglo xiv* (Pamplona, 1973).

Prosper Boissonade's work is entitled *Histoire de la réunion de la Navarre à la Castille* (Paris, 1893). More recently, José María Lacarra published *Historia política del reino de Navarra* (Pamplona, 1973) whose volume 3, pp. 345–436 addresses this period, and Luis Suárez Fernández has written *Fernando el católico y Navarra* (Madrid, 1985).

Historians who have written generally on medieval peninsular life have also mainly focused on Castile and Aragon, probably because the unity of these two kingdoms formed the core of the modern state of Spain. For a succinct analysis of this problem and the challenge it presents to the student of Iberian history, see Jocelyn N. Hillgarth, *The Spanish Kingdoms 1250–1516* (Oxford, 1976) 1:ix–x. See also his review of Joseph F. O'Callaghan, *A History of Medieval Spain* (Ithaca, 1975), which reflects an opposing viewpoint, in *Speculum* 52 (1977):722–726.

5. The following short precis of the history of Navarrese Jewry is based on the works listed in note 3.

6. This discussion is based on the relevant works cited in note 4; I have generally followed the interpretation of events given by Boissonade. See chapters four, five, and six below for additional data. Note my brief comment in note 61 to chapter four.

7. J. R. Castro and F. Idoate have assembled a catalogue of documents from the royal chamber of accounts (the *Cámara de Comptos*), now in the

Archivo General de Navarra entitled *Catálogo del archivo general de Navarra. Catálogo de la sección de comptos* (Pamplona, 1952–1970); it runs to fifty volumes. Florencio Idoate has authored volume 48 (Pamplona, 1968), which contains materials from the years 1461 to 1499 and is therefore most relevant to our study. The descriptions of the sources are brief, and often pertain only to the first folio of a document even when the source is longer than one page. Volumes 51 and 52 of the catalogue (Pamplona, 1974) contain short précis of the *registros* (registers, generally of tax collectors), which are perforce idiosyncratic in the information they provide glean from these large volumes.

Royal decrees are mainly found in the section of the *Cámara de Comptos* titled *Documentos* and the tax records in the *Registros*. The *Registro del Sello* for late 1494 to early 1495 is in the *Sección de Comptos, Documentos*, Cajón 165 Número 80 and Caj. 166 No. 7. Other documents relevant to this study were found in the *Papeles Sueltos* section of the *Cámara de Comptos*.

Another group of documents in the Archivo General de Navarra is found in the *Archivo del Reino* and it also contained valuable materials. So too the *Fondo de Monasterios,* especially the collection of Tulebras and Fitero. Other relevant church sources were in *Clero Regular,* specifically those of the Convento de Puente la Reina.

A general guide to the royal archives in Pamplona is provided by J. M. Lacarra, *Guía del archivo general de Navarra, Pamplona* (Madrid, 1953).

8. Francisco Fuentes Pascual has compiled a *Catálogo del archivo municipal de Tudela* (Tudela, 1947). The documents drawn by Jewish notaries were found by Julio Segura over the last few years. They are the property of the municipal archive but are not listed in this older catalogue. The city's notarial archive has no such guide. All the notarial registers I consulted there contained material on the Jews, and, significantly, registers from all notaries referred to in the notebooks are available. It is important to stress that materials from one notary are often interspersed within the register of another, and that the dates reflected in the notebook's title are often not borne out by the internal evidence of the source itself. The majority of the relevant material is from the 1490s; a lesser amount, from the previous decade. These volumes are all found in the Archivo de Protocolos de Tudela, although some of the notebooks originated outside of the city. The pagination of all these registers was done by my wife Miriam Schacter, who accompanied me in my research in Tudela. The notebooks I consulted were:

Pedro Latorre, Vols. 1492–1498; 1498–1501
Sancho Ezquerro, Vol. 1480–1500
Martín Novallas, Cascante, Vol. 1489–1496, 1490–1494

Juhan Pérez del Calvo, Vols. 1472–1499; 1502
Diego Martínez de Soria, Vol. 1455–1477
Pedro Jiménez de Castelruiz, Vols. 1478–1519; 1500–1541
Pedro de Rodas, Vols. 1463–1491; 1481–1491
Juhan de Cabanillas, Vol. 1490–1520
Pedro de Lesaca, Cortes, Vol. 1494–1523
Juhan Frias, Vol. 1496–1504
Miguel Martínez Cabero, Vol. 1498–1502
Juhan Aristoy y Navarro, Vol. 1494–1524
Juhan Martínez Cabero, Vols. 1467–1488–1489; 1490; 1491–
1492; 1493; 1492–1500; 1494–1500; 1498; 1496–1504

Only in the last few years have notarial registers been consistently used as a source for medieval Jewish history. The pioneers in this line of inquiry were Richard Emery, *The Jews of Perpignan in the Thirteenth Century* (New York, 1959) and Joseph Shatzmiller, *Recherches sur la communauté juive de Manosque au moyen age* (Paris, 1973). For the history of medieval Iberian Jewries, see the small volume by Klaus Wagner entitled *Regesta de documentos del archivo de protocolos de Sevilla referentes a judíos y moros* (Salamanca, 1978).

The Hebrew documents from the Jewish notaries are in the AMT. A description of these newly discovered documents is José Luis Lacave, "Importante hallazgo de documentos hebreos en Tudela," *Sefarad* 43 (1983): 169–79; Lacave is undertaking the publication of these documents. The *ketubbot* (marriage contracts), of which a couple are relevant to this work, will appear soon in his forthcoming book on Spanish *ketubbot*. I am grateful to him for sending me his early transcriptions of these sources.

9. The *Catálogos de los archivos eclesiásticos de Tudela* (Tudela, 1944) was also written by Francisco Fuentes Pascual. The archive contains for the purposes of this study *Tablas* for the years 1482 and 1488; some documents relating to the church and the Jews; and the *Libro Nuevo,* a notarial register kept by the Tudelan notary, Juhan Martínez Cabero.

F. Idoate has published *Catálogo documental de la ciudad de Corella* (Pamplona, 1964) and M. Clavero has compiled a typewritten *Catálogo de documentos 1129–1512* that is available at the Archivo Municipal de Pamplona.

1: Settlements and Population

1. There have been to date only three attempts to list the localities where Navarrese Jews established their residence; all are cartographic projects. The *Atlas de Navarra* (Pamplona, 1977), p. 52 has a map showing the Jewish and Muslim settlements during the fourteenth century. Its sources are the incomplete *Libro de fuegos,* 1366 (AGN) and the *Libro*

de monedaje of 1353 (AGN, *Cámara de comptos, Registros* Tomo 74).
Julio Caro Baroja's chapter on Jews in *Etnografía histórica de Navarra*
(Pamplona, 1971) 1:175–194 includes a map (p. 179) that indicates the
locations of the "juderías medievales" of the kingdom. Unfortunately,
Caro Baroja does not cite sources, nor does he define his use of the term
juderías, which leaves the reader wondering if he only included localities
that had specific living areas for their Jewish residents. Furthermore, there
is no indication which century (or centuries) the map reflects. Béatrice Leroy published a map of "the juderias of Navarre" in the thirteenth and
fourteenth centuries in her *The Jews of Navarre,* p. 254. It suffers from
some of the same inadequacies as Caro Baroja's work on the subject.

    2. The 1494 royal list is in AGN, *Registro* 516 fols. 161v–162v and
the Lerín report in AGN, *Archivo del reino (cortes y diputación): sección
de guerra* . . . Legajo 1 Carpeta 27.

    3. Jews also lived in Puente la Reina in the *merindad* of Pamplona, and
some resided in Ayuar, in the district of Sangüesa. See AGN, *Registro* 516
fols. 161v–162v.

    4. The nine new areas of settlement were those that had not contained
Jews in the "censuses" of 1353 and 1366. See note 1 above and the discussion of these sources in Juan Carrasco Pérez, *La población de Navarra en
el siglo xiv.* Neither is there any reference to Jewish settlement in these
locales in the secondary literature. It is possible that the new Jewish settlements in Mendabia and Muniain, located in areas in thrall to the conde
de Lerín, may have been established by the Castilian and Aragonese Jews
seeking refuge in Navarre during 1492. See chapter five.

    Evidence of Jewish settlement is sometimes thin. It is on the basis of
one document, for example, in AGN, *Fondo de monasterios: Monasterio
de Fitero,* Legajo 36 No. 406, Primero cuerpo, that we know of the existence of a Jew in Fitero. The catalogue of Fitero documents in AGN reflects
the possibility of another Jew living there, but the document, ibid., Leg. 2
No. 37 appears to have been lost.

    Sesma and Artajona are listed as having no Jews in the 1495 Lerín docu-
ment. The claim that seven other places lost their Jews relies on the negative finding that no Jews from these areas have been found in the extant
documentation. It should be noted that three other sites of Jewish settlement, the towns of Los Arcos, Laguardia, and San Vicente, were acquired
by Castile in the early 1460s.

    AGN, *Registro* 516 declares that no Jews reside in the *merindad* of Ul-
trapuertos. In the absence of any local documentation from the years 1479
to 1498, however, such a definitive statement cannot be justified. For a rare
reference in secondary literature to Jews living in this northernmost district
in the fourteenth century, see Javier Zabalo Zabalegui, *La administración
del reino de Navarra en el siglo xiv,* p. 221, note 1002. Zabalo does not
cite the source for his assertion.

5. AMC, Legajo 1. For other copies of this document and the reasons for the issuance of this order, see below, chapter six. Pace Carrasco, *La población,* p. 149 and Zabalo, *La administración,* p. 219; *juderías* were not founded to isolate Christians from the negative effects of contact with Jews.

6. José María Lacarra, in his article "El desarrollo urbano de las ciudades de Navarra y Aragón en la edad media," *Pirineos* 6 (1950):5, was one of the first to decry the lack of Spanish urban studies. He cited the need for detailed plans of the cities of medieval and modern Iberia and urged that local documentation be amassed so that serious work could begin. Lacarra's article was a major pioneering effort and thereby established the framework for any future attempts to chart the areas of Jewish settlement. He offered aerial maps and schematic overlays which illustrated where the Jewish quarters were in various Navarrese cities and towns, but did not supply supporting documentation, nor did he go beyond indicating the general areas of Jewish habitation.

Properties such as vineyards and orchards owned by Jews that were not used for residential purposes are not of concern here. Such parcels, and their sale and purchase, will be discussed in chapter two. Some data from earlier years on Jewish settlement in Estella, Funes, Pamplona, Tudela, and Viana can be found in Francisco Cantera Burgos, *Sinagogas españolas* (Madrid, 1955).

7. The Pontarrón section (probably named after a bridge that crossed over an irrigation canal) apparently contained a hospital. See APT, *Juhan Martínez Cabero, Vol.* 1490 fol. 49 r–v, and also Juan Ignacio Fernández Marco, *Cascante, ciudad de la Ribera* (Pamplona, 1978) 1:319. One notarial document reflects ownership by Jews of houses in a "barrio nuebo." See APT, *Pedro Latorre, Vol. 1492–1498* fol. 308v.

The main sources on the Jews' residence in Cascante, (they mostly reflect the activities of the Nazir family, Ezmel and Yento) are in APT, *Martín Novallas, Cascante, Vol. 1489–1496, 1490–1494* fols. 3r, 17v–18r, 22r–v, 29r–v, 30v–31r, and 31v–32r. In a *ketubbah* recently found in the municipal archives of Tudela (*Ketubbah* no. 1 and Hebrew document no. 3 in AMT), the bridegroom Moshe ben Levi ben Gabbai granted houses and a vineyard in Cascante to his bride Solbella, the daughter of Shmuel Sar Shalom, as a *mattanah lehud* (an especial gift to her alone). The abutments of the properties are listed; the vineyard was located in the Aguelas area and abutted several other parcels, including a vineyard belonging to the elder Don Yitzhak Nazir.

8. The sources for Puente la Reina are entries in a list of properties on which taxes were owed in 1491 to the local monastery of Santo Crucifijo: AGN, *Archivo del reino: Clero regular (Ordenes religiosas), Convento de*

Crucifijo de Puente la Reina, Sección 2a, No. 164. Jews appear in connection with the *censes* they owe and are mentioned as owning properties that abut those of others who paid imposts to Santo Crucifijo. According to the royal tax records of 1494—see below in this chapter—the village contained five Jewish hearths. It would appear, then, that the three people listed in the monastery's rolls (Jaco Bon, Peru Bon, and Salamon Jarra) constituted the majority of the population (or at least of the part of the population obliged to pay taxes).

The *hospital de peregrinos* of Puente la Reina was near the Church of the Crucifix (AGN, *Cámara de comptos, Documentos* Caj. 154 No. 58), as quoted in José Yanguas y Miranda, *Diccionario de antigüedades del reino de Navarra* (Pamplona, 1964) 2:479–481 and the hospital was in the southeast section of the medieval village (Lacarra, "Desarrollo urbano," Lámina V). It appears that the Jews lived near the church, which would place them in the same sector. The major thoroughfare mentioned in the sources might be the public street that bisects the village and ends at the famous Roman bridge.

9. See Ricardo Ciérvide Martinena, *Inventario de bienes de Olite* [1496] (Pamplona, 1979?), pp. 24–25. The map indicates that the Rua de la Judería is located in the northeast corner of the city near the Portal de Tafalla.

10. AGN, *Registro* 537 fol. 18v. This tax ledger was written in 1511 and notes that, because of the "converssion de los dichos judios," the synagogue was confiscated and the government was collecting taxes on its properties. That the houses may have been used for communal purposes is mere conjecture. It remains to be determined whether other Jews lived in this quarter, which contained the medieval castle. The synagogue also rented two vineyards and a "pieça" in the terminal of Seguero.

A map of Viana and the location of property owned by Jews in the fourteenth century can be found in Juan Carrasco Pérez, "Los judíos de Viana y Laguardia (1350–1408): Aspectos sociales y económicos," p. 438 (see also p. 439). When Navarre was incorporated into Castile, the castle, which had previously been used in defense against Castilian armies, was destroyed. A poorly drawn diagram of the location of the *judería* of Viana, "Plano de la iglesia [*sic*] de Viana," is in Cantera, *Sinagogas,* p. 335. The map is based on information relayed by one individual to Cantera.

11. For the sources on Jewish residence within Pamplona during 1479–1498, see below. A detailed description of the medieval city of Pamplona, including a trailblazing attempt to reconstruct its Jewish quarter, is given by Juan José Martinena Ruíz, *La Pamplona de los burgos y su evolución urbana (siglos xii–xvi)* (Pamplona, 1974); see especially pp. 177–89. Much has been added here to his account using late fifteenth-century documenta-

tion. As Martinena himself explained (p. 183), given the broad chronological range of his undertaking he had to be selective in his choice of sources. His work is graced by two important maps: a well-executed and clear representation of medieval Pamplona (between pp. 64 and 65) and a modest, though helpful, rough drawing of its *judería*.

The Latin word *vallam* used in a fourteenth-century document (AGN, *Documentos* Caj. 5 No. 131 as quoted in *La Pamplona*, p. 179 note 430) can best be translated as meaning a fortified fence or palisade; it probably did not mean a stone wall. The structure still existed in the late fifteenth century, for documents refer to the "portal de la juderia," which was an opening in the fence.

12. The *sarrazon de los canonigos* surrounded the *huerto de los canonigos*. See AGN, *Registro* 517 fol. 30v, and cf. the map in *La Pamplona*, p. 184. The convent is not mentioned in late fifteenth-century documents relating to the *judería* (cf. ibid., and pp. 136–138), the term *tejeria* is used to describe the western limits of the quarter (AGN, op cit., fol. 31v).

13. The best history of the Jewish quarter from the thirteenth century onward is given in *La Pamplona*, pp. 177–180. For a general survey of the evolution of Pamplona itself, see ibid., pp. 39–71. Martinena describes the separate development of the Navarrería, Población de San Nicolás (Población), and the Burgo de San Cernín (Burgo), and discusses the results of their unification in 1423.

Béatrice Leroy in her article "La juiverie de Tudela aux XIIIe et XIVe siècles sous les soverains français de Navarre," *Archives juives* 9:2, claims that, prior to the fourteenth century, each *burgo* had its own Jewish quarter. That seems unlikely. Leroy has published the document ordering the rebuilding of the Pamplona *judería* in 1336; see "Recherches sur les juifs de Navarre à la fin du moyen age," pp. 380–382.

14. The three gateways are in AGN, ibid., fols. 30r and 31v. The "portal de garcia marra" was also called the "portal del Rio." The path through the portal led to the mill of Garcí Marra situated on the banks of the Arga. The second gateway may have been named after the fountain (*fuent*) that existed outside the city's walls. The "fuent vieja" appears in AGN, ibid., fol. 32v and probably refers to the gate of that name. On all this, see *La Pamplona*, pp. 181–183 and 115–117.

15. Leonor was so titled already in 1466; see AGN, *Documentos* Caj. 159 No. 67 and as reported in Lacarra, *Historia política* 3:317. The edict itself, AGN, *Documentos* Caj. 160 No. 58, is now missing from the archive in Pamplona. Idoate in his *Catálogo . . . AGN* 48: 190 (No. 372) relied on a previous cataloguer for the capsule of the text, which had already disappeared.

Was the *judería* uninhabitable (ibid.)? Or was it simply in need of repair (Yanguas y Miranda, *Diccionario* 1:520)? The absence of the source leaves these questions unanswerable. The Jews were ordered to repair the houses, which leads to the conclusion that the royal treasury wished for financial reasons to restore the quarter, much of which it owned.

Julio Altadill, *Castillos medioevales de Navarra* (San Sebastián, 1936) 3:110, wrote that the Jews had occupied the Rua del Alfériz in 1469 on a royal permit. This I believe, is a misunderstanding. Martinena, *La Pamplona*, p. 179, wrote of this that the Jews had "escaped" from their quarter, but this was an unfortunate and misleading choice of words on his part.

16. The *compto* of 1467 (AGN, *Registro* 505), the only account prior to 1494 now extant, does not list any Jews living outside the *judería*, even though we know from Leonor's ordinance that they resided in the Rua del Alfériz. None of the Pamplonese royal tax ledgers after 1425 contain any data on Jews residing in neighborhoods other than their own. The houses they owned in these other sections, unlike those in the *judería*, apparently did not belong to the royal patrimony, and thus were free from royal taxation.

17. There are two copies of the 1494 register; they are AGN, *Registros* 517 and 518. Both are incomplete but the sections relating to the *judería* are intact. Although only *tomo* 518 contains the title page and the document commissioning Miguel de Beortegui to collect the taxes, references here are to *tomo* 517.

Although no changes in Jewish residence can be documented for the years 1479 to 1498, comparisons between the 1494 *compto* and those of 1467 and 1460, its immediate predecessors (*Registros* 505 and 499 respectively), are instructive. The latter was approved by the Cámara de Comptos, Chamber of Accounts, in 1462 and the former—interestingly—in 1490.

18. The size of the *judería* was arrived at by using the *cens* rate, which was 12 *dineros* (or 1 *sueldo*) per 30 square *codos*; see *Registro* 517 fol. 30r. The total *cens* was about 1358 *sueldos*, which gives at least 40,000 square *codos*. The houses and plazas that were not taxed are of course not included in this sum. Martinena, *La Pamplona*, p. 78, quotes a 14th-century definition of a *codo* as "cubitus terre in largo quod habeat sexaginta cubitus in longo," in other words, 60 square cubits. It is difficult to convert these measurements into modern equivalents. Zabalo, *La administración*, p. 231, follows Yanguas y Miranda, *Diccionario* 2:418, in citing a late sixteenth-century document found in the Archivo Municipal de Pamplona. Using this source, he claims that a *codo* of *tierra media* is 50 cm by 8 mm.

19. AGN, ibid., fol. 30r. These neighborhoods were listed since 1339 in the *comptos*. See *La Pamplona*, pp. 183, 185, and 186. It is not known why three separate districts were created or who initiated this division.

According to Martinena's map, p. 184, the southeast corner was part of the third *barrio*. There is no clear evidence to support this.

20. AGN, ibid., fol. 30r, v. This district rendered approximately 270

sueldos in taxes, as compared to 589 and 480 *sueldos* for the other *barrios*. The location of some of the shops and plazas within the *judería*, which would help determine the relative sizes of the neighborhoods, is unknown.

Although the average size of the houses was similar in all three *barrios*, in this district the houses were not subdivided, and so the dwellings tended to be somewhat larger. Still, no "large" houses (meaning one that was assessed for more than 30 *sueldos* tax) were located here. The most ample dwelling was occupied by a physician, Mastre Leon. Its previous owner was Mastre Abraham Comineto, called in 1450 the "fisigo del rey" (the king's physician). See AGN, *Registro* 479 fol. 214v. In 1367, *La Pamplona*, p. 183, there were twenty-six houses in this district.

21. On the synagogue, see *La Pamplona*, pp. 184–185 and 188–189. Its fate after 1498 is discussed in chapter six. According to the 1499 document cited there, the synagogue was located between two public streets and the orchard of an individual named Floristan, who probably was a New Christian. Martinena located the site of the synagogue in present-day Pamplona, near the home for retired priests and the Plaza de Santa María la Real.

The "sin[ag]oga mayor" does not appear in late fifteenth-century tax assessments, but various vacant plazas bordering it are mentioned (AGN, *Registro* 517 fol. 32r). The building was not located at the highest point of the *judería*; see the following note. Although the condition of the synagogue at that time is unknown, by 1521 it was in need of repairs (*La Pamplona*, p. 189).

22. AGN, ibid., fols. 30v and 31r. In previous years (*La Pamplona*, p. 185) this area was called "barrio de suso" and "vico superiori," probably because it was on a higher elevation than the other two districts. In fact, this street was said to "descend" from the *rua mayor* (AGN, ibid., fol. 31v). For more on this street, see *La Pamplona*, p. 184. As late as the *compto* of 1459 (AGN, *Registro* 497 fol. 25v), the phrase "de la otra part de la rua mayor" was inserted in the middle of the listing of houses for this *barrio*.

23. AGN, *Registro* 517 fol. 31r contains the reference to Juçe Orabuena (ms: Horabuena). Orabuena also had owned another smaller house in this district. For the two "casa[s] de oracion," see ibid., fols. 30v and 31r. The phrase is a translation of the Hebrew *bet tefillah*. In the *compto* of 1450, *Registro* 479 fol. 215r, the adjective "menor" (small) was appended. Although these houses were described as being privately owned, the *aljama* paid the taxes on Salamon Levi's house for that year. Also, according to *Registro* 495 fol. 27r, in 1458 Salamon Levi owned another house that was in use by the Jewish community.

Fernando de Mendoza, "Con los judíos de Estella," *Príncipe de Viana* 12 (1951):237–38, claims that there was more than one synagogue in

Pamplona, but it is not clear if he was referring to these two prayer houses. His work, it must be said, is generally unreliable.

24. AGN, *Registro* 517 fol. 31v. The neighborhood was sketched as follows: "el barrio del portal de garcia marra descendiendo de la Rua mayor de la Juderia que es enta el portal de la juderia enta la tejeria et por ay al derredor." In the parallel document in *Registro* 518 fol. 33r, the last phrase is shortened, thus: "que es enta el portal de la tejeria et por ally al derredor." As a look at the *compto* of 1412, *Registro* 320 fol. 197v as quoted in *La Pamplona*, p. 186, makes clear, the texts in both 517 and 518 are but further corruptions (especially 517) of its already opaque language: "el barrio del portal de Garci marra descendiendo de la rua menor [sic] de la juderia que es entroa el portal de la teilleria et por ailli al derredor."

The description in the text follows Martinena, who quotes a 1339 document, AGN, *Documentos* Caj. 8 No. 9, XXX, which reads "vico prope tegulariam iuxta portale fontis vetis." It is unlikely therefore that this neighborhood also encompassed the southeast corner of the Jewish quarter.

Without the subdivisions, the size of the dwellings was comparable to those in the first *barrio*. In 1367, *La Pamplona*, ibid., there were 25 houses in the district which was intersected by an unnamed street. The existence of this street is not even recognized in the 1494 documents.

25. AGN, *Registro* 517 fol. 31v. The association was not always headquartered at this address. In 1459, *Registro* 497 fol. 26v, it met in a house in the first district. The hospital was called "ospital de los baynos de la juderia." It is not mentioned in Martinena's discussion (*La Pamplona*, pp. 143–150) of Pamplona's hospitals. See chapter three, for more on these two institutions.

Registro 517 fol. 32v indicates that the *tiendas* (shops) were "enta la fuent vieja." These shops, it appears, were destroyed by the late 15th century.

26. *Registro* 517 fol. 26r. Martinena, p. 181, basing himself on a document from the AMP, explains that Christian artisans and laborers owned the surrounding vineyards. It appears that Jews also worked these lands.

There is evidence relating to other buildings in the Jewish quarter (AGN, ibid., fol. 32r–v). The exact location of these buildings, unfortunately, cannot be determined. These include the houses of the *alcaçeria* and its stalls and the shops of the silversmiths. Others—the royal ovens, the *costureros'* nine shops, the Jewish slaughter houses owned by the king, and other buildings—are listed as destroyed.

27. There is no monograph on the urban geography of medieval Tudela that compares with Martinena's study of Pamplona. The location of some of the Jews' property therefore cannot be determined, because it is not

known where some of the *terminos* or *puertas,* mentioned in the sources, were situated. There are two maps of Tudela that attempt to depict the city during the Middle Ages. One is the above-cited article by Lacarra, "El desarrollo urbano . . . ," p. XIX and the other in Basilo Pavón Maldonado's *Tudela, ciudad medieval: arte islámico y mudéjar* (Madrid, 1978), pp. 24–25.

Articles of interest on Tudela's history and its Jews also include B. Leroy's "La juiverie de Tudela . . . ," the entry on Tudela in Yanguas y Miranda's *Diccionario* 3:87–137 and generally the information in his *Diccionario histórico–político de Tudela* (reprinted Saragossa, 1828).

Pavón Maldonado, p. 15, argues convincingly that not all Jews transferred to the castle upon the order of King Sancho. For the royal order, see AGN, Documentos Caj. 1 No. 35, which is transcribed in F. Baer, *Die Juden im Christlichen Spanien* (Berlin, 1929) 1:933–35. There Baer cites several copies of this document.

28. No extant document from the late 15th century describes the Jews as living within the castle walls. Some Jewish houses are located "a la puyada del castillo" (ACT, Caj. 48 Letra J, No. 15). There were, however, Jewish shops within the castle; see note 30. Two recently found Hebrew documents—AMT, Hebrew documents nos. 1 and 2, dating from 1443 and 1441 (although this latter document is dated 1467, the location of the houses is quoted from an earlier marriage contract) respectively—refer to houses situated within the castle. Although there is evidence that the castle had been repaired in 1388 (AGN, *Registro* 212 fols. 1–11 as cited in Leroy, *The Jews of Navarre* pp. 90–91 and other sources noted on p. 54), it is possible that Jews were no longer living within the fortress toward the end of the following century.

Pavón Maldonado, pp. 15–16, suggests that Jews lived in both the *judería vieja* (the original quarter prior to the evacuation) and the *judería nueva* through the end of the fifteenth century. Although it may be true that they inhabited both locations in the early 1200s, data on Jewish residence from the late 1400s place them exclusively in the vicinity of the castle. On Jewish settlement in Tudela in Muslim and early Christian times, see Eliyahu Ashtor, *The Jews of Moslem Spain* (Philadelphia, 1979) 2:267 and 355–356.

29. See the aerial map in Lacarra, "El desarrollo urbano," Lámina VIII and the photograph in Luis María Marín Royo, *Guía Tudelana* (Tudela, 1974), p. 34. The monument to the Sagrada Corazón de Jesús was built on the site of the medieval castle. The *planilla* of the *judería* lay at the foot of the slope.

The small plain of the Jewish quarter was at a higher elevation than the other neighborhoods of the city. The references to the "puyada" of the *planilla* are in APT, *Juhan Martínez Cabero, Vol. 1467–1488–1489, 3/13/*

1486 fol. 2r; *Sancho Ezquerro, Vol. 1480–1500* fol. 406r; and in ACT, *Tabla 1482* fol. 42v par.6. The *planilla* itself is mentioned in APT, *Juhan Martínez Cabero,* ibid., 3/12/1487 fols. 12r 34v–36r; *Pedro Latorre, Vol. 1492–1498* fol. 55r; and *Martín Novallas, Cascante, Vol. 1489–1496, 1490–1494* fols. 307v–308r.

30. Information exists on a "sin[ag]oga mayor," a "sin[ag]oga menor," and a "sin[ag]oga chica." It is not clear whether the latter two synagogues were identical or whether either is to be identified with the Midrash Benei Orabuena, whose eleemosynary fund is cited in the above-mentioned AMT, Hebrew document no. 2. Documents (APT, *Novallas,* fols. 142r, 238r, 239v, 325v, and 326r) tell of the donation to the "sin[ag]oga menor" of a piece of land that abutted a wall of the castle and was situated below the synagogue. The *confraría* was described as being above the house of a Jew (APT, *Novallas,* fol. 325r–v). Cantera, *Sinagogas,* pp. 320–24 correctly wrote that there are no archaeological remains of Tudelan synagogues, but was mistaken in claiming that there is no mention of them in the city's documents.

The location of the *judería*'s textile workers' section is indicated in APT, *Pedro Jiménez de Castelruiz, Vol. 1500–1541* fol. 13r, pars. a and b. Jews were also to be found in the "barrio de los texedores" in the parish of San Miguel (ACT, *Tabla 1482* fol. 27v pars. 2 and 3 and *Tabla 1488* fol. 28v pars. 2 and 3). Possibly, these two areas were connected. Houses located in the *migrash ha-orgim* (textile workers' section) are listed in Hebrew document no. 6 (Ketubbah no. 2) of AMT, dated 1476.

There were shops of the *alcaçeria,* houses, and *tiendas* of the silversmiths and carpenters within and without the walls of the castle (AGN, *Registro 548* fols. 34v, par. 4 and 46r, par. 3).

31. For ownership of property by Christians and their presumed residence within the *judería,* see APT, *Juan Frias, Vol. 1496–1509* fols. 76r–77r and *Pedro Jiménez de Castelruiz,* fol. 13r pars. a and b. There is much evidence that Jews lived in other Tudelan neighborhoods. See, for example, APT, *Juhan Martínez Cabero, Vol. 1467–1488–1489,* 5/16/1489 for the parish of San Pedro; *Sancho Ezquerro,* fols. 233r–234v for San Miguel; and *Pedro Latorre,* fols. 4v–5r and 42v–43v for the district of San Salbador. A similar situation obtained in the 14th century; see Leroy, *The Jews of Navarre,* p. 127. Some houses were described in one source as situated in the *judería* and in another as located in Sant Pedro; compare ACT, *Tabla 1488* fol. 28, par. 4 with ACT, Caj. 48 Letra J, No. 15.

The "primera portal de la juderia" is mentioned in AGN, *Registro 548* fol. 32v par. 3. Because these tax registers often contain material from an earlier period, we cannot know for certain whether this gate still existed in the late 15th century. Indeed, this *compto* is for the year 1522, yet the Jews are described as they were before 1498. For a reference to a wall surrounding the Jewish quarter, see Yanguas y Miranda, *Diccionario* 3:103. No other writer mentions any walls besides those of the medieval castle. It cannot be determined whether Jews lived or owned property within the Muslim quarter of the city. The documents, as noted above, are mostly from Christian notaries, who would draw up a contract generally when at least one of the parties was Christian.

32. The area of Traslapuent encompassed many districts. Jews and Jewish institutions owned property there in the "soto del rey" bordering the Ebro (APT, *Juhan Martínez Cabero, Vol. 1491–1492* fol. 81r par. a; *Juhan Pérez del Calvo, Vol. 1472–1499* fols. 164r–165r and *Sancho Ezquerro*, fols. 166r and 190r–190v); in Campiello (*Juhan Frias, Vol. 1496–1509* fols. 18v–19r; *Juhan Martínez Cabero*, ibid., fols. 5r, 27r–28r and 87r; idem, *Vol. 1493* fol. 63r–v); in the *termino* of La Margelina in the Campiello section bordering callela Açach Franco (*Ezquerro*, fols. 46r–47r); in Valoria (*Juhan Frias*, fol. 31r); in Picadera *termino* (*Ezquerro*, fols. 97r–98v and 159r–160v); near the road to Cabanillas (ACT, *Tabla 1482* fol. 2r par. 1 and *Tabla 1488* fol. 1v par. 4); in the "sendero de medio" (APT, *Juhan Pérez del Calvo*, fol. 143r) near the terminus of Soladron (*Ezquerro*, fols. 105r–107v); abutting the road to Exea de la Calçada near the termini of Traslapuent (*Latorre*, fol. 25r–v); in the Ginestares terminus (*Juhan Martínez Cabero, Vol. 1490* fol. 28v and *Juhan Pérez del Calvo*, fols. 179r–181r); near the Mosquera terminus (*Cabero*, ibid., fols. 30r–31r and in *Vol. 1467–1488–1489*, 10/31/1487 fol. 43r); and generally in the area of Traslapuent (*Juhan Pérez del Calvo*, fols. 148r, 149r, 150v, 152r, and 152v and *Latorre, Vol. 1498–1501* fols. 1v–2r).

33. The following is a partial list of property owned by Jews in areas outside of Traslapuent. Unfortunately, some of the districts cannot be located. Yanguas y Miranda's *Diccionario histórico-político* is not of any help; he was addressing a 19th-century Tudelan audience who may have known where these places were situated.

Jews had holdings in Almarjales *termino* near Carra Borja (APT, *Cabero, Vol. 1467–1488–1489*, 1/31/1488 fol. 6r; ACT, *Libro Nuevo*, 9/27/1488); in Antera (*Cabero, Vol. 1493* fols. 22v–24r); near Puerta Calahorra (*Latorre*, fols. 42v–43v and *Cabero, Vol. 1490* fols. 30r–31r); in Beaxon *termino* (*Cabero, Vol. 1467–1488–1489* fols. 31v–32r and idem, *Vol. 1493* fol. 49r–v); in Cardet *termino* (*Latorre*, fol. 61r–v and *Cabero, Vol. 1490* fols. 30r–31r); in the terminus of Carr(er)a Borja (*Ezquerro*, fols. 256r–257v; *Cabero, Vol. 1467–1488–1489* 3/19/1489 fol. 10r; idem, *Vol. 1491–1492* fol. 45r–v; idem, *Vol. 1493* fol. 90v; and ACT, *Libro Nuevo*, 1/31/1496); near Carrera Fontellas (AGN, *Registro 548* fol. 32v par. 4); in Cartalobes *termino* (APT, *Ezquerro*, fols. 159r–160v); in Las Fuentes (AGN, ibid., fol. 25v par. 1); Guerta *termino* (APT, *Ezquerro*, fols. 153r–154v; *Cabero, Vol. 1493* fol. 54r–v; and *Juhan Pérez del Calvo*,

Vol. 1502 fol. 20r par. a); in the Guerto del Rax (?) (*Cabero, Vol. 1491–1492* fols. 43r–44v); in Lodares *termino* (*Cabero, Vol. 1490* fols. 30r–31r and *Latorre*, fol. 118r); in Manquiello (AGN, ibid., fol. 23r par. 2); in La Penyuela *termino* (APT, *Ezquerro*, fols. 141r–142v); in Poco de la Mora [on this name cf. Leroy, *The Jews of Navarre*, pp. 36 and 127] (*Latorre*, fol. 121v; *Cabero, Vol. 1491–1492* fols. 43r–44v; idem, *Vol. 1494–1500, 1494* fols. 2v–31; and *Pedro Jiménez de Castelruiz*, fol. 131 pars. a and b); in Valpertuna *termino* (*Latorre*, fols. 98r–v and 141r–v and *Cabero, Vol. 1467–1488–1489*, 5/13/1489 fols. 17v–18r); and in Vilela *termino* (*Pedro Jiménez de Castelruiz*, fol. 20r). One of the *ketubbot* in AMT (no. 3, Hebrew document no. 8) indicates that a Jew owned a vineyard in an area named Barbolanca; there is no other reference to this location.

A "torre de la judia" was located in Vilela *termino*; see *Cabero*, ibid., 11/23/1489 fols. 39v–40r. Yanguas, *Diccionario histórico-político*, p. 267, wrote that the *torre* was near the *tejería*, which suggests that the tower was part of the fortress walls entrusted to the Jews in 1170.

34. AGN, *Registro 516* fols. 161v–162v. The majority of Navarrese Jews lived within the kingdom's largest population centers, located in the southern and central sections of the country. See chapter five on how the number of Tudelan hearths compares with the number of Jewish houses in the city during the years 1484 and 1490.

35. AGN, *Archivo del reino (cortes y diputación): sección de guerra* Leg. 1 Car. 27. For the background of this document, see chapter five. Juan Carrasco, *La población*, p. 135, declares that there were 523 Jewish *fuegos* in the fourteenth century, excluding those of the Jews of Pamplona.

36. According to Bosquet, the city of Viana was under the control of the conde de Lerín and the village of Uxanavilla in thrall to the duque de Nágera. Larraga also was unlisted since it was part of the conde's property. Larraga and its *aldea* are mentioned in the Lerín report and said to contain only one Jewish inhabitant.

The proportion of taxpaying Jews to those unable to render imposts is unknown. Such data for Navarrese Christians during the fourteenth century can be found in *La población*, pp. 147–48. Until such calculations are made for Iberian Jewry, our knowledge of these matters will be incomplete.

Since both reports are dated post-1492, they include the Castilian and Aragonese Jewish exiles who fled to Navarre because of their expulsion in 1492. For data about these exiles, see chapter five.

37. Carrasco, pp. 33–34 and 152, cautions against using any coefficient without detailed analysis of the specific situation. Suárez Fernández, *Documentos acerca de la expulsión de los judíos* (Valladolid, 1964), p. 56, argued for a factor of six, based on a rather generous estimation of Jewish fecundity, and Tarsicio de Azcona, *Isabel la católica* (Madrid, 1964),

p. 626, followed suit. Javier Ruíz Almansa, "La población de España en el siglo xvi," *Revista internacional de sociología* 3:120, used a multiplier of six for all of Spain in the mid-sixteenth century. For our purposes, a coefficient of five, as employed, by among others, G. Desdevises du Dezert, *Don Carlos d'Aragon* (Paris, 1889), p. 14, for computing the general population of Navarre, is used. Carrasco's caveat is well taken, but informed estimates can be made and do have their uses.

38. Figures for the total population of Navarre are unreliable. Many scholars—including J. F. O'Callaghan, *A History of Medieval Spain*, p. 605; C. Clavería, *Historia del reino de Navarra* (Pamplona, 1971), p. 287; and J. Vicens Vives, *An Economic History of Spain* (Princeton, 1969), p. 291—estimate the number of inhabitants at from 80,000 to 100,000, and probably based their figures on Desdevises du Dezert's calculations for 1450; see *Don Carlos d'Aragon*, pp. 14–16 and the appendices on pp. 437–441. The latter's reasoning is highly tendentious and includes the dubious assumption that population increased in Navarre by an identical annual amount from the mid-fourteenth to the early nineteenth centuries.

Although Carrasco, p. 151, has argued that the Jews constituted 3.3 percent of the Navarrese population in the 14th century (not including those unable to pay taxes; see Yanguas, *Diccionario* 3:109 on Tudela), this figure cannot be easily adopted for the late 15th century. Pestilence, the civil war, and the economic depression that beset Navarre in the 1400s surely altered the demographic distribution of the entire Navarrese population. The number of Jews, in particular, was swelled by the arrival of the Castilian and Aragonese exiles in 1492.

There are other methods for determining population figures, but none of them can be successfully utilized here. For example, the number of Jews in Pamplona cannot be extrapolated using population–area coefficients, even if it were possible to ascertain the size of Pamplona's *judería*. As noted above, some of the dwellings were dilapidated and unlivable, others were subdivided, and even more problematic, some Jews lived outside their official quarter.

The size of the Jewish population of Navarre was not known by the royal treasury. In 1495, AGN, *Documentos* Caj. 166 No. 7 fol. 20r par. 3, the monarchs ordered the *recibidor* of the Jews, Mastre Ossua, to give an account of the *casas* of the native and foreign Jews of the entire kingdom. Ossua's report unfortunately is not extant.

On the difficulties involved in calculating the Jewish population of Castile-Aragon during the late fifteenth century, see Miguel Angel Ladero Quesada, "Le nombre des juifs dans la Castille du XVème siecle," in *Proceedings of the Sixth World Congress of Jewish Studies* (Jerusalem, 1975) 2:45–52 and below, chapter five. Until there are more precise figures, any judgments on the relative percentages of Jews in the various Iberian kingdoms are premature. Jocelyn Hillgarth, *The Spanish Kingdoms* 2:637, wrote that "no general study of population changes exists for this period" of the late Middle Ages. Much more complete information has been assembled for the sixteenth century; see F. Ruíz Martín, "La población española al comienzo de los tiempos modernos," *Cuadernos de historia. Anexos a la revista Hispania* 1 (1967):189–202 and, most recently, Carla Rahn Phillips, "Time and Duration: A Model for the Economy of Early Modern Spain," *American Historical Review* 92 (1987):531–562, particularly 536–541.

2: Economic Activities

1. A recent exploration of the Jews' role in the late 15th-century Castilian economy has been undertaken by Stephen Haliczer, "The Expulsion of the Jews and the Economic Development of Castile" in *Hispania Judaica, I: History* (Barcelona, n.d.), edited by Josep M. Solá-Solé et al., pp. 39–47. Miguel Angel Ladero Quesada has written important articles, among them, "Las juderías de Castilla según algunos 'servicios' fiscales del siglo xv," *Sefarad* 31 (1971):249–264 and "Los judíos castellanos del siglo xv en el arrendamiento de impuestos reales," *Cuadernos de Historia. Anexos de la revista Hispania* 6 (1975):417–439. See also Haim Beinart's brief remarks on Valmasedan Jewry in "The Expulsion of the Jews from Valmaseda," (Hebrew) *Zion* 46 (1981):39–40; Idem, *Trujillo: A Jewish Community in Extremadura on the Eve of the Expulsion from Spain* (Jerusalem 1980), pp. 35–47; and Luis Suárez Fernández, *Documentos acerca de la expulsión,* pp. 9–64, passim.

On Portuguese Jewry, one must consult Pimenta Ferro, *Os judeus . . . no século xv.* For Aragon, see the brief article by J. Ramón Magdalena, "Estructura socio-económica de las aljamas castellonenses a finales del siglo xv," *Sefarad* 32 (1972):341–370. I have not been able to acquire a copy of Maurice Kriegel's typewritten thesis titled *La communauté juive dans les Etats de la couronne d'Aragon sous Ferdinand le Catholique et son expulsion* to check for its relevance to our concerns here.

A valuable and convenient compilation of articles on Iberian Jews in the fifteenth century can be found in José Luis Lacave's Spanish translation of Y. Baer's "A History of the Jews in Christian Spain," *Historia de los judíos en la España cristiana* (Madrid, 1981) 2:762–763.

2. In addition to occupational descriptions, thirty-five of the Jews listed in the sources bore an honorable title beside their names. Eighteen were called rabbis, a distinction reflecting the bearer's possession of a high degree of Jewish learning; see chapter three below. Three carried the designation *don* and fifteen earned the title of *mastre,* this in spite of various 15th-

century peninsular attempts to deny Jews titles of courtesy. Among the *mastres,* eleven were listed as physicians and one as a hosiery maker. Two of the physicians were also rabbis. Another 15th-century list of Jewish occupations, based on notarial sources, can be found in Klaus Wagner, *Regesto de documentos del archivo de protocolos de Sevilla referentes a judíos y moros,* p. 7.

The reference to Mastre Ossua as royal physician is in AMT, Libro 43 No. 11, wherein he is also called Mastre Gabriel, the name he took after his conversion. He is probably the same Mastre Ossua who was physician to the princess in the years just prior to the period of this study; see APT, *Diego Martínez de Soria,* Vol. 1455–1477 fol. 45r.

The "cotamallero" might indeed be a maker of a coat of arms (*cota de malla*).

3. APT, *Pedro de Lesaca, Cortes,* Vol. 1494–1523 fol. 173r contains the April 1497 sale. According to ibid., fol. 178v, a Jew possessed property abutting the local mosque.

Interestingly, the Christians are the sellers and the Jews the buyers in the transactions documented during the years from 1490 to 1497 in the southern village of Cascante.

4. Often, once a newly planted vineyard was labeled a *majuelo,* it continued to be so classified even after the passage of many years.

5. On Jewish interest in viticulture in the peninsula during the Muslim period, see E. Ashtor, *The Jews of Moslem Spain* 2:190–300 passim. Navarrese Jews' involvement in the late 14th century is documented by Leroy, *The Jews of Navarre,* pp. 40–41. On Muslims as farm laborers, including vineyard workers, see M. García Arenal, "Los moros de Navarra en la baja edad media" in Mercedes García-Arenal and Béatrice Leroy, *Moros y judíos en Navarra en la baja edad media* (Madrid, 1984), p. 20. A learned discussion of some of the Jewish legal issues involved in wine manufacture can be found in H. Soloveitchik, "Can Halakhic Texts Talk History," *Association for Jewish Studies Review* 3 (1978):152–196. A recent treatment of other Iberian Jews' agricultural activities at the end of the fifteenth century is Miguel Angel Motis Dolader, "Explotaciones agrarias de los judíos de Tarazona (Zaragoza) a fines del siglo xv," *Sefarad* 45 (1985):353–390.

6. At times, one must be skeptical of the descriptions of property provided in a document (see above, note 3). According to APT, *Sancho Ezquerro, Vol. 1480–1500* fols. 233r–234v, a "palacio" and a yard in the Tudelan parish of Sant Miguel were sold on 2 October 1491 to Aym Çalama for thirty-five florins. A building and an animal pen were probably the real objects of the contract.

Information on Navarrese Muslims can be found in García Arenal, pp.

20–23, and Akio Ozaki, "El régimen tributario y la vida económica de los mudéjares de Navarra," *Príncipe de Viana* 178 (1986):480–482; for data on Jews gleaned from tax records, see below, chapter three.

7. The 1478 ordinances are in APT, *Juhan Pérez del Calvo, Vol. 1472–1499* fols. 148r, 149r, 150v and 152r,v; their effectiveness surely continued into our time period. For 14th-century data, see Leroy, *The Jews,* pp. 35–37. The record of the investigation of the roads in Traslapuente can be found in APT, *Latorre,* fol. 25r.

8. On these see below. Only in one case are *censes* paid to Jews or their institutions. In APT, *Latorre,* fol. 121v, Johan Degues sold a vineyard in Tudela to Habran Malach; the property was described as paying a yearly *cens* of one florin to the city's *sin[ag]oga mayor.*

9. The lowest sale price can be found in APT, *Juhan Martínez Cabero, Vol. 1467–1488–1489* fol. 32r for the year 1487 and the highest in *Juhan Pérez del Calvo, Vol. 1477–1499* fols. 39r, v, 66r–67v, 68r–69v, and 69v–71r. Those documents are dated 1477. All this evidence is from Tudela and its environs.

10. References to husbands having secured legal consent from their spouses—no actual documents of consent were found—are in APT, *Martín Novallas, Cascante, Vol. 1489–1496, 1490–1494* fols. 3r and 70r, and *Martínez Cabero, Vol. 1493* fol. 90v and *Vol. 1491–1492* fol. 87r. In a 1477 case, *Juhan Pérez del Calvo, Vol. 1472–1499* fol. 93r, a Jewish couple purchased a vineyard together. For unrelated reasons, the sale was cancelled.

Astruga's sale to Mayr Bendeut (ms: Bendebut) is in *Martínez Cabero, Vol. 1467–1488–1489* fol. 10r and ff.; also relevant are fols. 9r and 45v. There is no indication of whether she was married. The sale by the Falaquera sisters is in idem., *Vol. 1493* fol. 63r–v.

11. APT, *Novallas,* fols. 339v and 340r. It is noteworthy that two Muslims were chosen as arbiters.

12. See APT, *Martínez Cabero, Vol. 1467–1488–1489* fol. 36r for the Bendebut (ms: Bendeut) case: *Latorre, Vol. 1492–1498* fol. 308v is the record of the Çaraçaniel family transactions. See the case cited in note 22 where there is a possibility that the "sale" was effected in order to cover a debt.

13. In the documents, the verbs *cambiar* and *permutar* both mean to barter, and such a transaction is called a *truça.* The relevant sources, respectively, are APT, *Juhan Pérez del Calvo, Vol. 1472–1499* fol. 143r (fols. 179r–181r show the sale of the property by the Jew on the same day); *Ezquerro,* fols. 159r–160v; and *Martínez Cabero, Vol. 1467–1488–1489* fols. 31v–32r.

14. APT, *Martínez Cabero, Vol. 1494–1500, 1494* fol. 19r, v and

ACT, *Libro Nuevo*, 4/22/1494. Other documents of *relinquimiento* are in *Martínez Cabero*, Vol. *1467–1488–1489* fol. 23v; Vol. *1491–1492* fol. 83v; and ACT, *Libro Nuevo*, 6/20/1492 and 5/4/1496.

15. The two *tablas* extant in ACT are from the years 1482 and 1488; all the Jewish payments were due on St. John's day. When Aym Çalama remitted the six shillings he owed on a vineyard and two other parcels, as stipulated in a contract of January 1488, his payment was recorded with the other Christian lessees. The *tabla* described him however as a *tendero,* a term that suggests that he was an agent acting on behalf of a Christian tenant. See APT, *Martínez Cabero*, Vol. *1467–1488–1489* fol. 6r; ACT, *Libro Nuevo*, 1/31/1488; and *Tabla 1488* fol. 3r. The *tabla* notation of three shillings is half of the rental recorded in the notarial document and presumably is an entry of a semiannual payment.

16. The history of the ownership of the parcels can be traced through ACT, *Tabla 1482* fol. 27v; Caj. 48, Letra J. No. 15; *Libro Nuevo*, 11/23/1487 and 5/4/1496; and APT, *Martínez Cabero*, op. cit., fols. 23v and 38r.

17. The Levis' contract is recorded in APT, *Ezquerro*, fol. 406r. The *primiçieros* Johan de Villafranca and Johan de Sorio, in the name of all the parishioners, also required the Levis to invest fifteen florins' worth of improvements over the course of four years. Parcels abutting the stockyard also reflected Jewish *cens* payments to the church.

The Gamiz payment is documented in *Martínez Cabero*, op. cit., fols. 12r and 34v–36r. Andreu de Rueda, the *procurador* of the prior and monks of the House of the Virgin St. Mary, was appointed in Pamplona on 6 June 1487.

18. AGN, *Archivo del reino, Clero regular (Ordenes religiosas), Convento de Crucifijo de Puente la Reina, Sección 2a,* No. 164. Further discussion of this document can be found in chapter one.

19. The Corellan account is in AGN, *Cámara de comptos, Documentos* Caj. 166 No. 30 fol. 1r; the Tudelan, in *Registros,* 548 fols. 22v, 23v and 25v.

20. AGN, *Registro* 517 fols. 30r–32v. Further discussion of these rents can be found in chapter one.

21. There do not appear to be any cases in which Jews were the renters. APT, *Latorre,* fol. 138r, v records that Juhan Ferandez (ms: Fferandez), a Christian, paid a wheat rental on certain lands to Rabí Mayr Bendebut.

De Sesma and Šalomon Ortelano first appear in ACT, *Libro Nuevo,* 8/17/1486. De Sesma was the *raçionero* of the *yglesia collegial* and acquired the orchard only after much legal maneuvering with the executors of the estate of Pedro de Torralba, its previous owner. Ortelano is called the "tributor" (*tributador*) of the property. The document that records the agreement, concluded in 1487, is in APT, *Martínez Cabero*, op. cit., fol. 43r; a parallel source is ACT, *Libro Nuevo,* 10/30/1487. The payment schedule indicated that half of the annual sum was to be paid on All Saints' Day and the rest in January. Originally de Sesma had merely "placed the orchard in the hands" of Ortelano.

22. APT, *Novallas,* fols. 29r, v and 31v–32r. The lease may well have been a smokescreen for a covert loan; see below.

Earlier that year in Cascante, a Christian rented a number of houses to a newly arrived refugee from Castile-Aragon for seventeen florins per year. See below, chapter five.

23. APT, *Latorre,* fols. 4v–5r and 42v–43v. The house of Juliana de Magallon carried a *cens* of ten *groses* payable to the church of Santa María in Tudela. Juliana, not Mosse Mazal, paid the sum.

24. Jacob Macuren's default is recorded in AGN, *Documentos* Caj. 165 No. 80 fol. 45r. The sources for Yento Nazir are cited in note 22, above; on Jews and wine, generally, see above, note 5. That 15th-century Portuguese Jews sold wine and oil is documented by Pimenta Ferro, *Os Judeus,* pp. 296–297.

25. The small riding horse purchased by Simuel Benaçan is called a "rocin" in APT, *Pedro de Lesaca, Cortes, Vol. 1494–1523* fol. 178r and is probably equivalent to the Latin *rocinus* and the English rouncey. Simuel Azamel's purchase is noted in *Novallas,* fol. 315v; for the foreclosure on Jacob Macuren's property, see the previous note. Navarrese Muslims were heavily involved in the sale of animals; see García Arenal, pp. 22–23.

26. The purchase from the *judería*'s abbatoir is recorded in APT, *Latorre,* fol. 111v; the sale of skins is in *Ezquerro,* fols. 413v–414r. Fines were collected from Christians who purchased meat from Jewish and Muslim slaughterhouses; see below, chapter three.

27. Habran Farag's purchase is recorded in APT, *Latorre,* fol. 117v; the meaning of the term *gabineros* is not clear to me. Mataron is mentioned in ibid., fols. 140v–141r; the items sold to him were *corderinas* (shorn lamb skins). Jews such as the *remendones* (cobblers) in Tudela, AGN, *Registro 548* fol. 34v, and the shoemakers in Pamplona, *Registro 517* fol. 32v, needed animal skins. The term used for Shrovetide was *carnestalendas* [*sic*], the three carnival days before Ash Wednesday and the beginning of the Lenten season.

28. The contract of May 1497 is in APT, *Latorre,* fol. 304r. Habran Aboçach probably had an arrangement with the slaughterhouses. The baby lambs were called *borregos* and *borregas,* the wool and skins, *lana suzia.* The contract ran through the "dia de carnal" of 1498, and the terms were twenty-eight and a half *groses* per *roua;* thirty-four florins were to be paid on St. John's day in June, twenty florins on St. Bartholomew's day, and the rest on *carnestalendas.*

The payment of the Tudelan city officials is noted in AMT, *Libro de cuentas de propios, Vol. 1480–1521* fol. 12v. The messenger also confiscated the woolen products, called simply *lanas*, that had been imported from Logroño. For a general discussion of the wool trade in the peninsula, see Hillgarth, *The Spanish Kingdoms* 2:36–38.

29. The 1494 case is in APT, *Latorre* fol. 61r. Full payment was expected within fifteen days of the execution of the contract. In AMC, *Legajo* 22, 1491–1492, the Corellan village council paid Ezmel Falaquera for quantities of hemp and for the cost of transporting it to Tudela. The document of 1490 is in APT, *Novallas*, fols. 7r–8r. Seven florins were due on the day of San Miguel and the rest at the end of the year. *Latorre*, fols. 12or, v and 195v records a Jew commissioning clothing to be made, and *Aristoy y Navarro, Vol. 1499–1524* fol. 236r (see chapter five, below), indicates that cloth was sequestered from both *aljamas* of the Jews. This information shows that Jews were involved in the clothing trade. On the situation in the previous century, see Leroy, *The Jews*, pp. 44–46, and for 15th-century Portugal, Pimenta Ferro, pp. 294–296.

30. AGN, *Registro* 548 fol. 34v documents the silversmith shops in Tudela. *Registro* 517 fol. 32v is the source for Pamplona. The findings of the arbitrators, Rabí (ms: Raby) Mayr Bendebut and Mahoma Alozeria, dated February 1486, are in APT, *Latorre*, fols. 245v–r and 246r. Yuçe Çaraçaniel may or may not be the same person as Juçe Çaraçaniel mentioned earlier in this chapter. See Leroy, pp. 47–48 for the 14th century.

31. Op. cit., fols. 3or and 28v. Jehuda Bendebut was heavily involved in transactions of this kind, and his family frequently used Latorre as its notary. L. Suárez Fernández, *Judíos españoles en la edad media* (Madrid, 1980), pp. 102 and 255 discusses peninsular Jews' involvement in the sale of fish during the late Middle Ages. On this trade, generally, during the early modern period, see Fernand Braudel, *The Structures of Everyday Life* (New York, 1985), pp. 214–20.

32. *Latorre*, fols. 25v, 28v, 3or, and 41v. On these agreements, see *inter alia* Robert S. Lopez and Irving W. Raymond, *Medieval Trade in the Mediterranean World* (New York and London, 1955), pp. 212ff.

Cargas were the measurements in volume, and *dozenas*, containing twelve pounds, the measures in weight. According to Ricardo Ciérvide, *Inventario de bienes de Olite*, one *dozena* is equivalent to 4.464 kilograms. The amount of fish noted in fol. 3or, then, is 533 pounds.

Prices in the documents vary. It is probable that fish prices were lower in May because the Lenten season was over.

33. *Latorre*, fol. 106r. The name appears in the ms. as "Bendeut."

34. Ibid., fols. 57v–58r and 57v margin. Although Jews are not permitted according to their law to eat eel, they may derive profit from its sale.

35. Ibid., fol. 106v.

36. Ibid., fols. 112r and margin and fols. 208v–209r.

37. A statement of obligation, APT, *Ezquerro*, fols. 413v–414r, could also reflect an overdue payment on a past sale. This underscores how hazy was the distinction between commerce and money or commodity lending.

38. The document referring to the activities of the village of Lerín is in *Latorre*, fol. 192r, that of the Muslims of Ablitas in idem, Vol. *1498–1501* fol. 7r–v and that of the church in *Juan Frias, Vol. 1496–1509* fol. 54r. In ibid., fol. 34v, a *labrador* of Murillo is also described as being a *vezino* of Tudela. On those who patronized Jewish moneylenders in the 14th century, see Leroy, *The Jews*, pp. 73–78. See also the two fine articles by Juan Carrasco Pérez: "Acerca del préstamo judío en Tudela a fines del siglo xiv," pp. 909–948 and "La actividad crediticia de los judíos en Pamplona (1349–1387)," pp. 221–263.

39. There are no works that give modern equivalents to 15th-century Navarrese units of measurement. That there was great diversity in the definition of certain units in 14th-century Navarre, see Zabalo, *La administración*, pp. 228ff. Leroy, p. 65, notes that a *kafiz* contained 164 liters and that a *robo*, one fourth of a *kafiz*, would contain 41 liters.

The prohibition in Jewish law against doing business with non-Jews such that payments would fall due on non-Jewish religious festivals was mitigated in the Middle Ages. See the Franco-German Tosafists' commentary on the Babylonian Talmud, *Avodah Zarah* fol. 2a and Jacob Katz, *Exclusiveness and Tolerance* (Oxford, 1961), pp. 24–36, *passim.*

40. On the taxes, see chapter three. The 1497 documents are in APT, *Latorre, Vol. 1492–1498* fols. 299r, v and 347r–v. Orabuena may have also collected rent on the use of the *granero* (silo).

41. APT, *Juhan Pérez del Calvo, Vol. 1472–1499* fols. 82v and 86r and *Martínez Cabero, Vol. 1490* fols. 18v–19r are examples of *comandas* and contain no mention of the amounts to be repaid, the need for guarantors, and the like. It is difficult to explain the nature of this contract precisely. As Robert S. Lopez and Irving W. Raymond, *Medieval Trade in the Mediterranean World*, p. 175, have written, "to describe the *commenda* is easier than to define it."

The contracts of obligation, were said to "guardar el derecho" (guard the rights) of the Jew; some agreements, though, are described as being with or without contracts of obligation; see *Latorre*, fol. 142v. The documents often note that the loans cannot be collected by means of the creditor's oath but only by displaying a seal appended by a public notary; on this, see Y. F. Baer, *The Jews of Christian Spain* 1:147.

Profits were probably not realized through listed penalties or interest rates. For a discussion of this issue, see below on moneylending.

42. The relevant cases are in APT, *Latorre*, fol. 192r; *Diego Martínez de Soria, Vol. 1455–1477* fol. 37r; and *Latorre, Vol. 1498–1501* fol. 7r–v.

43. *Martínez Cabero, Vol.* 1467–1488–1489 fols. 13v, 15v, and 27v. The arbiters were Miguel de Guaras and Abraham Bendebut (ms: Bendeut).

44. All these transactions were recorded in the registers of Latorre and Martínez Cabero. The hemp was variously measured under the supervision of local overseers (*behedores*). On the same day of the transaction recorded in *Latorre, Vol. 1492–1498* fol. 115r–v, the Jewish lender sold houses in Corella to the Christian borrower; on the same day of ibid., fols. 123v–124r, Jehuda (ms: Gehuda) Bendebut lent money to some Muslims to whom he had delivered hemp.

45. A *comanda* can be found in *Latorre,* fol. 27v. In one case, ibid., fol. 112v, the hemp was "graciously lent." Fol. 234v records a case where grain and hemp were leased; the grain was due, as was the custom, on August 15, whereas the hemp was to be repaid in November. Due dates, generally, ranged from September to December. The borrower, *Martínez Cabero, Vol. 1490* fol. 85r, could also return the value of the object instead of the actual item that was lent. On the average schedule of repayments in an earlier century, see Leroy, p. 65, and the articles by Carrasco cited in note 38, *passim.*

Other items were leased by Navarrese Jews, and here too the distinction between commission selling and outright loans is unclear. See *Latorre,* fols. 120r, v and 195v; *Juhan Pérez del Calvo, Vol. 1472–1499* fol. 93v for dealings with cloth; and *Latorre,* ibid., fols. 127v and 138v for the trade in *geso* (plaster).

46. On medieval theological conceptions of usury, see John T. Noonan, Jr., *The Scholastic Analysis of Usury* (Cambridge, 1957), especially the introduction, pp. 1–8.

In the last few years, several fine studies have addressed the topic of moneylending by medieval Jews. The pathbreaking works in this field have been Richard Emery's *The Jews of Perpignan in the Thirteenth Century* and Joseph Shatzmiller's *Recherches sur la communauté juive de Manosque au moyen age.* On moneylending by Navarre Jews, the works of Leroy and Carrasco Pérez have already been cited.

47. In the case recorded in APT, *Juhan Frias, Vol. 1496–1509* fols. 18r–19r, a Jew was accused of usury in the sale of a vineyard. *Latorre,* fol. 135r–v, records a Jew witnessing a loan from one Christian to another; *Novallas,* fol. 79v lists a Jew's property in the abutments of a parcel offered as collateral by a borrower from the local church. In ibid., fol. 116r, a Jew transferred to a Christian a number of his outstanding loans that remained to be collected; the latter surely made full use of these notes. The Yuçe Falaquera loan is recorded in *Latorre,* fols. 194r–295r.

48. Although the notebooks of Jewish notaries have been lost, indica-

tions that they once existed appear in the registers of Christian notaries. There are a few references to *quinyans* (literally, purchase agreements; see Leroy, p. 61) in the sources; they may well have included moneylending contracts. In *Novallas*, fol. 316v, a Christian *procurador* (appointed by a Christian) demanded satisfaction from a Jew because of an outstanding *quinyan* written in what the author calls "judayco." For others, see ibid., 316v–317r, 346r and related documents on 190r and 317r. *Martínez Cabero, Vol. 1467–1488–1489* fol. 3v notes that on 9 September, 1487, a Christian ordered some Jews to pay their debts and adduced a *quinyan* as evidence.

Carrasco notes the preponderance of members of certain families in moneylending during the previous century. See his "Acerca del préstamo judío," p. 917, "La actividad crediticia," pp. 231–39, and his "Los judíos de Viana y Laguardia," pp. 427–29.

49. Although moneylending documents found in the notarial registers do not append occupational descriptions to the Jews' names (see earlier in this chapter), one Jewish creditor is labeled a surgeon in the *Registro del Sello* of the royal chancellery, AGN, *Documentos* Caj. 165 No. 80 fol. 55r. Muslim debtors can be found in APT, *Latorre*, fols. 62r, 122v, and 123v. The "sennor de Ablitas" and the village of Larraga appear as borrowers in ibid., fols. 113r,v, and 192r, respectively. As for Christian creditors, the *escudero* is in *Novallas*, fols. 17v–18r; the Sangüesan cleric in AGN, op cit., Caj. 166 No. 7, fol. 28r; the *estudiant* in Caj. 165 No. 80 fol. 31r; and the "alcalde de Monreal" in ibid., fol. 10r. Some borrowers, of course, were repeaters; in APT, *Latorre*, fol. 31r, two loans involving the same individuals were negotiated on the same day.

For an analysis of individuals who in previous years were in debt to Navarrese Jews, see Leroy, pp. 73–78, and Carrasco's, "Acerca del préstamo judío," pp. 921–922 and ff., "La actividad creditícia," pp. 239–44, and "Los judíos de Viana. . . ," pp. 429–431.

50. E. J. Hamilton, *Money, Prices and Wages in Valencia, Aragon and Navarre, 1351–1500* (Cambridge, Mass., 1936), pp. 120–42 and Jorge Marín de la Salud, *La moneda navarra y su documentación* (Madrid, 1975), pp. 11–24 discuss the money that circulated in Navarre. The phrase "bewildering monetary diversity" is from Hamilton, p. 137.

The second most common currency mentioned in the sources was *solidas jaquenses* from Aragon; Castilian currency appears much less often. The value of the transactions negotiated in these coins did not vary much from those business dealings in which Navarrese currency was used. Baer, *Christian Spain* 1:201 wrote that most Jewish loans were petty and the sums involved were used for everyday business. Cf. Pimenta Ferro, pp. 310–330 for Portugal, and for fourteenth-century Navarre, Leroy, pp.

68–69, and Carrasco, "Acerca del préstamo judío," pp. 916–919, "La actividad creditícia," pp. 225–230 passim, and "Los judíos de Viana," pp. 426–429.

51. Cf. the tables in "Acerca del préstamo," p. 927 and those in "Los judíos de Viana," p. 443.

52. The terms employed were "deuda y obligaçion," "carta de obligaçion," and most frequently and simply, "obligaçion." APT, *Latorre*, fol. 42r contains the phrase "comanda y obligaçion." On *commendas*, see note 41, above.

For euphemisms of an earlier period, see "Acerca," pp. 925–926. For a discussion of those employed in Jewish law, see Haym Soloveitchik, "Pawnbroking: A Study in Ribbit and of the Halakhah in Exile," *Proceedings of the American Academy for Jewish Research* 38–39 (1970–1971):203ff. and now idem, *Pawnbroking, A Study in the Inter-Relationship between Halakhah, Economic Activity and Communal Self-Image* [Hebrew] (Jerusalem, 1985), passim.

Duenya Alazar's loan is recorded in *Latorre*, fol. 301v. *Novallas*, fols. 17v–18r records a transaction in which the lender was Christian and the same terms were used. Despite the use of the word *oçio* (pleasure), it is hardly likely that this was an interest-free loan.

53. The source for Juhan de Leyça's loan is *Latorre*, fols. 99v and 200r. Ibid., fols. 42r, 50v and 107r records other cases in which *tragineros* borrowed from Jews. These loans were due either within the month of the transaction or during the following month. For the case involving Mastre Mosse, see *Martínez Cabero, Vol. 1467–1488–1489* fol. 24v. The loan may well have been negotiated before the date listed in this document. At the request of the creditor, loans were often recorded by a notary a number of times after the original loan contract was drawn. On penalties, see Leroy, p. 62.

54. See also Lopez and Raymond, *Medieval Trade*, pp. 156 and 160–161.

55. In APT, *Latorre*, fol. 46r, v, the penalty was equal to the principal.

56. *Novallas*, fol. 176r; *Juhan Pérez del Calvo, Vol. 1472–1499* fol. 141r; and *Martínez Cabero, Vol. 1490* fols., 84r and 85r. On interest rates at the turn of the fifteenth century, see Pedro López Elum. "Datos sobre la usura en Navarra en los comienzos del siglo xiv," *Príncipe de Viana* 124–125 (1971):257–262. See Leroy, p. 62, for the late fourteenth century.

57. The three documents are in APT, *Ezquerro*, fols. 375r–376v; *Martínez Cabero, Vol. 1493* fols. 27v–29r; and *Novallas*, fol. 116r, v, respectively.

58. The identification of a specific parcel can be found in *Latorre*, fols.

6r, 27r–v, and 126v–127r; *Novallas,* fols. 2r, 17v–18r and 75v; and *Pedro de Lesaca, Cortes, Vol. 1494–1523* fol. 12r–v. Cf. Leroy, pp. 60–61. Pedro de Salbatierra as guarantor appears in *Latorre,* fol. 49r, v. Instances of others in this role are in ibid., fols. 58v–59r and *Pedro Jiménez de la Castelruiz, Vol. 1478–1519* fol. 19v.

59. Ximeno de Sant Juhan's transaction with Abraham (ms: Habran) Chinillo is referred to as a "prestamo con oçio" in *Latorre,* fols. 121–122r. Salamon Lebi's complaint is in *Juhan Pérez del Calvo, Vol.* 1502 fols. 12v–13r. The "vrumeta" [*sic*] was to be returned by the "domingo del casimodo."

60. The 1494 document describing Salamon Bendebut's (ms: Bendeut) pledge is in AGN, *Documentos* Caj. 165 No. 80 fol. 67r and is discussed in chapter three. The 1482 pledge for the salary of the *cavalleros* (ms: *caballeros*) salary is recorded in AMT, *Libro de cuentas de propios, Vol. 1480–1521* fol. 30r.

61. On Jewish agents in fourteenth-century Navarre, see Béatrice Leroy, "Les comptes d'Abraham Enxoep au début de XVe siècle," *Príncipe de Viana* 146–147 (1977):177–205; idem, *The Jews of Navarre,* pp. 92–106; Meyer Kayserling, "Das Handelshaus Ezmel in Ablitas," *Jahrbuch für Israeliten 5620* (Vienna 1859):40–44; and idem, *Die Juden in Navarra, den Baskenlaendern und auf den Balearen,* pp. 47–59. Now see José Enrique Avila Palet, "Don Ezmel de Ablitas, 'El Viejo', su muerte, y los problemas de su herencia," *Sefarad* 45 (1985):281–314.

On such Jews in the rest of the peninsula during the late 15th century, see Pimenta Ferro, *Os Judeus em Portugal,* pp. 310–330; and the important article by Miguel Angel Ladero Quesada, "Los judíos castellanos del siglo xv en el arrendamiento de impuestos reales."

62. On Jews as *procuradores,* see APT, *Latorre,* fols. 2v, 192r; and *Martínez Cabero, Vol. 1491–1492* fol. 81r. As arbiters, see AMC, *Legajo* 22, 1496–1497, for a case in which they were asked to render a decision on the same day. *Pedro Jiménez de Castelruiz, Vol. 1478–1519* fols. 8r–11v is a case in which the Jewish party to the dispute paid a pair of stockings to the Christian arbiter, who also received a ten-pound reduction in his *pecha* tax from the *procurador* of Johan de Beamont, the *prior* and *canciller* of Navarre.

63. *Juhan Pérez del Calvo, Vol. 1502* fol. 12r. Ms: Abraham.

64. AGN, *Fondo de Monasterios: Tulebras,* Legajo 14 No. 252 (A) and (B). Ms: Sancta María de La Caridat de Tuluebras.

On 19 March 1483, APT, *Juhan Pérez del Calvo, Vol. 1502* fol. 9r–v, the Christian litigants Johan de Leba and Jayme Segura of Cascante chose Salamon Bendebut as their sole arbiter.

65. The sources for Abraham (ms: Abram) Chinillo's activities in 1492

and 1497 are *Juhan Frias, Vol. 1496–1509* fols. 4r and 34v, respectively. In 1497, the creditor had already sequestered some cattle; in 1492, an ass had been taken before the *jurados* intervened. The case involving Yento Nazir is in *Novallas,* fol. 11r.

66. *Martínez Cabero, Vol. 1467–1488–1489* fol. 6v, dated 19 January 1489. On the marriage of Johana Dezpeleta, the infante ordered the church to pay a specified sum. The officials were Johan de Berrozpe, prior of Falces, and Pero de Iracheta.

67. On 29 October, 1492, *Novallas,* fol. 31r, Yento Nazir was released from his tax-farming contract, which had already run for three years. His appointment by Urban de Valladolit is in ibid., fol. 33r, v and his release in ibid., fol. 81r. According to that agreement, Yento was to pay thirteen golden florins (from the Aragonese mint) in January and an identical sum the following year. Juçe Çaraçaniel's contract with Miguel Garçeys (ms: Garçez), *Martínez Cabero, Vol. 1491–1492* fols. 30v and 32r, was signed on 17 June, 1491.

68. The 1482 lease between Abraham (ms: Abram) Farach and Johan de Durango can be found in *Martínez Cabero, Vol. 1467–1488–1489* fol. 9r; the 1495 agreement is in *Novallas,* fols. 108v–109r. According to AMT, *Libro de cuentas de propios, 1480–1521* fol. 120v, Mossen Pierres de Peralta was the "tributador de las mesuras del almudi" in 1490. See below, chapter three, on the relationship of some Jews to the house of the *almudy.* The 1477 sources are *Juhan Pérez del Calvo, Vol. 1472–1499* fols. 38r–v and 66r–67v; fols. 39r, v and 68r–69v; and 69v–71r. Salamon Bendebut is alternately called therein *regidor, ministrador,* and *fazedor.*

69. The meeting between Mayr Bendebut (ms: Bendeut) and Simuel Chinillo is recorded in *Latorre, Vol. 1492–1498* fol. 333r.

70. The 1483 and 1487 payments are in AMT, *Libro de cuentas,* fols. 33r and 85v (ms: Levi). The *sello de seguro* was needed because Tudela "no fiziessen marcas y no cobran marcas." Abençox was to bring a *desespada* for the city officials. A study of Tudela's financial administration based on this first volume of the *Libro de cuentas* by Juan Carrasco Pérez, "La hacienda municipal de Tudela a fines de la Edad Media (1480–1521)," is in Emilio Sáez, Cristina Segura Graíño, and Margarita Cantera Montenegro, eds., *La ciudad hispánica durante los siglos XIII al XVI.* (Actas del coloquio celebrado en la Rábida y Sevilla del 14 al 19 de septiembre de 1981, Madrid, 1985) 2:1663–1697. Salamon Bendebut's (ms: Bendeut) mission is recorded in *Libro de cuentas,* fol. 84r and is discussed below in chapter four.

71. *Libro de cuentas,* fols. 20r, 29r, 54v, 80r, 120r, and 131r for Mosse Cardeniel's collections; fol. 28r for his 1482 bids; and fols. 150r and 206v for Gento Azamel and Aym Çalama, respectively. See also Leroy, *The Jews,* p. 97.

72. All the information is from the *Libro de cuentas* whose first volume begins with the year 1480. The *tajo* and *cornado* were the two imposts on fresh fish; candles called "candelas de seno" were subject to a tax. For the *panaterias*, see fols. 149r, 151r, 156v, 160v, 161r, 180r, 200r, 206r, and 208r. Açach Çaraçaniel's bid is in fol. 118v, and the relevant bids on salted fish are in fols. 161r and 163r.

73. APT, *Martínez Cabero, Vol. 1490* fols. 75v–76r for Salamon Bendebut (ms: Bendeut) and *Latorre, Vol. 1492–1498* fol. 100r for Açach Çaraçaniel.

74. AMT, *Libro de cuentas,* fols. 6v, 17r, v, 21r, 38v, 52r, 64r, and 91r. Cf. the appointment of a Jew as Murcia's official surgeon in the 1480s; see Hillgarth, *The Spanish Kingdoms* 2:440.

75. The ledger of receipts and expenses of the village of Corella is AMC, *Legajo 22.* This document is inconsistently paginated and the yearly reports do not follow chronologically. Locating a specific entry requires searching for the appropriate yearly ledger and then for the relevant comment. References therefore will be made to the year, and to a folio number if one exists.

For business agreements between Jews and the village, such as the purchase of animals or the sale of hemp, see above in this chapter.

76. See note 61 and those works, especially of Américo Castro and Claudio Sánchez-Albornoz, cited in the article of Ladero Quesada.

77. *The Jews,* pp. 80–106, *passim.*

78. The orders to sequester property are in AGN, *Registro 509* fols. 1r and 87v. These folios surround a register of the treasurer of Navarre.

Jews involved in the *alcabala* (ms: *alcavala*) collection in the early 1460s are mentioned in APT, *Diego Martínez de Soria, Vol. 1455–1477* fols. 14r and 53v. According to J. Cabezudo Astraín, "Los conversos aragoneses según los procesos de la Inquisición," *Sefarad* 18 (1958):176, Jehuda Almeredi of Tudela farmed the *rentas* of Valdonsela.

79. AGN, *Documentos* Caj. 164 No. 27. MS: Mayr Bendeut.

80. *Registro 509* fol. 1v. This document is written in a different hand than the sources cited above in note 78.

81. APT, *Pedro de Rodas, Vol. 1463–1491* fols. 12r, v and 14r (ms: Juçe). Mosse Vita and Pedro de Berrozpe were *guardas del derecho* of the "tablas, saca y peage."

82. AGN, *Registro 516* fol. 165v. MS: Salamon Bendeut.

83. The sequestration order was issued on November 24, AGN, *Documentos,* Caj. 165 No. 80 fol. 47v. The agreement to submit to arbitration is in APT, *Latorre,* fol. 24v.

Just prior to the years of this study, problems existed with tax collection in Buñuel. In a series of documents, APT, *Diego Martínez de Soria, Vol. 1455–1477* fols. 14v–15v, Mayr Bendebut, as *siseno* (collector of the *sisa*) and *tributador* of the village of Cortes and its environs, sequestered the property of a number of tax delinquents from Buñuel. On these issues in an earlier period, see Leroy, pp. 95–96.

84. The 1498 document is in *Latorre, Vol. 1498–1501* fols. 13r–14r; the sentence was executed by a Jew and a Christian. The two Christian arbiters chosen in 1488 had to deliver their sentence by Christmas of that year; *Martínez Cabero, Vol. 1467–1488–1489* fol. 6or–v. Mss: Bendeut.

85. AMC, *Legajo*, 22 1481. Bendebut received fifty-five pounds as his share. He also collected the *alcabala* (ms: *alcavala*) of the *yerba* (ms: *yerua*) of Araciel.

86. Ibid., the relevant years. In these documents, Bendebut is called "don Salamon." Bendebut was not in charge of the wool-tax collection in 1487.

87. Ibid., the relevant years. Ms: Symuel Bendebut.

88. Ibid., 1495–1496 and 1496–1497 fol. 506v. Ms: alcavala.

89. Ibid., the relevant years. For 1496, see fol. 507.

90. Ibid., the relevant years. Fortunyo might be Fortuño de Bunuel, *vezino* of Corella mentioned in APT, *Pedro de Rodas, Vol. 1463–1491* fol. 10r.

91. Jento Cardeniel's position is noted in Ricardo Ciérvide, *Inventario*, p. 148. For Ybray de la Rabiça, see APT, *Pedro Jiménez de Castelruiz, Vol. 1478–1519* fols. 8r–v and 9v–11v. Jews' involvement in the collection of the *alcabala* and *saca* just prior to our period of study is evidenced by *Juhan Pérez del Calvo, Vol. 1472–1499* fols. 16v and 24v and in *Diego Martínez de Soria, Vol. 1455–1477* fol. 14r.

92. AMC, *Legajo* 50. Ybray de la Rabiça and Abraham (ms: Abrahan) de la Rabiça do not appear to be the same person.

Legajo 22, 1481 preserves an instance of a Jew nicknamed "tuerto" (one-eyed) who traveled to Tarazona to collect an outstanding tax debt for the village.

93. Any quantitative evaluation must await detailed studies of 15th-century Iberian Jewry and the 15th-century peninsular economy generally; see notes 1 and 61, above. Hardly any research has been done on the Navarrese economy of the late fifteenth century. Hamilton's *Prices, Money, and Wages* treats Navarre only up to 1450. The brief overview by Pedro López Elum, "La depresión navarra en el siglo xv," *Príncipe de Viana* 126–127 (1972):151–68 is just a beginning.

3: Communities, Structure, Activities, and Taxation

1. For a survey of Jewish communal organization throughout history, see Salo W. Baron, *The Jewish Community*, 3 vols. (Philadelphia, 1943). To be sure, Jews in various countries over time exhibited differences in

communal structure and organization. On Iberian Jewish communities, see Abraham A. Neuman, *The Jews in Spain*, 2 vols. (Philadelphia, 1942) and H. Beinart's article, "Hispano-Jewish Society" in H. H. Ben-Sasson and S. Ettinger, eds., *Jewish Society through the Ages* (New York, 1971), pp. 220–238.

The word *aljama* has its roots in Arabic; it means assembly or gathering and is used to refer either to the Muslim or Jewish communities under Iberian Christian rule. See David Romano, "Aljama frente a judería, call y sus sinónimos," *Sefarad* 39 (1979):347–354 and I. de la Cacigas, "Tres cartas públicas de comanda," *Sefarad* 6 (1946):91. *Kahal*, a Hebrew term, has the same import within this context. As Romano points out, *aljama* is a juridical expression and should not be confused with *judería*, a term denoting the Jewish quarter, as many, including some students of Navarrese Jewish history, have done. Fifteenth-century Navarrese documentation clearly supports Romano's argument.

2. The earliest charters referring to Navarrese Jewry are the *fueros* of Tudela (1170) and Funes (1171). These texts can be found in Fritz Baer, *Die Juden* 1:933–937. All stipulations regarding Navarrese Jews in the *fueros* have yet to be thoroughly examined. Baer's "Die auf Juden Bezüglichen Gesetze in den Alteren Rechtscompilationen von Aragonien und Navarra," ibid., 1:1024–1043, is an important introduction.

Zabalo, *La administración*, pp. 221–224, describes the situation of the five super-communities vis-à-vis the royal government in the 14th century. AGN, *Registro* 506 fol. 52r-v, dated 1451, reports the collection of the *pecha* from the six *aljamas*. Investigation of early 15th-century sources will yield the reasons why the sixth *aljama* was added and indicate when it was established.

3. The 14th-century material is in AGN, *Documentos* Caj. 192 Nos. 5, 15, 16, and 21 and is written in Hebrew. Baer published these texts and appended critical notes in *Die Juden* 1:949–958 and 983–986. There is a 14th-century Romance "translation," probably a simultaneous rendition, of numbers 5 and 21, in *Cámara de comptos, Papeles sueltos*, Leg. 2 Car. 7, published by José Yanguas y Miranda, *Diccionario de antigüedades* 3:319–24. Yanguas incorrectly dated the document and his mistake was repeated by those who followed him. See Meyer Kayserling *Die Juden in Navarra*, pp. 76–80 and Julio Caro Baroja, *Etnografía histórica de Navarra* 2:189. In my brief analysis of these documents, I have followed Baer, *A History* 1:220–222, with small departures from his interpretation.

4. According to *Die Juden* 1:957, prior to the writing of this document, seven members of seven families evidently possessed veto power. Yanguas, *Diccionario* 3:95 includes a document that indicates the functions of the twenty council members of the Tudelan municipality. Baer, *A History*, p. 222, noted parallels with Aragonese city councils. The Hebrew terms

for these officials were "הָעִיר   גְּדוּלֵי" and "הַקָּהָל   גְּדוּלֵי
מְנַהִיגֵיה" Baer, p. 217, uses the Romance term *jurados* although this
parallel does not appear in the sources.

5. On the office of *bedin* in northern Castile and in Aragon, see Baer,
A History, p. 212. The office declined in the fourteenth century. According
to Zabalo, *La administración*, p. 208, note 935, the *bedin* collected taxes
from Jews, which would make him equivalent to the Christian *baile*. José
Luis Lacave has indicated in an article titled "Un interesante documento
hebreo de Tudela," to be published in a jubilee volume in honor of Haim
Beinart, that he intends to write an essay on the word *bedin*.

6. AMT, as yet unnumbered. Julio Segura, the archivist, has graciously
provided me with his transcription of the document.

7. Notaries were often imprecise in their descriptions; particularly, it
seems, when the communal positions described were designated by Hebrew terms, which needed to be translated. Nevertheless, there are sources
testifying to the existence of *jurados* in the Tudelan *aljama*: APT, *Pedro
Latorre, Vol. 1492–1498* fols. 20v–21v; *Juhan Martínez Cabero, Vol.
1467–1488–1489* fol. 46r; idem, *Vol. 1490* fols. 30r–31r, and ACT, *Libro
Nuevo*, November 23, 1487; and AGN, *Documentos* Caj. 165 No. 80 fols.
29r and 30r. Other sources document *regidores: Latorre*, fols. 20v–21v;
Juhan Aristoy y Navarro, Vol. 1499–1524 fol. 236r–v; and *Juhan Martínez Cabero, Vol. 1490* fols. 30r–31r. *Adelantados* are documented in
Latorre, fols. 20v–21v and *Cabero, Vol. 1467–1488–1489* fol. 23v; *ordenadores* in AGN, *Documentos* Caj. 165 No. 80 fol. 30r; and *ministros* in
Cabero, Vol. 1467–1488–1489 fol. 5v.

Ordenadores, in *Juhan Pérez del Calvo, Vol. 1472–1499* fol. 11v, and
jurados and *regidores*, in ibid., fol. 12r, are recorded for the *aljama* of Cascante in 1474. The community of Cortes had *adelantados*, as indicated in
Pedro de Lesaca, Cortes, Vol. 1494–1523 fols. 177v–178r, and *jurados*
and *regidores* are noted for Corella, AGN, op. cit., fol. 31v. In Estella,
there were *jurados, regidores*, and *ordenadores* of the *aljama*, according
to *Documentos* Caj. 166 No. 7 fol. 15r, and the Sangüesan Jewish community was served by the *regidores* of the foreigners and the *jurados* of the
natives, as indicated in ibid., Caj. 165 No. 80 fol. 57r. When the royal
chancellery referred to all the *aljama* officials in the kingdom, they were
called "jurados, regidores, and ordenadores," ibid., fol. 24r.

Adelantados of the Tudelan *aljama* mentioned in *Cabero, Vol. 1467–
1488–1489* fol. 23v were called *jurados* in another document referring to
the same transaction, ibid., fol. 38r. *Ordenadores* may have been those
councillors who were involved in tax collection, as when the *ordenadores*
of the *pecha* of the Tudelan *aljama* had to submit certain sums, AGN,
Documentos Caj. 164 No. 28. *Ministro* was a term that probably referred
generally to any member of the *aljama*'s council, *Cabero*, op. cit., fol. 5v.

The nomenclature of Navarrese municipal officials was also hazy; *Ju-*

rados and *regidores* appear to have fulfilled similar (if not identical) functions. The term *regidores* may have referred to any rulers of a municipality; for Tudela, see *Martín Novallas, Cascante, Vol. 1489–1496, 1490–1494* fols. 278r–284v and AGN, *Documentos* Caj. 193 No. 34 fol. 11v.

8. "One *jurado* and three other Tudelan Jews" arranged a tax-farming agreement with a local church, *Cabero, Vol. 1467–1488–1489* fol. 46r, and the "lieutenant of an *adelantado* and *regidor,* two *regidores,* seven *jurados* and other *regidores*" were present at the induction of the new *baile* (ms: *bayle*) of the Jews and Muslims of Tudela, *Latorre,* fols. 20v–21v. Evidence for fourteenth-century Navarrese Jewry is in Leroy, *The Jews of Navarre,* pp. 17–18, and for fifteenth-century Portugal in Pimenta Ferro, *Os judeus,* p. 118.

According to Yanguas, *Diccionario* 1:189, the number of Christian *jurados* varied with each *pueblo.* According to María Angeles Irurita Lusarreta, *El municipio de Pamplona en la edad media* (Pamplona, 1959), p. 66, the number of Pamplonese *jurados* was constantly changing.

9. *Cabero, Vol. 1490* fols. 30r–31r and a parallel document on 38r–39v, dated June 17. Another variant between the two sources is the number and names of Jews listed as present at the sale. Rabí Jaco de la Rabiça, the communal notary, appears in fols. 38r–39v and probably transcribed the proceedings for his own records. The document of sale contained all the standard stipulations expected in such contracts and was signed by two Christian and two Jewish witnesses. These Jews were not residents of the Tudelan *judería.* For parallel situations in the rest of the peninsula, see Neuman 1:42.

10. The Tudelan *aljama*'s activities are described in AGN, *Registro* 548 fols. 22v, 34v, and 46r. According to Baer, *A History* 1:83, the *aljama* had leased these shops from the crown since the late thirteenth century. The Cortes issue is in APT, *Pedro de Lesaca,* fols. 177v–178r, where three *adelantados* are also described as being officials of the entire village. If true, this would be quite remarkable: Could it be that after 1492 the overwhelming majority of the town's population was Jewish? See chapter five. Other Christians were employed by the Jewish communities, as when, *Cabero, Vol. 1490* fol. 65r, the *aljama* of Tafalla settled an account with a rich Tudelan Jew through a Christian agent.

11. *Cabero, Vol. 1490* fol. 23v. In halakhic terminology, Jeuda Bennaçan was named an *apotropos.* Jewish legal sources often quoted the *Babylonia Talmud, Gittin fol.* 37a that the court was the "father of orphans." See inter alia, Moses ben Maimon (Maimonides), "Laws of Inheritance" 10:5 in his *Mishneh Torah* (Vilna, 1928) and Jacob ben Asher, *Tur Ḥoshen Mishpat* (Vilna, 1928), chapter 290, paragraphs 1 and ff. Cf. Lacave's "Un interesante documento hebreo de Tudela" (as yet unpublished), Leroy, pp. 19–20, and Pimenta Ferro, pp. 118–119.

12. On the "sin[ag]oga mayor" of Tudela, see *Latorre,* fol. 121v; *San-*

cho Ezquerro, Vol. 1480–1500 fols. 105r–107v, where the congregants are
called parroquianos, (parishioners); Juhan Pérez del Calvo, fol. 152v; and
Pedro Jiménez de Castelruiz, Vol. 1478–1519 fol. 4r and Vol. 1500–1541
fol. 13r. The "sin[ag]oga menor" is mentioned in Novallas, fols. 142r
and 238r–239v; and Pedro Jiménez de Castelruiz, fol. 4r. The "sin[ag]oga
chica" is referred to in Cabero, Vol. 1490 fol. 28r. A "Midrash Benei Ora
Buena" is attested to in a Hebrew document of 1467; it cannot be determined if this institution is identical with the smaller synagogue. See AMT,
Hebrew document no. 2, which will be published by Lacave in the aforementioned Beinart Jubilee Volume.

The "casas de oraçion" and the "confraria de la teba" of Pamplona are
in AGN, Registro 517 fols. 30v and 31r. On the relationship between con-
frarías and the Jewish ḥevras, see the articles cited in Baron, Jewish Community 3:90–91.

The Corellan synagogue can be found in AGN, ibid., fol. 55r; that of
Viana in Registro 537 fols. 18v and 28r. On synagogues and their activities
within the Iberian peninsula, see Neuman 2, chapter 17.

13. The Tudelan document is in APT, Sancho Ezquerro, fols. 105r–
107v (ms: Bendeut, Malac), that of Viana in AGN, Registro 537 fol. 18v.

14. The Alcalaer donation is labeled in APT, Novallas, fols. 142r,
238r–239v, and 325r–326r as "pura perfect intervivos." For more on this
see below, chapter four. Examples of parcels containing rentals payable to
the synagogue (ms: sinoga mayor) are in Latorre, fol. 121v and Pedro
Jiménez de Castelruiz, Vol. 1500–1541 fol. 13r. The irrigation improvements were effected in 1478; see Juhan Pérez del Calvo, Vol. 1472–1499
fol. 152v.

15. The evidence for Tudela is in Ezquerro, fols. 25r–28v and Pedro
Jiménez de Castelruiz, Vol. 1478–1519 fol. 4r; for Corella see ibid., fols.
3v–4r.

16. On Jewish charities in medieval Christian Iberia, see Neuman 2,
chapter 18, and Shimon Shtover, "Charitable Organizations in Medieval
Christian Spain" (Hebrew), in Aryeh Morgenshtern, ed., Sefer Zikkaron
l'Avraham Spiegelman, 151–168. The almosna of Cascante is mentioned
in Juhan Pérez del Calvo, fol. 12r. The Tudelan almosnas are mentioned
in Latorre, fols. 42v–43v, 118r, and 121v; Diego Martínez de Soria, Vol.
1455–1477 fol. 53r; Pedro Jiménez de Castelruiz, Vol. 1500–1541 fol.
13r; and Cabero, Vol. 1491–1492 fol. 45r, v. Also relevant are ACT, Tabla
1482 fols. 30r, 49r, and 55r and Tabla 1488 fols. 19v and 34r. The "Midrash Benei Ora Buena" also had a hekdesh (probably equivalent to almosna) attached to it; see note 12. The ministers of the various almosnas
came from the ruling families; see below.

17. The January 1482 document is in Ezquerro, fols. 46r–47r and that
of April 1490 is in Cabero, Vol. 1490 fol. 28r. The evidences for fines and

the like being funneled into the *almosna*'s treasury is from AMT, the 1482 Francisco Febo *privilegium*.

18. *Cabero, Vol. 1491–1492* fol. 13r–v.

19. Latorre, fol. 111v (ms: Salamon Bendeut), for the Tudelan slaughterhouses; and AMT, *Libro de cuentas de propios, Vol. 1480–1521* fols. 9v, 29r, 40v, 42r, 54v, 118r, and 120v for the fines paid by Christians for frequenting them. H. Beinart, *Trujillo*, p. 88 presents a parallel situation for late 15th–century Castile. The evidence for Corella is in *Latorre*, fol. 117v, for Pamplona, in AGN, *Registro* 517 fol. 32v. APT, *Novallas*, fol. 322r may contain a reference to a Jewish *carnicería* in Cintruénigo; it is unclear if there were open-air shambles. See also José Luis Lacave, "La carnicería de la aljama zaragozana a fines del siglo xv," *Sefarad* 35 (1975):3–35.

20. *Cabero, Vol. 1467–1488–1489* fol. 64r for Tudela; AGN, *Registro* 517 fol. 26r for Pamplona; and *Registro* 519 fol. 55r–v for Corella.

21. Pamplona's *baynos* are mentioned in *Registro* 517 fol. 31v, and the *confraría* in charge of Tudela's baths in APT, *Novallas*, fols. 42r and 325r–v. The issue of mixed bathing is succinctly discussed in Dwayne E. Carpenter, *Alfonso X and the Jews: An Edition of and Commentary on Siete Partidas 7.24 "De los judíos"* (Berkeley and Los Angeles, 1986), p. 87. For the particular situation in Tortosa, see D. Romano, "Los judíos en los baños de Tortosa (siglos xiii-xiv)," *Sefarad* 40 (1980):57–64.

22. *Ezquerro*, fols. 385r and 386r; *Novallas*, fols. 100v–101r and 346r; *Cabero, Vol. 1467–1488–1489* fol. 23v: idem, *Vol. 1490* fols. 38r–39r and 65r; and ACT, *Libro Nuevo*, 11/23/1487 document the activities of the notary of the Tudelan *judería*. The newly found documents are part of AMT; they are to be published by José Luis Lacave as part of a larger volume on medieval Iberian *ketubbot*.

On the Jewish courts and their jurisdiction in medieval Iberia, see Neuman 1, chapter 7. *Juhan de Cabanillas, Vol. 1490–1520* fol. 7r–8r appears to indicate that the court also met at night. *Novallas*, fol. 316v is a case wherein the *nunçio* was a witness in support of a Christian's complaint of a Jew's indebtedness; a "quinyan" written in "Judayco" was used as evidence. See Lacave, "Pleito judío por una herencia en aragonés y caracteres hebreos," *Sefarad* 30 (1970):325–37. The question of whether a *nunçio* is permitted to announce the forthcoming sale of land on the Sabbath was asked of R. Nissim Gerondi; his response, which includes a reference to the *nunçio* of Tudela, can be found in Leon A. Feldman's recent edition of *Teshuvot ha-Ran* (Jerusalem, 1984), pp. 381–382.

23. AMT, the 1482 *privilegium*. On the external political ramifications of this charter, see chapter six. A recent article on slanderers and their punishment in the peninsula is E. Ben-Zimra, "Ha-Malshinut ve-ha-Mesirah be-Mishnatam shel Ḥakhmei Sefarad," in Meir Benayahu, ed., *Studies in*

Memory of the Rishon Le-Zion R. Yitzhak Nissim (Jerusalem, 1984–85)
1:297–321. See also Neuman 1:130ff; Baer, *A History* 2:69, 263–266, and
323; and Leroy, pp. 26–27 for Navarre.
  24. Johan de Tuledo and Açach Malach appear in APT, *Cabero, Vol.
1492–1500* fol. 15r, v, Muça Rabaniel and Açach Malach (ms: Açac
Malac) in AGN, *Documentos* Caj. 165 No. 80 fol. 29v. A Christian initiated a legal action before the *bayle,* as documented in *Novallas,* fols.
289r–290r. The *bayle* of the Jews of Sangüesa (no Muslims officially lived
within this district) can be found in AGN, *Registro* 495 fol. 8v.
  In the 13th and 14th centuries, the *baile* (sometimes spelled *bayle*),
called *senescal* in Estella and Pamplona and *merino* in Sangüesa, was a
financial officer. See, inter alia, Baer *Die Juden,* 1:941–948; Yanguas, *Diccionario* 1:517; and Zabalo, *La administración,* pp. 114ff. and 220.
  25. APT, *Latorre,* fols. 20r–21v. In the ms, the names of Abraham Bendebut and Abraham de la Rabiça are given as Habran Bendebut and Habran de la Rabiça. The document has been published with some minor
errors by Mercedes García-Arenal, "Los moros de Navarra en la baja edad
media," pp. 119–20. García Pérez de Verayz held several offices during his
career. He was the *alcayde* of the Tudelan *castillo,* and served again as *baile*
(ms: *bayle*) in late October 1494, AGN, *Documentos* Caj. 65 No. 80 fol.
29v.
  26. In 1492, the *portero* of the bailiff was ordered to foreclose on the
property of Tudelan Jews because of the *pecha* owed by the *aljama, Documentos* Caj. 164 No. 28. On the *porteros'* activities and individual Jews,
see chapter two, above.
  27. The three cases, respectively, are in ACT, Caj. 48 Letra J. No. 15:
AMT, *Libro de cuentas de propios,* fol. 14r; and APT, *Cabero, Vol. 1467–
1488–1489* fol. 5v.
  28. See note 11; a parallel document is in ACT, *Libro Nuevo,* 11/23/
1487. De la Rabiça's petition is in *Cabero, Vol. 1467–1488–1489* fol. 38r;
it may well have been used as official testimony.
  29. The rabbinate was not a communal post; the rabbis were men of
considerable Jewish learning. They were not attached to a synagogue, *pace*
Zabalo, *La administración* p. 220. R. Yoel ibn Shuaib, preacher and Bible
commentator, lived some years in Tudela in the late 15th century but apparently had no official position within the community.
  A comprehensive list of all the offices within the *aljamas* can be found
above, note 7; the activities, generally, of these officers are reported in
chapter two. For an Iberian parallel, see Pimenta Ferro, *Os judeus,* pp.
129–136.
  30. See Baer, *Die Juden* 1:953 for the late 13th century. The composition of a *bet din* in 1467 Tudela can be found in José Luis Lacave, "Un

interesante documento hebreo." The family names of the court members were Levi, de la Rabiça, and Minir.

31. In 1490, APT, *Cabero, Vol. 1490* fols. 30r–31r, Mosse Malach, Juçe Falaquera, Juçe Bembolat, Mosse Xani, and Jaco Farag were *regidores*; Rabí Habran de la Rabiça, Rabí Sento Benjamin, Rabí Mayr Bendebut, Mastre Mosse Bendebut, Abram Memenir, Sento Farag, Yuce Albelia, Jaco Lebi, and Simuel Gamiz were listed in this position in 1494, *Latorre,* fols. 20v–21v. The *regidores* of the native *aljama* in 1497 were Abram Malach, Sento Falaquera, Jaco Lebi, Simuel Vencyda, and Salamon Veniamin, *Juhan Aristory y Navarro, Vol. 1499–1524* fol. 236r. Juçe Atortox and Simuel Feci held that position among the *foranos,* ibid., fol. 236v.

32. The 1451 arrangement is in AGN, *Registro* 509 fol. 52v. The details of the apportionment of the two thousand *libras,* down from five thousand in 1449, among the six *aljamas* is not known. Fol. 52r indicates that the 1449 sum had been reduced from seven thousand *libras,* and this obligation was distributed by the representatives of the *aljamas* meeting in Tafalla. The rules regarding *pecha* collection are from AMT, the 1482 *privilegium.*

There is some information about local collections. According to *Registro* 519 fol. 38v, the tax in Corella was called the "pecha ordinaria"; in Tudela, the *pecha* was rendered in a special "tendiella" (probably means a stall), *Registro* 548 fol. 32v. The situation in Cascante and Tudela in the 1470s is reflected in APT, *Juhan Pérez del Calvo, Vol. 1472–1499* fols. 11v, 164r–165v and 166r.

On taxes rendered by Jews in medieval Iberia, generally, see Neuman 1, chapters 6 and 7. Leroy, pp. 80–83 discusses the *pecha* in the 14th century and, pp. 83–92, other taxes the Jew paid. See, for Castile, M. A. Ladero Quesada, "Las juderías de Castilla según algunos 'servicios' fiscales del siglo xv," pp. 249–64 and Pimenta Ferro, pp. 159–214, for Portugal.

33. The pre-1494 collection of Mastre Ossua is documented in AGN, *Registro* 516 fol. 12r and v; the 1495 *pecha* is in Documentos Caj. 165 No. 80 fol. 55v. The *pecha* of all the *aljamas* was rendered in a lump sum. The new collection surely was for more than two thousand *libras*; a tax per *casa* instead of a lump sum was probably ordered because of the increase in Jewish population just prior to 1494. See chapter five.

Kayserling, *Die Juden,* p. 59, was mistaken when he claimed, following Padre Alesón, *Anales de Navarra* (Viana, 1715) 2, 1, 106, that the 14th-century Naçan Gabay was the last general tax collector of Navarrese Jewish imposts. There is even evidence, albeit inconclusive, *Registro* 519 fol. 38v, that Ossua was also the *rabí mayor* (chief rabbi) of the kingdom. Cf. Neuman 1:114–115; Leroy, p. 28; and Pimenta Ferro, pp. 107ff.

34. AGN, Caj. 165 No. 80 fol. 55v records the release of Mastre Ossua

and the other officials and the order to Bendebut (ms: Bendeut) and Mataron. Bendebut's activities in December are noted in ibid., fol. 67r.

35. Caj. 166 No. 7 fols. 20r and 16r; these documents are also discussed in chapters one, four, and five. See also Neuman 1:71.

36. The Cortes decision on the *quarteres* is extant in a number of copies: Caj. 193 No. 42; Caj. 165 No. 60; *Registro* 516 fol. 56r–v; and AMT, Libro 4 No. 6. Another fourteen *quarteres* were also authorized, but the Jews, the Muslims, and the others were exempt. On extra taxes that Navarrese Jews were required to pay, see Leroy, pp. 88ff.; on these taxes generally, see Yanguas y Miranda, *Diccionario* 2: s.v. *pechas*.

37. The Tudelan priests' rendition is discussed in AGN, *Registro* 516 fol. 156r. Caj. 165 No. 80 fol. 30r discusses the payment of the half florin by the native and foreign Jews and the Muslims in successive paragraphs. According to Caj. 193 No. 34 fol. 11v, the city, even after the imposition of this tax, was unable to remit its share of the *quarteres*.

38. *Registro* 516 fols. 161v–162v records the payment of the Jews, and fol. 163r that of the Muslims.

39. Caj. 165 No. 80 fol. 24r.

40. Ibid., fol. 25v. The *camas* that were requested were more than simple beds. Although, see note 32, Navarrese *aljamas* did meet at times to discuss tax appropriations, it is unclear if this was a regular occurrence. See, generally, Baer, *A History* 1:215 and Neuman 1:60.

41. There is no study on the *hermandat* in Navarre; see, however, the brief summaries of relevant documents cited in Florencio Idoate, *Catálogo del archivo general de Navarra*: 48: s.v. *Hermandad del Reino*, and the items cited in Yanguas, *Diccionario* 1:466. On the institution in Castile-Aragon, see Hillgarth, *The Spanish Kingdoms* 2:504–508 and M. Lunenfeld, *The Council of the Santa Hermandad* (Coral Gables, 1970). For the years 1488, 1489, and 1490, the relevant documents are in AGN, *Documentos* Caj. 193 No. 29; Caj. 165 No. 21; *Archivo del reino. sección de cuarteles, alcabalas* Legajo 1 Carpeta 12. For subsequent years, see, for example, *Documentos* Caj. 165 Nos. 59 and 65.

42. On the *alcabala* in Navarre, see Yanguas, *Diccionario* 2:368–70; Zabalo, p. 208; P. López Elum, "La depresión navarra en el siglo xv," pp. 151–68; and Leroy, pp. 45ff. for the Jews' involvement. AMT, *Libro de cuentas de propios* is the source for the Jews' payment of the 150 libras. Fols. 1v, 9v, 20v, and 29v contain the references for the years 1480 to 1483. The Muslims paid 350 *libras* annually and the *clerizia* (clergy) paid 50. Fol. 120v, for the year 1490, clearly indicates the reason for this payment. The relevant folios for 1488 through 1493 are 96v, 109v, 120v, 131r, 142r, and 152r.

43. Ibid., fol. 163v, and fol. 220r for 1498.

44. The annual payment of the Pamplonese Jews was sixty-seven *libras carlines*; AGN, Caj. 165 No. 80 fol. 22v. Queen Leonor's leniency is recorded in AMT, the 1482 *privilegium*.

45. *Registro* 548 fols. 18r and 35v contains the material on Pamplonese Jews, *Registro* 517 fols. 26r and 32v material on the Tudelans. For Açach Orabuena, see APT, *Latorre,* fol. 117r.

46. Caj. 164 No. 28 contains the document of 1492. Other instances of problems with the rendition of the royal taxes are documented in Caj. 165 No. 80 fol. 31v, where the *aljama* of Corella was the complainant; and in APT, *Juhan Pérez del Calvo, Vol. 1472–1499* fol. 11v, where a commission was established in the village of Cascante to determine if the Jews paid their *pecha* and other taxes. *Juhan Martínez Cabero, Vol. 1491–1492* fol. 97r contains a reference to a tax paid by Tudelan Jews in connection with their *judería.*

The reference to New Christians is in AGN, *Archivo del reino: sección de legislación general y contrafueros* Leg. 1 Car. 13.

47. AGN, *Archivo del reino: sección de legislación general y contrafueros* Leg. 1 Car. 13. Queen Leonor's reasoning in reducing the Jews' burden was that the Jews suffered more harm to their persons and property when captured, AMT, 1482 *privilegium.*

48. See AMT, *Libro de cuentas,* fol. 40v for 1484; and fol. 67r for 1486. In a meeting of the municipality in 1472. APT, *Ezquerro,* fol. 15v, in protesting a new tax levied for the city's defense, the Jews argued that they as "buenos vezinos" always contributed toward the military security of the city.

49. For Larraga, AMT, ibid., fol. 165r; for Melida, fol. 209r. According to *Registro* 516 fol. 161v, Larraga was in the hands of the conde de Lerín in 1494. Also relevant is Caj. 165 No. 80 fols. 22 and 25.

50. The documents for 1487 and 1491 are in AMT, ibid., fols. 80v and 131v, respectively. In the latter year, the Muslims paid twenty *libras* for the same tax; in 1492, ibid., fol. 142r, they paid the same amount. In the 1493 example, fol. 153r, the Muslims and Jews rendered the same amount. The Jews received a rebate of fifteen florins later that year, whereas 13 florins and 5 *groats* were returned to the Muslims. The Muslims paid thirty-seven *libras* and ten *sueldos* toward the 1494 burial; see fol. 184r.

51. The building in 1486 of a "samantada debro" (meaning unclear to me) was done on October 15, ibid., fol. 67r; the "calçada" that went to the "bebradero debro" (probably a path that led to a spot where water was drawn for drinking) was supported by the Jews in 1493, fol. 152r; and the Muslims also paid for the bridge repairs in 1489, fol. 115r. Also relevant are fols. 84r and 125v.

52. See ibid., fol. 132r for 1491; fol. 163v for 1494, one trip to "la guerta" and another to Bunyuel; and fol. 195v for 1496 when the Jews contributed to "concejar y cobrar la saca del trigo y salir la bandera a venidos con los senores jurados."

53. On the institution of the *almudi* (also spelled *almudy,* called the *chapitel* in the rest of Navarre), see Yanguas 2:348 and Zabalo, pp. 171–173. The payment of the *franqueza* from 1490 to 1494 is recorded in

AMT, ibid., fols. 120v, 132r, 164v, 151v, and 163v. The reason given for the granting of the *franqueza* in 1490 was that the Jews had already contributed to an "ayuda of the tributo of the almody." The Jews as well as the municipality employed *mutallafes* to oversee weights and measures, AMT, 1482 *privilegium*. The *motalfía* of the Jews of Tudela is recorded in AGN, *Registro* 548 fol. 35r.

54. See ACT, *Libro Nuevo* 10/7/1485 for the grape tithes in 1485; APT, *Cabero, Vol. 1467–1488–1489* fol. 46r and ACT, *Libro Nuevo* 3/10/ 1486 for 1488; and *Libro Nuevo* 1488 (document undated) for tithes on lambs. For Portugal, see Pimenta Ferro, p. 193.

55. APT, *Cabero, Vol. 1490* fol. 15v and ACT, *Libro Nuevo* 3/11/ 1490. The church's decision was made with the consent of the "chantre, vicario general and the bishop of Taraçona, the dean of this church." The same two arbiters decided another case together; see earlier in this chapter. The Muslims and the church were involved in a parallel case: *Cabero, Vol. 1467–1488–1489* fol. 30 and ff. as published in Mercedes García-Arenal, "Los moros en Navarra," pp. 118–119. The 1459 inventory is in the AGN, *Clero, Tudela* No. 21 and has been published by Béatrice Leroy for the first time in "Recherches sur les juifs de Navarre à la fin du moyen age," pp. 424–430.

On the issue of ecclesiastical authorities attempting to impose church taxes on Iberian Jews, see Neuman, 1:84–85. As Cantera Burgos rightfully noted in his article "Christian Spain," *The Dark Ages*, Cecil Roth, ed., (Ramat Gan, 1966), p. 379, this was a constant preoccupation of the medieval church. Already in 1068, the Council of Gerona ordered Jews to continue paying tithes on land they bought from Christians; see inter alia, L. Suárez Fernández, *Judíos españoles en la edad media*, pp. 49 and 93. For payments of *diezmas* and *primiçias* by Navarrese Jews, see Zabalo, p. 224 and J. M. Lacarra and A. J. Martín Duque, eds., *Fueros de Navarra* 2 (Pamplona, 1975):302–303. On the issue, generally, in the late Middle Ages, see Solomon Grayzel, *The Church and the Jews in the Thirteenth Century* (Philadelphia, 1933), pp. 36–38.

56. APT, ibid., fols. 16r–17r and ACT, ibid., 3/19/1490; the church was listed as the plaintiff and the *aljama* as the defendant. The agreement stated that the arbiters were paid two golden florins apiece for their efforts. It should be noted that the case was not brought before the *baile* of the Jews.

57. *A Social and Religious History of the Jews* (2nd ed.: New York and London, 1965) 10:199.

4: New Christians and the Struggle
   Over the Inquisition

1. For the best survey of these troubled years for Iberian Jewry, see Y. F. Baer, *A History of the Jews in Christian Spain* 2:95–243.

2. A convenient summary of the history of Iberian New Christians in the fifteenth century is H. Beinart, "The Converso Problem in 15th Century Spain" in R. D. Barnett, ed., *The Sephardi Heritage* (London, 1971), pp. 425–56.

3. During the 15th century, the overwhelming majority of the *conversos* were Jews; on Muslims who converted in the sixteenth century in Navarre, see AGN, *Archivo del reino: sección de negocios eclesiásticos* Legajo 1, Carpeta 39. See also the documents in Mercedes García-Arenal, "Los moros de Navarra," pp. 130–33 and the discussion of Navarrese moriscos in Iñaki Reguera, *La inquisición española en el país vasco* (San Sebastian, 1986?), pp. 179–188.

It should be remembered that the beginnings of a Navarrese *converso* community is not to be dated from 1391. The persecutions of that time do not appear to have directly affected Navarrese Jewry. Haim Beinart in his *Conversos on Trial* (Jerusalem, 1981), p. 37 explains that New Christians fled to the north of the peninsula because they were unrecognized there and because the Inquisition was not active in those areas. On this latter point, see below. Portuguese Jewry also did not suffer from the 1391 pogroms; on the New Christians there up through 1497, see Pimenta Ferro, *Os judeus em Portugal no século xv* 1:431–47 and 2 (Lisbon, 1984): 870–907.

4. On Johan Daybar being originally from Huesa, see APT, *Ezquerro,* fol. 385v. According to fols. 436v–437r, Daybar served in the capacity of arbiter for a New Christian. In his role as *procurador,* see AMT, *Libro de cuentas de propios, Vol. 1480–1521,* the year 1497; as father-in-law of Johan Miguel de Munarriz, see APT, *Pedro Jiménez de Castelruiz, Vol. 1478–1519* fol. 19v. The name of the Daybar clan was also spelled de Ayvar and de Aybar.

Alonso and Miguel were related and both came from Huesa; see APT, *Ezquerro,* fol. 385v. On Johan Miguel de Munarriz as *procurador,* see AMT, op. cit., the years 1480 and 1484; as an official of Tudela, see APT, *Diego Martínez de Soria, Vol. 1455–1477* fol. 31r. Garcia Daybar was *procurador* in Tudela, AMT, op. cit., the year 1481, and *jurado,* ibid., fol. 262r.

5. On Miguel, see APT, *Juhan Martínez de Soria, Vol. 1490* fol. 15v and many other documents from 1486 through 1494. For Johan, see ibid., and idem., *Vol. 1492–1500* fol. 15r and v. As a *justiçia* and member of the *plega,* see APT, *Diego Martínez de Soria,* fol. 31r.

On Ferdinand's appointments, see Amador de los Ríos, *Historia social, política y religiosa de los judíos de España y Portugal* (new edition, Madrid, 1960), p. 632. On their families, see below on the Inquisition. Two articles by José Cabezudo Astraín are relevant here; see "Los conversos aragoneses según los procesos de la Inquisición," especially pp. 275–276, and "Los conversos de Barbastro y el apellido 'Santángel'," *Sefarad* 23

(1963):265–84. On the penetration of *conversos* into municipal offices, especially in Castile, see F. Márquez Villanueva, "Conversos y cargos concejiles en el siglo XV," *Revista de archivos, bibliotecas y museos* 63 (1957):503–40.

6. APT, *Pedro Latorre, Vol. 1492–1498* fol. 233r and v. The sheep were to be slaughtered in the abbatoir in Alfaro, and Abraham (ms: Habran) Farag was to send a messenger there to collect the skins, from which the skulls were already to have been removed. Farag then was to give a *roua* of hemp to a Falces agent who would come to Tudela. For more on the activities of Farag, see chapter two.

For another survey of New Christian occupations, here as documented in the notarial documents of Seville, see K. Wagner, *Regesto de documentos del archivo de protocolos de Sevilla referentes a judíos y moros,* pp. 10–11.

7. APT, *Pedro Latorre, Vol. 1498–1501* fol. 1v, from the year 1498. On March 5 of that year, Juhan Pérez de Cascant, a New Christian, was referred to as the *ar[r]endador* of the baking ovens of the village of Cascante; see ibid., fol. 7r. Jobs such as these were also held by Jews.

8. APT, *Sancho Ezquerro, Vol. 1480–1500* fol. 385r. The Hebrew document of *quinyan* was dated 25, Marḥeshvan, 5254; for more on such documents, which were meant to hide moneylending and speculation, see chapter 2. On Alonso and his conversion, see APT, ibid., fols. 348r–349v; on Paçagon, formerly of Calatayut in Aragon, see APT, *Latorre, Vol. 1482–1498* fols. 16v–17r, and chapter five, below. The document of release here was signed by Jew and a Christian and also by Johan Daybar, presumably a relative and a New Christian.

9. The document in APT, *Ezquerro,* fols. 385v–386r is an "encomienda y puro deposito." For more on these, see chapter two.

10. APT, *Latorre, Vol. 1492–1498* fol. 279r, v. On the same date, Sancho de Legasa was named the guarantor of the funds Mauleon owed to the merchant Alonso Daybar. In this document, there were two Christian witnesses and one New Christian (the action took place after Daybar's conversion). See ibid., fols. 348r–349v.

11. Ibid., fol. 300r and margin. For other moneylending documents involving Simuel Çadoque, see ibid., fols. 99v (where he is mistakenly called Habran) and 200r.

Other converted Jews attempted to recover outstanding sums owed by their former coreligionists. Pedro de Miranda, formerly Aziz, appointed Johan de Linyan as his agent to collect monies from Abram Benabez. And the merchant García Daybar, probably a relation of the aforementioned Alonso, asked the canon Johan de Castro to retrieve 18 golden florins from Salamon Almeredi. See APT, *Martín Novallas, Cascante, Vol. 1486–1496, 1490–1494* fols. 319r and 346r.

12. APT, *Juhan Martínez Cabero, Vol. 1493* fol. 3v.

13. Ibid., fols. 3v and 4v–5r. In order to encourage conversion, the church, throughout the Middle Ages attempted to prevent Jews from disinheriting relatives who had converted to Christianity.

14. Ibid., fols. 5r–v and 6r–7v where the items were to be delivered at eight hours ("a las ocho horas") on Monday. The sentence was also read to Johan Royz in Saragossa; see fol. 7r. Each arbiter received the substantial sum of three golden florins. For cases between New Christians and Jews who were *foranos,* see chapter five.

15. APT, *Novallas,* fol. 100v–101r. For cases of New Christian *foranos,* see chapter five.

16. APT, *Latorre, Vol. 1492–1498* fol. 55r and v. On arguments between New Christians and Jews in which Muslims served as arbiters, see chapter two.

17. APT, *Juan de Cabanillas, Vol. 1490–1520 1494,* fols. 7r–8r (ms. Ginilla. Gracian remembered that the compromise was read at night. The other witness, Rabi Huçe Vilforat also gave testimony. Other parties to the conflict were the son of Vidal, his widow, and the widow's sister. Since the *alcalde* was absent, the case was heard by the *justiçia.*

18. AGN, *Cámara de comptos, Documentos* Caj. 166 No. 7 fol. 16r. This ruling was made at the *instançia* (legal request) of Mastre Ossua.

19. See APT, *Novallas,* fols. 142r, 238r–239v, 325r–326r. The *mayorales* or *regidores* of the *confraría* (on the brotherhoods, see chapter three) received the property. With the chamber came a "pasaje convertizo," which may have connected the *mikveh* with the synagogue. The donation was called "irrevocable . . . pura perfecta de para luego de present intervivos."

20. On alms by New Christians to Jewish organizations, see, generally, J. N. Hillgarth, *The Spanish Kingdoms* 2:433. In this case, it is not clear why the property was not sold together for the price of the chamber.

21. APT, *Juhan Martínez Cabero, Vol. 1491–1492* fols. 105r, v and 105v–106r. The settlement also included claims on Mastre Mosse's estate. The church considered the case to be under its jurisdiction; see note 13 on the Royz issue. Master Mosse would not have chosen a church official as his arbiter. In fol. 106r, the two Caritats are called "judiantes" which, if it means that they were judaizers, might explain the church's special interest in the case. Mastre Mosse might have been deemed guilty of teaching Judaism to his son and therefore ordered to pay for his Christian studies.

22. APT, *Novallas,* fol. 351r. Alonso also was owed 1,000 *sueldos* from another source.

A reference to R. Yoel ibn Shuaib, who lived in Tudela sometime in the 1480s, and his opinions of *marranos* must be included here. On his views, see H. H. Ben-Sasson, "The Generation of the Spanish Exiles on Its Fate," (Hebrew) in *Zion* 26 (1961): 23–42, *passim*; B. Netanyahu, *The Marranos of Spain* (New York, 1966), pp. 172–75; and Baer, *A History of the Jews in Christian Spain* 2:507. Whether the opinions of ibn Shuaib reflected Iberian realities or how long he lived in Tudela is unclear. Suffice it to say that Netanyahu, Baer, and Ben-Sasson all have different opinions on both issues. M. Kayserling's statement in *Die Juden in Navarra*, p. 85, that ibn Shuaib lived in Tudela from 1469 to 1489 is erroneous. Kayserling based himself on Conforte's *Kore ha-Dorot* ed. D. Kasell (Berlin, 1846), p. 28a, who only writes that ibn Shuaib was in Tudela in 1485. R. Yoel does not appear in any of the documents of the period, although other members of his family do. While not conclusive, this omission is significant.

23. See H. C. Lea, *A History of the Inquisition of Spain* (New York, 1906–07) 1:223, and most recently Reguera, *Inquisición*, pp. 13–15.

24. The papal bull of 1 November 1478 can be found in B. Llorca, *Bulario pontificio de la inquisición española*, vol. xv of Miscellanea Historiae Pontificiae (Rome, 1949):51–54 and, generally, pp. 48–59. On the bull, see Lea, *History* 1:158, and ibid., p. 160 on the first tribunal in Seville.

Previously, there was a papal Inquisition in Aragon; see Lea, p. 147. Much has been written on this subject but it does not concern us here. On later events in Aragon, see ibid., pp. 236, 238, and 244.

25. Baer, *History* 2:363–64 and 365–67 and Lea, pp. 245–49. The two inquisitors named were Fray Gaspar Juglar and Pedro de Arbués. For a brief reprise of the important data, see José Angel Sesma Muñoz, *La diputación del reino de Aragón en la época de Fernando II (1479–1516)* (Saragossa, 1977), pp. 329–342 and Angel Alcalá Galve, *Los orígines de la inquisición en Aragón* (Saragossa ?, 1984 ?), pp. 31–62.

26. Lea, pp. 249–51, Amador, *Historia*, pp. 692–695, and a narrative retelling of events in Alcalá Galve, pp. 62–67.

27. Lea, pp. 252–253. On the trials and those involved, see Baer, *History* 2:368–379, Lea, pp. 254ff, and Alcalá Galve, pp. 68–72.

28. Lea, p. 254. Béatrice Leroy in *Revue des études juives* 138 (1979): 493, is mistaken in placing this event in 1488.

29. ACA, Registro 3684, fol. 75, in Lea, ibid. For a recent benign interpretation of Ferdinand's political goals, see Luis Suárez Fernández, *Fernando el católico y Navarra*, pp. 125–130. See my introductory chapter and chapter six, below, for a more expansive treatment of Castile-Aragon's policies toward Navarre.

30. This probably is AMT, Lib. 10 No. 33, which J. Yanguas y Miranda quotes from in *Diccionario* 1:496. Yanguas dated this document as belonging to 1481; I have not been able to locate it.

31. AMT, Lib. 16 No. 53 and a copy in AGN, *Archivo del reino: sección de negocios eclesiásticos* Leg. 1 Car. 13. The document was published by Yanguas in *Diccionario* 1:496–498.

32. Lea, p. 543, wrote that the tribunal of Barbastro functioned only "as early as 1488." This shows that it existed in 1486.

33. AMT, ibid.

34. AMT, ibid. The language employed here appears to suggest that Suárez Fernández is mistaken in arguing that Ferdinand did not become forceful with Navarre until December 1487.

35. On this, see chapter six.

36. As to the "supporters of the heretics," Cabezudo Astraín, "Los conversos aragoneses," pp. 275–76, quotes an Aragonese inquisitorial document that illustrates the connection before 1485 of the Sánchez clan, one of the families accused of the murder of Arbués, to important Tudelan Jews, specifically Mair de la Rabi[t]a and Jeuda Almere[c]í. The Sánchezes, according to the source, observed Jewish rituals and disregarded Christian customs while visiting Tudela. It will be seen in the next chapter how the Saragossa–Tudela road was also used by Jews fleeing Castile and Aragon in 1492. For a New Christian in Tudela who arrived from a much further distance, see Y. F. Baer, *Die Juden im Christlichen Spanien* 2:495.

37. ACA, Reg. 3684, fols. 102 and 103 in Lea, p. 254. The inquisitors' request was dated July 22. Martín de Santángel was not caught and was burned in effigy on 28 July 1486.

38. Pascual de Magallon was called in other documents the president of the *hermandat,* a *jurado* of the city, and presbyter of the church of St. Mary. According to APT, *Juhan Martínez Cabero, Vol. 1491–1492* fols. 105r–106r, he had connections to New Christians.

39. AMT, *Libro de cuentas de propios,* fol. 72r. The governor general was in the kingdom in Pamplona as late as November 9; see AGN, *Cámara de comptos, Documentos* Caj. 176 No. 14.

On Johan de Miranda, see earlier in this chapter, Xymeno de Villa-franca was *procurador* of Tudela in 1491, AMT, op. cit. the year 1491.

40. Ibid. *Confessos* was another name for the New Christians; see also APT, *Novallas,* fols. 289r–295v.

41. Stephen Haliczer has argued that Castilian *conversos* initially welcomed the Inquisition; see his "The Castilian Urban Patriciate and the Jewish Expulsions of 1480–92" *American Historical Review* 78 (1973): 42ff. and the corrective provided by a number of other scholars in later issues of the journal, 79:623–626 and 1163–1166.

For a comparison with Aragon's staunch, though equally unsuccessful, defense of its judicial system, see Alcalá Galve, p. 79.

Navarre's fear of the Catholic Monarchs influenced other political decisions regarding the Jews; see chapter six.

42. APT, *Juhan Martínez Cabero, Vol. 1467–1488–1489* fol. 14v. Juan de Pero Sánchez was named a substitute agent on 10 March 1486,

standing in for Alonso Sánchez, who was described as a doctor in laws and citizen of Saragossa. The lease was negotiated for three years at 100 golden florins annually. According to Juan Antonio Llorente, *Historia crítica de la inquisición de España* (Barcelona, 1870), pp. 125–26, Juan de Pero Sánchez fled from Saragossa to Toulouse in France where he was held by the local Inquisition and then released, much to the consternation of the Aragonese Inquisition. Sánchez probably then settled in Tudela. See also Sesma Muñoz, *La diputación,* p. 349 citing A. de la Torre, *Documentos sobre relaciones internacionales de los reyes católicos* (Barcelona, 1950)2:389–390.

On the "heretics," see Cabezudo Astraín, "Los conversos," pp. 275–276 and Baer, *History* 2:367–371. According to Cabezudo Astraín, the prior of Arguedas was a member of the New Christian Sánchez family. In his desire to clear himself before the Inquisition, he implicated himself further.

43. See in this chapter the section on New Christians and the Royz and Caritat cases.

44. APT, *Martínez Cabero,* ibid., fols. 14v–15r. Strikingly, this document immediately follows the lease described above. The petition was witnessed by two presbyters of the church, who, together with the authors of the lease, appear to be the minority that disagreed with the imprudent stand of their church against the Inquisition. There is no information regarding to whom the petition was addressed.

45. According to Lea, p. 254, Ferdinand and Isabella returned to Salamanca, and their campaign was postponed until the spring.

46. ACA, Reg. 3609, fols. 148v–150. The document was published by A. de la Torre, *Documentos sobre relaciones internacionales* 2:384. The document was written in Salamanca. It is unclear whether Juan de Ribera had changed his mind about military action against Navarre.

47. See Llorca, *Bulario pontificio,* pp. 132–137 for the document published from Archivo Histórico Nacional, Madrid, Inquisición, Cód. 1 Num. 35. The source was first published by Fidel Fita in *Boletín de la real academia de historia* 16 (1890):368–71.

48. AMT, *Libro de cuentas de propios,* fol. 84v. According to Lea, p. 253, note 3, the bull was officially received in Cordova on 31 May 1487; probably, the Navarrese knew of its impending arrival. For other political issues at this time between Navarre and Aragon, see AMT, ibid., fols. 84r and 85r, to be discussed in the following chapter.

49. AMT, ibid., fol. 84v.

50. AMT, ibid., fols. 85r, 85v and 89v record the payments for the writings, among which was the "scriptura de apilacion" (appeal). It had taken until 7 May 1488, for Innocent VIII to clearly declare that

all the orders, including Cistercians who had a monastery at Fitero, were subject to the Inquisition; see Lea 2:30–31.

51. APT, *Juhan Martínez Cabero*, ibid., fol. 17v. On his connection to the Arbués assassination, see Lea, p. 256.

52. APT, ibid., fols. 43v–44v. The "contrato de reclamaçion" did not specify what they did.

53. AMC, *Legajo* 22 fol. 478 of the year 1487–88. Copies were also taken to the "prior"; this may be a reference to the prior de Santa Cruz, Fray Tomás de Torquemada.

54. AMC, ibid., 1487–1488. For the characterization of Castile-Aragon's policies toward Navarre as menacing, see Suárez Fernández, *Fernando y Navarra*, p. 135.

55. Ibid., dated February 17.

56. The document appears in AGN, *Archivo del reino: sección de negocios eclesiásticos* Leg. 1 Car. 12 and in AMT, Lib. 38 No. 27; the latter was transcribed from the former, which is also a copy. It was executed by Pedro Rodet (probably the Tudelan notary Pedro de Rodas) on 27 February 1488. The document has been published by Yanguas in Diccionario 1:498–499.

Pedro Gómez was a *jurado* of Tudela and often was used as the city's messenger. See chapter five.

57. The agents were the *procurador fiscal* and the *receptor*.

58. Lea, p. 601, taken from *Memorias de diversos autos,* Auto 27 No. 3. For a description of this source and a discussion of its provenance, see ibid., p. 592. Also see p. 256 of Lea and Llorente, *Historia crítica* 1:124–125.

59. See Lea, *Memorias,* p. 610 (Auto 29, Nos. 8–16) for the list of names. Against this background, the Navarrese royal order separating the Jews of Corella from the rest of the inhabitants of the village should be understood. On this, see chapter six.

On the fugitives who by this time had left Navarre, see Lea, pp. 254–260 and Llorente, *Historia crítica*: 125–127. Also check Fidel Fita's article "La inquisición española y el derecho internacional en 1487. Bula inédita de Inocencio VIII," *Boletín de la real academia de historia* 16 (1890): 368, where he argues that the papal bull of 1487 did have practical effects.

60. On prevailing ideas about the Inquisition in Navarre, see, inter alia, Lea, p. 233. On early precedents for the Inquisition in Portugal, see Pimenta Ferro, *Os Judeus,* pp. 445–447.

61. See A. de la Torre, *Documentos sobre relaciones internacionales* 3:181–184; 1489, Nos. 8–13. On money for the war against Granada, see, generally, Hillgarth, *Spanish Kingdoms* 2:379–381.

The conflicting interpretations of the Treaty of Valencia—and indeed of this period of Navarrese history—can be found in Prosper Boissonade, *Histoire de la Réunion de la Navarre á la Castile*, pp. 74–77, arguing that Navarre was a Castilian protectorate and Suárez Fernández, *Fernando y Navarra*, pp. 136–37, arguing that the treaty was a natural outgrowth of the relations between the kingdoms. [That both of these opinions are but natural outgrowths of their authors' own political views goes without saying.]

62. APT, *Juhan Martínez Cabero*, ibid., fol. 7r. The document contains an inventory of the clothing. Johana was taken from the home of the merchant Martin Degues and may have wanted her friend Johanes de Soria to take the clothing so that the Inquisition would not sequester the items and confiscate them when the trial was completed.

63. AMT, *Libro de cuentas de propios*, fol. 113r.

64. Ibid.

65. Lea, p. 259.

66. *Enquestas* are already mentioned in AMT, op. cit., fol. 85r from the year 1487 and in AMC, *Legajo 22*, 1487–88. On the political turmoil, see chapter five. It should be noted that the case of the Alcalaer-Munyoz donation (see above) also took place in 1495. See also in chapter five how Fray Miguel acted as an arbiter in a case between a Jewish immigrant and Castilian New Christians.

67. APT, *Martín Novallas*, fols. 292r–295v. The *justiçia* Johan de la Cambra was substituting for the *alcalde*. The *nunçio* was Sancho Çereso. The *acesor*, mentioned in the document, was the Inquisition's legal guide, who evaluated the nature of the accusation. All these officials participated in inquisitional functions in Ciudad Real in the 1480s; see Beinart, *Conversos on Trial*.

A list of the questions asked of the witnesses can be found in *Novallas*, fol. 291r–v. Defense questionnaires were also used in Ciudad Real and included the introductory phrase "sy saben," which is contained in the documents here. See Beinart, *Conversos*, pp. 179–185 and p. 140, note 129.

The documents in the Novallas register from fol. 278r through 295v all concern investigations before various authorities. APT, *Juan de Cabanillas*, fols. 7r–8r, which contains the Chinillo family debate discussed above, appears to be of the same style and by the same hand as the Novallas documents. It too recorded an investigation that took place before the *justiçia* of the city.

Novallas, fols. 278r–284v is the record of an investigation of coin clipping before the *marixal* of the monarchs. The accused was a Jew named Dabit Alazar, and several members of the Daybar clan and Pedro de Quintanilla appeared as witnesses. The inquiry was held soon after 1 April 1495. A close analysis of this document and the whole group of investigatory reports should be made.

68. Quintanilla never appears to have been tried for his actions. Indeed on 18 October 1495, he witnessed a business contract in Tudela; see APT, *Latorre*, Vol. *1492–1498* fols. 120v–121r. On Johan de Linyan, see note 7.

69. APT, *Novallas*, fols. 289r–291v. Fol. 291r–v is a list of the questions and a summary of the responses. On the issue of Jewish witnesses appearing before the Inquisition, see, generally, Haim Beinart, "Jewish Witnesses for the Prosecution of the Spanish Inquisition" in *Essays in Honour of Ben Beinart, Acta Juridica* (Capetown, 1978), pp. 37–46 and idem, *Conversos*, especially the items cited in note 123 on p. 137. Beinart did not find any testimony given by Jews before the tribunal in Ciudad Real. Recently, John Edwards has published "Jewish Testimony to the Spanish Inquisition: Teruel 1484–1487," *Revue des études juives* 143 (1984):333–350. In our case, Salton the Jew is a witness, but he was called before a separate judicial authority.

On García Pérez de Verayz, see above in this chapter; and on his role as bailiff, see chapter three.

70. Salton appears in documents relating to the Benamias case, where he has some connection with Castile. See APT, *Novallas*, fols. 263r–270r and the discussion of these sources in chapter five. To judge from the dates in those documents, it is possible that Baquedano traveled to the royal court between the first investigation in January and the date of this testimony. His trip may have been intended as an attempt to quash this investigation into his affairs.

Baquedano was present during Salton's testimony. This was permissible when defense witnesses were called; see Beinart, *Conversos*, p. 117.

71. If it were a bribe, then the money was not, as the other witnesses claimed, intended for food. It was not explained why Salton would have authored a brief against Baquedano. Fray Miguel may have called Salton as a witness to find out if he had a part in stimulating the Inquisitor's interest in his case. Fernando de Pulgar, the *converso* chronicler of the reign of Ferdinand and Isabella, claimed (as quoted in Beinart, p. 137) that Jews testified against *conversos* to take revenge on them.

5: Castilian and Aragonese Jewish Exiles in Navarre

1. See his preface to I Kings in *Perush al Nevi'im Rishonim*, p. 422, where he wrote " ‏מהם הלכו למלכות פורטוגאל‎ ‏ולמלכות נבארה הקרובים אליהם‎". Solomon ibn Verga, author of the sixteenth century *Shevet Yehudah*, quoted Abravanel extensively on the expulsion and so cited his brief remark that some of the exiles emigrated to Navarre. See, with some minor variants, p. 121 in the edition of Azriel Shoḥat (Jerusalem, 1946–47).

2. He wrote in *Sefer Divrei ha-Yamim le-Malkhei Zarefat u-Mal-*

khei Beit Ottoman ha-Togar (Amsterdam, 1733) part 1, p. 47a and b:
"לא גרשם מלך נבא"רה מארצו וילכו שם מהיהודים אשר
באראָ"גון רבים לשבת."
An almost identical passage can be found in his *Emek ha-Bakha,*
ed. M. Letteris (Cracow, 1895), pp. 101–102 and now in the new edition of Karin Almbladh (Uppsala, 1981), pp. 61–62. Indeed, it appears
from Yosef's chronicles that members of his family were among these
immigrants.

3. Andres Bernáldez, *Historia de los reyes católicos,* eds. Fernando de
Gabriel and Ruíz de Apodaca (Sevilla, 1870) 1:339. Alonso de Santa Cruz,
writing later in 1550 about the reign of the Catholic Monarchs, faithfully
followed Bernáldez. See his *Crónica de los reyes católicos,* ed. J. de M. Carriazo (Seville, 1951) 1:61. The editors show (p. 60, note 22) that Santa
Cruz based himself here on chapters 110–114 of Bernáldez.

Surprisingly, the noted seventeenth-century Navarrese chronicler, Francisco de Alesón, did not allude to this influx of Jews. See J. Moret and
F. de Alesón, *Annales del reyno de Navarra,* reprint of the Pamplona 1766
edition (Bilbao, 1969). Volume five, which covers these years, was written
by Alesón.

4. AMT, Libro 41 No. 38. A copy of this document, transcribed by
José Yanguas y Miranda, the nineteenth-century Navarrese historian and
archivist, is to be found in AGN, *Archivo del reino: sección de negocios
eclesiásticos* Legajo 1 Carpeta 13. Yanguas published the document in his
Diccionario de antigüedades 1:499–500, and Meyer Kayserling copied it
from Yanguas in his *Die Juden in Navarra,* Anhang L, pp. 212–213. He
translated the letter into German on pp. 106–107. Salo Baron has included
most of the document in English in his *A Social and Religious History of
the Jews* 11:242–243.

5. Kayserling, *Die Juden,* p. 105. Amador de los Ríos, *Historia social
política y religiosa,* p. 730, note 2, quotes "algunos escritores hebreos" to
the effect that Aragonese rabbis requested permission from the king of
Navarra to settle within his kingdom. I could not find such a contention
in the Hebrew writers of the period, and it may well be that Amador mis-
interpreted Kayserling's remarks. What may have prompted Kayserling's
remark was that Castilian Jews petitioned the Portuguese king, João II,
to be allowed entrance into his kingdom. See the sixteenth-century author
Gedaliah ibn Yaḥya, *Shalshelet ha-Kabbalah* (Jerusalem, 1962), pp. 272–
273, and cf. the letter of a relative named David to Yeshaiah Messini re-
published by J. Hacker, "Some Letters on the Expulsion of the Jews from
Spain and Sicily" in *Studies in the History of Jewish Society Presented to
Professor Jacob Katz,* pp. 95–97. See also Pimenta Ferro, *Os Judeus em
Portugal,* p. 252.

6. According to Yitzhak Baer, the edict of expulsion was made public

between April 29 and May 1; see *A History* 2:434. He suggests that from March 31 through May 1, the decree was an open secret. Jews, though, may have waited for the official promulgation before departing, hoping that negotiations with Ferdinand and Isabella would be successful. Bernáldez stated, *Historia,* 1:339, that Jews did not begin to leave until the first week of July; this letter from Tafalla obviously disproves his contention.

7. Graetz, who elsewhere on this issue closely followed Kayserling, stated this clearly in *Geschichte der Juden* (Leipzig, 1897–1911) 8:365.

8. (London, 1848), p. 287.

9. Kayserling, *Die Juden,* p. 107, note 2. He did not point out that 1328, the year of the pogroms in Estella, was not "exactly a century before" the events of 1492. Lindo's statement does not seem to refer to the widespread massacres of 1391, which incidentally does not appear to have directly affected Navarrese Jewry. Kayserling leveled a much more sweeping accusation against Lindo and his imaginary manuscripts earlier in his book on Navarre; see pp. 16–17, note 1.

10. Ibid., p. 107, and Amador de los Ríos, *Historia,* p. 730.

11. AMT, *Libro de cuentas de propios,* 1480–1521 fol. 144v par. 1.

12. See note 6. Tudela may not have been sure that the expulsion would take place until the formal proclamation of the decree.

13. It is not known why the governor, Gabriel de Avenas, was then in Estella. He was in the city at least from April 10 through April 17, when the Cortes was congregated there. See Florencio Idoate, *Catálogo del archivo general de Navarra* 48: Nos. 862 and 865. There is no indication whether the Cortes continued meeting through the end of May. They did have much to discuss; for a review of events during these months, see Boissonade, *Histoire de la Réunion de la Navarre à la Castille,* pp. 78–92 and Suárez Fernández, *Fernando y Navarra,* pp. 146–148. For more on this meeting of the Cortes and its pronouncements regarding Navarrese Jews, see chapter six.

It seems doubtful that the messengers, already in Tudela, were that city's representatives to the Cortes. Most likely, they were sent because of the issue of the Jewish refugees.

14. AMT, *Libro de cuentas,* fol. 144v par. 3.

15. Ibid., par. 9.

16. The position taken by Olite is unclear. Although Olite did not receive the latest missive according to the list, the meeting was to take place there. It cannot be determined whether this reflects Olite's agreement with Tudela's initiatives or if the meeting was scheduled there because of the Cortes.

Since the courier had one less place to visit, the payment of the *jurados* was four pounds four shillings (*sueldos*). On June 2, the payment was four pounds ten shillings.

17. AMT, *Libro de cuentas,* fol. 144v par. 10.

18. Pedro Gómez probably is Pedro Gómez de Peralta, who later was a *jurado* of Tudela. See APT, *Juan Frias, Vol. 1496–1509* fol. 4r. If so, this indicates that Tudela sent a high-ranking delegation, thus underscoring the importance of the mission.

19. AMT, op. cit. The cost for Gómez' mission, including the payment for a mule, was seven pounds four shillings.

20. AMT, *Libros de cuentas,* fol. 145r par. 2.
The prior de Santa Cruz was the *inquisidor general,* Tomás de Torquemada. Although he is not mentioned in the expulsion edict, a document of May 2, published by Baer in *Die Juden im Christlichen Spanien* 2:516, indicates that the Jews were expelled by order of both Torquemada and the monarchs. The mention of the prior de Santa Cruz in our document shows that he was perceived, in Navarre too, as a prime mover behind the expulsion.

21. AMT, ibid., fol. 145r par. 3.

22. Pascual de Magallon was a *jurado* of Tudela (APT, *Diego Martínez de Soria, Vol. 1455–77* fol. 31r par. a.) and a member of its *plega* (ibid., fol. 42v, margin of par.b.), was called *escudero* (APT, *Juhan Martínez Cabero, Vol. 1490* fols. 75v–76r), and was probably president of the *hermandat* (APT, *Martín Novallas, Cascante, Vol. 1489–96, 1490–1494* fol. 237v).

23. According to the *Libro de cuentas,* Mezquita waited ten days for Magallon. From June 15, when Pedro Gómez probably left, he was alone in Olite.
There is no indication that anyone else joined Magallon and Mezquita. Although Tafalla had requested to be kept in touch by Tudela, the Tafallans may not have wanted to send a representative of their own. The *Libro de cuentas* did not record any contact on this issue between Tudela and Tafalla after June 2.

24. AMT, ibid., fol. 145r par. 3.

25. See chapter six.

26. APT, *Martín Novallas,* fol. 204r–v. "que si por caso los Judios se fuessen que pagado vaya por pagado. Et si por caso los Judios estabarra de no se yr ata passado el tiempo que montaria la dicha tercera parte y empues se yban ante de cumplir el dicho annyo que contassen a rata temporis por lo que abrian estado el dicho Respecto. . . ."
It must be noted that Jews are referred to here in the plural. Could this clause reflect a standard formula included, during these months, in contracts where one of the parties was a Jewish refugee from Castile-Aragon? This, however, is our only source for this insertion. Another possibility is that Constantos had purchased these houses on behalf of several Jews. For more on his activities in Navarre, see below.

27. AMT, *Libro de cuentas,* fol. 146r par. 7.

28. AMT, ibid., fol. 142v par. 6. Instead of *bienvenido,* the scribe wrote "bienvendido." Whether this was an unintentional mistake or a deliberate pun, it may reflect the opinion of the author, who could have believed that the Jews' commercial abilities persuaded the rulers to let them enter.

29. Yanguas, *Diccionario* 1:499. Interestingly, he included the Tafalla–Tudela letter and his own remarks on it in his entry "Inquisición." Graetz, *Geschichte der Juden* 8:366, followed Yanguas, and mentioned the spirit of hatred toward Jews as the causative factor. See the discussion by Salo Baron in *Social and Religious* 11:242–243 and 406.

30. Amador de los Ríos, *Historia,* pp. 729–730.

31. Kayserling, *Die Juden,* pp. 105–107. Exemptions were made for doctors and surgeons to visit their Christian patients. See chapter six, where it is shown that this document is not to be dated to 1482, and that the Cortes meeting was not held in Tafalla.

32. The growth of anti-Judaism in Navarre during the years 1479 to 1498 is discussed in chapter six. The relevant documents are analyzed there and appropriate citations given.

33. On the attempt to establish the Inquisition in Navarre, see chapter four. There is another way to understand the resistance of Tudela to the Inquisition and their superficially contradictory efforts to keep out the immigrant Jews. If the prime movers behind both actions were *conversos,* it would not be surprising for them to combat the Inquisition and yet attempt to stem an influx of Jews, which could possibly raise the specter of more accusations of judaizing. Native Navarrese Jews would also fear that indigent immigrants might prove to be a drain on communal finances. That such, allegedly, was the attitude of the Portuguese Jews to their immigrant coreligionists during the negotiations in 1492, see, among others, Graetz, *Geschichte der Juden* 8:374; Kayserling, *Geschichte der Juden in Portugal* (Leipzig, 1867), pp. 110–111; and Baron, *Social and Religious* 11:246 and p. 408 for the sources. Also consult the primary sources listed in note 5.

There is, however, no evidence here for the attitudes of either the *conversos* or the Jews to the entry of the émigrés. (See chapter four, note 41 on similar arguments surrounding the Inquisition.) In fact, the Tafalla–Tudela letter is the only source reflecting the attitudes of any of the Navarrese people. The original Tudelan missive is not extant.

34. It may not be coincidental that "damage to the *republiquas*" was a phrase used by Ferdinand and Isabella in their expulsion document and also by Tudela in its arguments to Tafalla. The Castilian-Aragonese expulsion document can be found in, inter alia, Baer, *Die Juden,* pp. 404–407 (see p. 406, line 4) and Suárez Fernández, *Documentos acerca de la expulsión de los judíos,* pp. 391–393.

The kingdom of Navarre, since 1479, and indeed throughout the previous three centuries was often at the mercy of its Spanish and French neighbors. See the introductory chapter. Charles VIII was more interested in his Italian campaigns, however, thus letting Ferdinand gain the upper hand in Navarre. The Convención de Granada in May 1492 and the Entrevista de Zaragoza on August 18 of the same year underscored Ferdinand's influence in the Pyrenean kingdom. On the political history of Navarre during these months, see again the sources listed in note 13 and José María Lacarra, *Historia política del reino de Navarra* 3:373–378. Unfortunately, there is a lacuna in historical documentation for events between those at Granada and Saragossa.

35. For a treatment of the Navarrese civil war and the shifting alliances, see the books cited in note 34 and the introductory chapter to this book. On the behavior of Ferdinand and Isabella, see this chapter.

Although Pamplona was in the Beaumontes camp, it does not appear that many immigrants settled there. Inasmuch as Tudela did send letters to Pamplona, perhaps these issues transcended the civil war.

See note 80 on the duque de Nágera and the Jews.

36. It is unlikely that the differences in policy toward the Jews stemmed from the fact that Tudela was part of the diocese of Tarazona (Aragon) whereas all the other participants in these events were subject to Pamplona. That Tafalla joined Tudela in its efforts shows that there was no divergence on this issue between the dioceses. Moreover, the diocese of Pamplona incorporated areas of Castile from where the Jews were expelled.

37. On help to previous Jewish immigrants in Navarre, see for example, Kayserling, *Die Juden,* p. 91; Baer, *A History* 2:118; Amador de los Ríos, *Historia,* p. 661; B. Leroy, "Le royaume de Navarre et les juifs aux XIVe et XVe siècles," pp. 278 and 280 and idem., "Recherches sur les juifs de Navarre à la fin du moyen age," pp. 333 and 360.

It is interesting to note that while both Navarre and Portugal (see Pimenta Ferro, pp. 252 and 427) allowed the Castilian-Aragonese refugees to enter, there is no evidence to suggest that the Navarrese monarchs exacted high entrance fees as did their Portuguese counterparts. Johan and Catalina may have had greater need for additional inhabitants in the kingdom.

38. For the document of 30 July 1493, see Suárez Fernández, *Documentos acerca de la expulsión,* pp. 526–27.

Additionally, Ferdinand and Isabella, working toward the eventual unification of Navarre with their kingdoms, were surely concerned with religious homogeneity, which would require an absence of Jews in Navarre. On this, see below in this chapter on the convoy to Mallén in 1493. They did attempt to keep the Castilian and Aragonese Jews from entering Portugal: see, inter alia, Baron, *Social and Religious* 10:216.

39. See the passages from Yosef ha-Kohen's works cited above in note 2.

40. Andres Bernáldez, *Historia* 1:339.

41. The following are names of those who can be definitely identified as immigrants who came to Navarre in 1492 and whose place of origin is known (all but one of the names have been taken from documents in the notarial archives of Tudela): Astruch Carillo, Almaçan (Castile), (*Juhan Martínez Cabero, Vol. 1491–92* fol. 89v par. b); Mayr Abenrrodija, Almaçan, (ibid., fol. 89v par. c); Jaco Benrraui, Calatayut, (ibid., fol. 89v par. d); Mastre Vidal, Çaragoça, (*Juhan Martínez Cabero, Vol. 1493* fol. 3v par. a); Simuel de Cort—Namias, Çaragoça, (ibid., fols. 5r–7v); Ezmel Aunarrabi, Çaragoça, (ibid., fol. 10v); Çulema Arruesi, Mores (Aragon), (ibid., fol. 13r); Bonafox Constantos, Soria, (*Martín Novallas*, fols. 20r–v and 21v par. b); Astruch, Agreda (Castile), (ibid., fols. 33v–34r); Vida and Rabí Abram Benamias, Cornago (Castile), (ibid., fols. 263r–270v); Abram Orabuena, Taraçona (Aragon), (ibid., fol. 315v); Mosse Baço, Çaragoça, (*Sancho Ezquerro, Vol. 1480–1500* fols. 413v–414r); and Soli Gotyna, Çaragoça, (*Pedro de Lesaca, Cortes*, fols. 49r–50v).
The document from the municipal archives of Tudela (Libro 41 No. 32) contains a Mosse de Leon from Saragossa (Çaragoça). It also notes that many Jews from Saragossa fled to Tudela in 1492. On Jews who arrived from Soria, see David Gonzalo Maeso, "Aportaciones a la historia de la judería de Soria," *Celtiberia* 56 (1978):153–168.

42. Lindo, *History*, p. 287; Kayserling, *Die Juden*, p. 107; Graetz, *Geschichte der Juden* 8:366; and Baron, *Social and Religious* 11:243.

43. Bernáldez, *Historia*, p. 339.

44. If Lindo, the earliest of the authors, had made this error, Kayserling et al. would have checked it. Earlier in this chapter it was seen how Kayserling was skeptical of another of Lindo's assertions.

45. Kayserling, *Die Juden*, p. 108; for Graetz and Baron, see note 42. Also check Yanguas, *Diccionario*, s.v.; *Andosilla, Lerín, Mendavia*, and *Sant Adrian*.

46. AGN, *Archivo del reino (cortes y diputación): sección de guerra* Legajo 1 Carpeta 27. The copy was made by the order of the king in Madrid. It was needed for a case that was pending between the then conde de Lerín and the village of Artajona in the Consejo de Navarra.

47. Although the number of Jews was clearly 77, their population given at the conclusion of the document is 86. If a mistake was made in the number of Jewish inhabitants of Lerín, it being *setenta* (70) rather than *sesenta* (60)—and such an emendation is warranted by the figure given for the taxes—the final number would be 87.
Kayserling recorded 66 Jews for Lerín, and Yanguas noted twenty-five Christians in Sant Adrian. Both figures are incorrect. Incidentally, Larraga

also listed sixty-four absentees (*ausentes*), a decrease in population surely caused by the civil conflict. Did the conde wish to increase his population by admitting Jews? The *Libro de fuegos* of 1366 (AGN) has 215 *vecinos* for Lerín, of whom four were Jews. We have no indication when this marked rise in the number of Jews occurred.

The report also lists a ten thousand [BLANK in text] tax paid by the Jews of Pamplona. Since no rate of taxation is listed and we do not know how many of these Pamplonese Jews were newly arrived immigrants, the report cannot help us here.

48. AMT, *Libro de cuentas,* 1484 fol. 40v pars. 5 and 6. The tax, according to the entry, is for a "caballero."
    For a full discussion of the taxes that the Jews paid, see chapter three.

49. AMT, *Libro de cuentas,* 1490 fol. 120v pars. 9 and 10. Here the payment was for the "tributo de la franqueza del almudi."

50. AGN, *Registro* 516 fols. 161v–162v for the Jews, and fol. 163r, for the Muslims.

51. Although tax records cannot be easily used for population information, they should be utilized to discern any trends, especially in the absence of any other data.

52. For a treatment of this problem, see Juan Carrasco Pérez, *La población de Navarra,* pp. 33–35, and my discussion in chapter one.

53. On the tabulations of 1353 and 1366 see, generally, Carrasco, ibid., pp. 76–86. Research still remains to be done to collect all extant information pertaining to the fifteenth-century populations.

54. The texts for the numbers given for 1353 and 1366 are in Carrasco, ibid., pp. 149–50; for 1494, see AGN, *Registro* 516 fols. 161v–162v.
    We have information from the royal archives that the population of both Corella and Cascante fell dramatically by the mid-15th century, mainly because of plagues and the Navarrese civil war. In 1447, Cascante was given a remission in taxes because of a population decline that resulted in an almost total depopulation of the town. Corella was given a similar exemption in 1448 because it too was depopulated. See AGN, *Cámara de comptos, Documentos* Caj. 151 No. 41 and Caj. 154 No. 52, as quoted in G. Desdevises du Dezert, *Don Carlos D'Aragon,* Appendix III, p. 439.
    The rise of the Jewish population must have taken place after the late 1440s and therefore points strongly to the possibility that the émigrés of 1492 were the cause of the increase.

55. Carrasco, *La población,* pp. 151–152 for the 1353 and 1366 count; for 1494, AGN, *Registro* 516 fol. 163r. The comparison between Jews and Muslims is advanced cautiously, because other factors could have affected these figures.

56. AMT, *Libro de cuentas,* 1493 fol. 151v pars. 6, 8, and 10. On this *franqueza,* see chapter two.

57. AMT, ibid., fols. 152r pars. 11 and 12, and 152v par. 1.

58. AMT, *Libro de cuentas,* 1495 fol. 184r pars. 6, 7, and 8.

59. AGN, *Documentos* Caj. 165 No. 80 fol. 55v par. 5. It is difficult to judge whether "otras tantas" was a large or insignificant sum.

60. AGN, *Documentos* Caj. 166 No. 7 fol. 20r par. 3.

61. Occasionally in documents in the Navarrese archives, appended to names of Jews is a reference that the individual is an émigré *(forano)* or that he was formerly of another locale, such as Saragossa. This information, though useful for other sections of this chapter, cannot help in making population estimates.

62. Sometimes they do appear in other collections such as the 1495 report on the property of the conde de Lerín. For more on immigrant Jews in these areas, see below in this chapter.

63. For a recent opinion, see J. N. Hillgarth, *The Spanish Kingdoms* 2:449. See also F. Cantera Burgos, "Los judíos expulsados de San Martin de Valdeiglesias" in I. Hassan, ed., *Actas del I Simposio de Estudios Sefardíes* (Madrid, 1970), pp. 23ff. H. C. Lea had long ago cast doubt on the figures that were advanced in his time; see *A History of the Inquisition of Spain* 1:142.

64. Baer, *A History* 2:510 ff, and Suárez Fernández, *Documentos,* pp. 55–56.

65. See Baron, *Social and Religious* 11:245, and especially p. 407. M. Kayserling in his *Geschichte der Juden in Portugal,* pp. 111–112 argues that the number may have been higher.

Pimenta Ferro's assertions can be found in her *Os judeus em Portugal no século xv,* pp. 253–56.

66. See the table in J. H. Elliot, *Imperial Spain 1469–1716* (London, 1963), p. 13. He cites Javier Ruiz Almansa, "La población española en el siglo xvi," pp. 115–136.

Pimenta Ferro, pp. 424–426 shows graphically that the plague and fear of it were major ingredients of Portuguese life in the last quarter of the fifteenth century.

67. Kayserling, *Die Juden,* p. 108, wrote "jedoch nur die wenigsten von ihnen liessen sich haüslich nieder."

68. Ha-Kohen in his chronicles, *Sefer Divrei ha-Yamim,* p. 49 a and b, *Emek ha-Bakha,* p. 101 in Letteris edition, wrote

"ויהי לתקופת השנה ויבקשו האנשים ... לצאת ... ויתנם מלך ארא"גון
" עבור ויבואו באוניות עד פרובינצ'יה...

These Jews should not be confused with a group of immigrants who left the peninsula for Marseilles in 1492 and also were kidnapped. See I. Loeb, "Un convoi d'exilés d'Espagne à Marseille en 1492," *Revue des études juives* 9 (1884):66–76 and especially idem, "Les exilés d'Espagne en France," *REJ* 10 (1885):236–237.

Pimenta Ferro briefly talks of refugees who left Portugal for North Africa and the Levant. See *Os judeus . . . século XV,* pp. 252 and 427.

69. ACA, *Archivo real: cancillería (registros) itinerum* No. 3647, fols. 154r–155v. This document was published by A. de la Torre, *Documentos sobre relaciónes internacionales de los reyes católicos* 4:137–140.

It would appear that to travel through Aragon was the only way for any Jews in Navarre to leave the Iberian peninsula. Yosef's family traveled to Provence; surely a land route through what is today southern France would have been shorter. The trip through Aragon, however, only required permission from one ruler and once on the shores of the Mediterranean, the Jews had many options of places to which they could travel and settle. On this problem in 1498, see chapter six.

70. See Suárez Fernández, *Documentos,* pp. 58–59, where he seems to argue that the two thousand Jews (following Bernáldez) who crossed into Navarre all asked permission to pass through Aragon. He also contends, based on no discernible source, that these Jews set sail for Italy; the experience of Yosef's family shows that this was not true.

71. See the citation in note 69. On the latter assertion, see chapter six.

72. AGS, *Registro general del sello, 1493–VIII,* fol. 51 as quoted in Suárez Fernández, *Documentos,* pp. 56–57. Another group was dealt with in the document: Those who had already returned to Castile-Aragon as Christians and now, in reaction to hardships they had encountered, intended to emigrate to other lands.

73. AGS, ibid., *1492–XI,* fol. 40 as published in Suárez Fernández, ibid., p. 489. This letter was written to Zamora, a city on the Castilian border with Portugal. Its issuance was occasioned by a specific request of a Jew from Segovia (AGS, ibid., fol. 26; Suárez Fernández, ibid., p. 489).

Other documents support this information on the conditions whereby Jews from Portugal could return as Christians to Castile-Aragon. A January 1493 order from Ferdinand and Isabella repeated the above stipulations about the return of the erstwhile Jews' property and dealt with a request by these *conversos* to keep books in Hebrew and Arabic, excepting those of the "Mosaic law or glosses and commentaries thereon." The monarchs agreed to books of science written in Hebrew and Arabic and forbade the ownership of volumes of the Talmud, or "Brivia," or "other works of Mosaic law" (AGS, ibid., *1493–I,* fol. 52; Suárez Fernández, ibid., pp. 504–505).

74. Suárez Fernández cites eight other documents dated October 1493 that order the restitution of property to returning *conversos* from Portugal (ibid., p. 528 and citations there). All the documents are from the *Registro del sello* in Simancas; that corpus itself needs to be investigated to extract information on those who returned from Navarre. A Jew who converted and reentered through the village of Alfaro most likely came from Navarre. See ibid., pp. 469–470.

75. AMT, Libro 41 No. 32.

76. Ibid., "su grande infidelidat por hauerse reduzido . . . a la sancta madre yglesia y ffe cristiana."

77. The *jurados* briefly added that in the majority of similar cases, they had responded favorably to Tudelan requests. Although not spelled out, this could possibly refer to properties of former Saragossan Jews who fled to Navarre, converted there to Christianity and petitioned to regain their former possessions.

Because the response of the Tudelan officials to this letter is not extant, we cannot report on the disposition of the request.

78. Yosef ha-Kohen's remark can be found in *Sefer Divrei ha-Yamim*, p. 49b and in *Emek ha-Bakha* (ed. Letteris), p. 101. The term "iron furnace" (*kur ha-barzel*) is occasionally used in the Hebrew Bible to refer to Egypt. Kayserling's contention is in *Die Juden*, p. 108, and Amador de los Ríos' remarks are in *Historia*, p. 730.

The negative comments by Abravanel in *Perush al Nevi'im Rishonim*, p. 188 should be understood as referring to Portugal.

79. Baron, *Social and Religious* 11:243.

80. AGN, *Registro* 516 fol. 161v. It is interesting that the duque, a powerful figure whose territories straddled the border of Navarre and who was a partisan of Ferdinand and Isabella, had a number of immigrant Jews on his property; see above.

Viana may not have been controlled by the conde de Lerín in 1492 but the émigrés eventually may have moved there. What happened to these Jews after 1495 is unclear.

81. Suárez Fernández, *Documentos*, pp. 485–459. This document will be analyzed later in this chapter.

82. See below in this chapter.

83. See chapter one.

84. Immigrants, though sometimes considered apart from the native population, were not accordęd the status of a separate community. For example, in 1492, AGN, *Cámara de comptos, Documentos* Caj. 164 No. 28 [A], Jews were forbidden to walk outside their homes during mass on Sunday and special holidays. The law also included itinerant visitors (*estrangeros*) who found themselves in the kingdom. This was the standard reference to transients.

85. It is not known whether during the years 1492 to 1497 in Portugal, the immigrants from Castile-Aragon also established their particular institutions. Once outside the Iberian peninsula, however, according to abundant evidence, exiled Jews formed their own congregations and communities with coreligionists from their former towns, cities, or kingdom.

86. For 1493, see AMT, *Libro de cuentas*, fols. 151v par. 10, 152v par. 1, 153r par. 5, and 156r par. 6. In 1494, the relevant entries are fols. 163v par. 11 and 164r par. 1.

87. AGN, *Documentos* Caj. 165 No. 80 fol. 30r par. 6.

88. AGN, ibid., fol. 55v par. 5.

89. There is no indication when precisely the shift took place. The documents of the *Registro del Sello* are extant only from September 1494 through February 1495.

In the following years (1495 to 1498), the Tudelan tax records never refer to the Jewish communities without the extra appellation of native or foreign. Although the term *aljama* was not consistently applied, the immigrant community was seen as and acted as a settled, organized group.

90. Two coexisting *aljamas* are recorded only for Tudela, Sangüesa, and the kingdom of Navarre as a whole. The few references in the *Registro del Sello* to the *aljamas* of Pamplona (AGN, *Documentos* Caj. 165 No. 80 fol. 22v par. 1 and fol. 25v par. 1); Corella (AGN, ibid., fol. 31v par. 4); and Estella (AGN, *Documentos* Caj. 166 No. 7 fol. 15r par. 6) during 1494 to 1495 make no distinctions between *nativos* and *foranos*, using simply the phrase, "aljama de los judios." There is no evidence whether or why there was only one Jewish community in these three locations.

91. AGN, *Documentos* Caj. 165 No. 80 fol. 57r par. 5.

92. APT, *Juan Aristoy y Navarro, 1499–1524* fol. 236v.

93. Rabí Çarça can be identified as Açac Çarça, who appears in four documents from December 1494 to January 1495 in regard to liens on his property arising from lawsuits in which he was involved. See AGN, *Documentos* Caj. 165 No. 80 fols. 63v par. 1 and 64r par. 6; Caj. 166 No. 7 fols. 18v par. 1 and 21v par. 5. They are unconnected to his communal activities.

94. We also know that Juçe Atortox of Tudela carried the title *mastre* and was a surgeon by profession, APT, *Juhan Martínez Cabero, 1493* fol. 10v.

Given the slenderness of the evidence and its tax-related character, we cannot determine if there was a sophisticated communal structure as in the native community, or if the immigrant communities of Tudela and Sangüesa had a comparable organizational framework.

95. One may speculate that the royal government did have a hand in the *foranos'* change of status. Early in 1494, King Johan and Queen Catalina were finally allowed to enter the kingdom and were crowned. They may have wished to reform the tax system to make it more efficient, which led to the designation of the *forano* group as an *aljama*.

96. The information comes only from the municipal receipts of Tudela and the occasional citations in the *Registro del sello*. While there are other sources on the taxes of Jews during the period 1492 to 1498, there is no way to ascertain if these imposts were solely the burden of the native group or if the immigrants were included in their assessment and payment.

97. For an additional comparison, record will be made below of the

payments of the Muslims. For an analysis of the native Jewish contribution to all these taxes, see chapter three.

98. It is not known if the right to levy this fee was the result of the negotiations the city had with the Navarrese monarchs nor if this tax was paid in the other localities of the kingdom. Navarrese historical precedent does not indicate a royal tradition of exacting such a fee; the monarchs were satisfied with the additional standard revenues to be collected. In fact, it seems that most imposts were suspended for the newcomers, who had to pay only a prescribed few taxes. See Amador de los Ríos, *Historia,* pp. 423ff. on the situation in 1370.

The policy in Portugal in 1492 was more complex, and based on available evidence, far more oppressive than in Navarre. The Jewish émigrés had to pay an entrance fee as high as eight *cruzados* of gold per capita, according to some reports. This only entitled the immigrant to remain for eight months. Six hundred families, able to afford 150 ducats apiece, received permission to settle permanently in the kingdom. See, inter alia, Baron, *Social and Religious:* 10:216 and 11:245. See also the new information provided by Pimenta Ferro, *Os judeus . . . século xv,* pp. 253–256.

99. This is the first explicit tax recorded for the *foranos,* AMT, *Libro de cuentas, 1493* fol. 151v par. 10 and *1494* fol. 163v par. 11. These two years were the only ones in which the "franqueza del almody" was granted to the Jews and Muslims. Again a discussion of all the taxes mentioned below can be found in chapter three.

100. AMT, *Libro de cuentas,* 1493 fol. 151v pars. 8 and 9; 1494 fol. 163v pars. 6 and 9.

101. AMT, ibid., fol. 153r pars. 4 and 5.

102. AMT, *Libro de cuentas,* 1494 fol. 179r par. 2.

103. They were first, a special impost toward the city's expenses in the siege of Larraga (AMT, ibid., fol. 165r par. 9); second, fees for *salir la bandera,* once to *la guerta* and one time to the village of Buñuel (AMT, ibid., fol. 163v par. 8); third, a contribution to the *concellar de la placa* (AMT, *Libro de cuentas,* 1493 fol. 152v par. 8); and, fourth, the payment by the *aljamas* of both the Muslims and the Jews of 22 pounds 10 shillings apiece, for the *calçada del bedradero* that went to the Ebro (AMT, ibid., fol. 152v pars. 1 and 2).

104. AMT, ibid., fol. 152r pars. 11 and 12; 1494 fol. 163v par. 7. The Muslims paid 300 pounds annually (ibid., 1493 fol. 152r par. 10 and *1494* fol. 163v par. 6). As to whether these payments were for the *alcabala,* see the chapter on taxation. For the annual remittances, see the *Libro de cuentas, Vol. 1480–1521.*

105. AMT, ibid., 1493 fol. 152v par. 1 and fol. 153r par. 5. The latter reference is to the second payment, which was 150 pounds. It is fair to assume that this reflects the total of both payments that year.

106. AMT, ibid., 1494 fol. 164r par. 1.
107. AMT, ibid., fol. 163v par. 10.
108. APT, *Pedro Latorre, Vol. 1492–98* fol. 43v.
109. AMT, *Libro de cuentas,* fol. 195v par. 9.
110. Tudela might have faced a shortage of funds, as shown by the fact that the native community advanced two years' payment of the *alcabala.* Although there is no evidence for Kayserling's contention (*Die Juden,* p. 108, note 1 on Lerín) that the major reason the émigrés were admitted was for the extra tax revenues they would generate, no government would have overlooked broadening their tax base with imposts on the new immigrants.

111. On 24 October 1494, the *gentes de finanças* (the financial officers of the kingdom) issued three rulings to Pedro de Valejo, the *portero real,* in favor of the *recibidor* of Tudela. They ordered the *aljamas* of the native Jews and of the Muslims, and the newly arrived Jews to pay a half florin of gold *per casa* to fulfill their obligations toward the four *quarteres,* designated for the arrival of the Navarrese monarchs, AGN, *Documentos* Caj. 165 No. 80 fol. 30r pars. 3, 4, and 5. This is the document, referred to earlier, wherein the indigenous group is first called *nativos.* Although treated separately, all three groups had equal obligations. For more on these taxes, see chapter three.

112. AGN, *Documentos* Caj. 165 No. 80 fol. 55v par. 5. As noted above, the natives were to pay eight pounds per house and the immigrants, the sum of 750 pounds and "otras tantas."

113. AGN, ibid., fol. 55v par. 4. MS: Salamon Bendeut.

114. AGN, ibid., fol. 67r par. 4. According to this same document, Salamon was repaid 200 golden *escudos* that he had lent the queen while she was in Sant Johan in the district of Ultrapuertos. The monarchs also gave him 200 golden florins so he could redeem the items he pledged. Bendebut (ms: Bendeut) was able to recover the pawns because the Jews finally had remitted the 100 *ducados* to the king as promised (AGN, ibid., fol. 67r par. 5).

A few issues still remain unclear: we do not know if Bendebut pawned his own belongings and if he was then acting in his role as a royal official or as the representative of the Jews.

115. AGN, ibid., fol. 57r par. 5.

116. AGN, *Documentos* Caj. 166 No. 7 fol. 20r par. 3. Because the *nativos* were to pay *per casa* for the *pechas,* it was necessary to determine their precise number. For the *foranos,* who were to render a flat sum, a census was immaterial. This information, however, was vital for any future imposts. As noted in chapter one, the census is not extant.

117. AMT, *Libro de cuentas,* 1495 fol. 184r pars. 6, 7, and 8. As noted earlier in the chapter, the Muslims paid 37 pounds 10 shillings; the *nativos,* 30 pounds; and the *foranos,* 22 pounds 10 shillings.

118. On the *alcabala,* see above in this chapter. On the export taxes, see AMT, *Libro de cuentas,* 1496 fol. 19v pars. 9 and 10.

119. So did the *aljama* of the Muslims. See AMT, *Libro de cuentas,* 1497 fol. 209r pars. 3, 4, and 5. The native Jews paid 181 pounds 5 shillings and the immigrants remitted 143 pounds 5 shillings.

120. AMT, ibid., fol. 209r par. 6. In this entry, "dichos judíos" refers to both groups.

121. APT, *Juan Aristoy y Navarro* fol. 236r and v. The *foranos* owed 21 golden florins and the *naturales* 140. These documents also indicate that the two groups were involved in the same enterprises. The *fiadors* (ms: *fyadores*) for the immigrants were Mosse Arrueti and Ayzca Çury, both of whom were apparently natives.

122. The *foranos* are listed in the 1497 records as paying 22 pounds 10 shillings (AMT, *Libro de cuentas,* 1497 fol. 209v par. 4) but the entry was crossed out and a scribal insertion refers to the 1498 receipts. The amount is repeated in the latter account.

123. AMT, *Libro de cuentas,* 1498 fol. 220r par. 7.

124. Because the *alcabala* was collected on sales within the city, non-residents were considered to be equally liable. See Yanguas y Miranda, *Diccionario* 1:365 and 3:113.

125. The immigrants (see note 122) paid 22 pounds ten shillings, which is a substantial decrease from the 150 pounds for the *alcabala.* But the natives paid only 25 pounds, AMT, *Libro de cuentas,* 1498 fol. 220r par. 8. Upon reflection, it can be seen that the sum was precisely one-sixth of their year's due. Recalling that the Jews were expelled in March 1498, both groups must have paid for only two months. On whether they paid this amount at the end of the year when they were officially Christians and whether this reflects the unofficial continuation of the Jewish community, see chapter six. The Muslims paid their annual sum of 300 florins for the *alcabala* (AMT, ibid., fol. 220r par. 4) since they were not expelled in 1498. The Muslims also rendered monies for the support of the knights ("ayuda de los cavaleros") (AMT, ibid., fol. 220r par. 5), whereas the Jewish communities did not.

It must be pointed out that since there is no parallel information on the internal communal taxation of the Jews, it is not known if the immigrants contributed to the native Jewish community before they became an *aljama,* in their own right, nor what taxes the *foranos* demanded of their own, after the granting of official legal status to their group.

126. The overwhelming number of documents used for this section were found in the APT. When the notaries summarized a contract they had just drawn up, however, they rarely indicated that the Jewish principals were immigrants. Occasionally, they do note that an individual was formerly of Saragossa, Soria, and the like. This alone is not sufficient evidence that these were Jews who left Castile-Aragon specifically because of the ex-

pulsion decree and who subsequently formed the *forano* community. There had always been Jews, prior to 1492, who crossed the borders in either direction to establish residence in the neighboring kingdoms.

127. The edict of expulsion has been published many times. See, among other references, the citations in note 34.

128. See Bernáldez, *Historia* 1:338.

129. For a description of these problems as recorded in a royal document, see AGS, *Registro del sello*, 1492, X, fol. 57, as published in Suárez Fernández, *Documentos*, pp. 473–476. Obviously, those who needed ready cash could not afford to wait.

130. APT, *Juhan Martínez Cabero, 1491–92* fol. 89v par. a, Ezmel (ms: Avnarabi) is described here as a "residente" of Tudela. We know from another document that he is from Saragossa, APT, *Juhan Martínez Cabero, 1493* fol. 13r.

By July 26, Ezmel had already received the money. The debts were not itemized, and so it cannot be determined if the price was fair. Pascual de Ayenssa appears in the documentation of this period as a *mercadero, scudero*, and as the procurador of Tudela in 1485 and 1494. See APT, *Pedro Latorre, 1492–98* fols. 39r–v and 135r–v, and *Juhan Martínez Cabero, 1493* fol. 3v par. a, 4v–5r and 5r–7v. Also see AMT, *Libro de cuentas*, the years 1485 and 1494.

There does not appear any indication of why Martínez Cabero was chosen as the notary. Not enough is known about why certain notaries had their specific clientele. In idem., *Vol. 1491–92* fol. 81r, a case is recorded of a Jew of Prexano who appointed another Jew from his home town in Castile as his *procurador* in May of 1492.

131. APT, *Juhan Martínez Cabero, 1491–92* fol. 89v pars. b, c, and d. It may be supposed that the three immigrants were connected, because of the proximity of their places of origin and because the same common *procurador* appeared in pars. b and d. It would be pure speculation to argue that the *procuradores* were Jews who had chosen to convert.

132. APT, *Martín Novallas*, fol. 21v par. b. For problems with the collection of Jewish credits in Soria in August 1492, see AGS, *Registro del sello*, 1492, VIII, fol. 16, as published in Suárez Fernández, *Documentos*, pp. 463–464. It cannot be ascertained if Constantos waited until September, when the issue may have been resolved.

133. APT, *Juhan Martínez Cabero, 1493* fol. 13r. The ass had been rented by Arrueti and evidently was not returned before his flight to Navarre.

134. AGS, *Registro del sello*, 1492, VIII, fol. 107, as published in Suárez Fernández, *Documentos*, pp. 458–459. Laguardia had been part of Navarre but was incorporated into Castile in 1461, so Osua may have returned to his former homeland. Osua is not to be confused with Mastre Ossua, the *receptor* of the Jews.

This is one of many indications that Ferdinand and Isabella were not intent on "robbing" Jews of their possessions.

135. AGS, ibid., X, fol. 57, published in Suárez Fernández, ibid., pp. 473–476. For the accusations, see the relevant documents in Suárez Fernández.

Juan de Ribera, a major influence in Navarrese politics (see the previous chapter) was also *corregidor* of the province of Guipúzcoa and the royal assistant in Calahorra, Logroño, Alfaro, and Santo Domingo (towns immediately outside of Navarre).

136. APT, *Novallas*, fol. 315r. Another case involving a Christian of Agreda and a Jew named Estru, who fled to Tudela, can be found in A. de la Torre, *Documentos* (1965) 5:527–528. Ferdinand and Isabella came to the aid of the Christian Diego de Vera.

137. APT, ibid., fols. 33v–34r. We do not have the actual sale document but only the loan agreements. Gonçalez, ibid., fol. 21v par. a evidently owed a rental to a Jew, who had on September 12 appointed a *procurador* to collect it.

138. APT, *Pedro Latorre, 1492–98* fol. 49v. It must have been extended litigation because Barçeloni is said to be "reparto" in Tudela. The document does not clearly describe the relationships among the participants.

For a somewhat parallel situation in Portugal, see AGS, *Registro del sello, 1493,* III, fol. 299, published in Suárez Fernández, *Documentos,* pp. 509–510.

139. The documents on this issue are in APT, *Novallas,* fols. 263r–270v. A few more details need to be reported. Sánchez was Martínez' *procurador* and the *primo* of Benamias; Martínez's connection is not known. Fols. 268r–v contain a statement by Vida (27 March 1495) that she will pay Ferrán Sánchez. Here the debt in the amount of 3,000 *maravedís* is listed as being in the amount of 3,279 *maravedís*. This is probably the more exact figure. Both of the debtors lived in Castile, one being the *frayre* of a church in Cornago. The gold ring and parchment belt were described as originally belonging to Sánchez and Rogat, his father-in-law. They were to be taken out of pawn and given to them so that Rogat "who is here, be content."

Folio 270v contains an interesting document that appears to be a scratch sheet for Novallas, the notary. It is not the actual compromise. It is extremely difficult to read, because the handwriting of Novallas is miniscule and there are frequent crossings-out. It can be learned, though, that Rabí Abraham (ms: Abram) attempted to bypass his legal inheritors by giving his property as a "donaçion" to his wife. These holdings originally seem to have been part of the dowry that Vida brought to the marriage. Sánchez claimed that the "donaçion" was illegal and refused to be satisfied with the 100 *maravedís* allotted to each of the legitimate inheritors. It appears that nieces of Rabí Abraham were involved, but we cannot tell where they stood in the litigation.

Fray Miguel de Baquedano was involved in an inquisitorial process at this time; see chapter four. This may well explain the delay in the arbiters' ruling.

140. APT, *Pedro de Lesaca, Cortes, 1494–1523* fols. 49r–50v. It is striking that two Jews and one Christian were chosen as arbiters. Presumably, this was done because the relevant documents were in Hebrew. María chose one Jewish arbiter, Osua Bienbenis, who was the *adelantado* not only of the *aljama* of the Jews of Cortes but also of the city (ibid., fols. 177v–178r). Bienbenis and his family converted in 1498 (ibid., fol. 170r par. c). So did Simuel Gotyna, the Jewish arbiter for Salamon Gotyna, and presumably a relative of his (ibid., fol. 170r par. a).

The document contains a reference to the parents of María, who were living in Saragossa, apparently as Christians. In one line, the meaning of which is obscure, it appears that María's parents threatened the Christians of Cortes with excommunication unless they satisfied their daughter's demands. María's and Salamon's children are also mentioned as part of the litigation but no details are given.

Pedro de Lesaca is described here as a *notario apostolico* in the kingdoms of Aragon and Navarre but there is no indication that this was a religious proceeding. The *alcaldes* and *officiales reales* mentioned at the beginning of the document apparently were officials of Cortes.

141. Bernáldez, *Historia* 1:338. For the royal order, see AGS, *Registro del sello, 1492,* IX, fol. 228, published in Suárez Fernández, *Documentos,* pp. 465–467. The area under investigation included Logroño, Calahorra, Alfaro, and Agreda. For an accusation against a Jew, formerly of Agreda, see the citation in note 136.

142. APT, *Novallas,* fol. 20r–v; for a discussion of this rental, see above in this chapter.

143. In the five clear cases of loans (four *obligaçiones* and one *comanda*), the Christians who borrowed from Jews all paid their debts. See APT, *Juhan Martínez Cabero, 1493* fol. 10v, and *Pedro Latorre, 1492–98* fol. 6r par. a and margin, fol. 46r–v, and fols. 110v–111r and margin. The sums range from 15 florins to 50 pounds and mainly represent activities on the part of Ezmel Abnarrabi and Habran Orabuena.

The case of the Jewish borrower is found in APT, *Sancho Ezquerro,* fols. 372v–373r. Anton de [BLANK in document] freed his "aguelo" [*sic*] from the obligation to pay.

There are other documents involving *foranos* that should be noted briefly: They record a purchase of 200 sheep for their wool (APT, *Novallas,* fol. 315v); a payment to a Christian for instruction in the craft of tailoring (APT, *Latorre, 1492–98* fol. 37r–v); the granting to a *forano* exemption from the *panateria* of Tudela (AMT, *Libro de cuentas,* 1493 fol. 160v par. 4); and an order to sequester the property of a *forano* and the subsequent lifting of that directive (AGN, *Documentos* Caj. 165 No. 80 fols. 63v par. 1 and 64r par. 6; Caj. 166 No. 7 fols. 18v par. 1 and 21v par. 5).

6: The Road to Expulsion

1. The document that refers to "one day in March" as the final date of residence for professing Jews can be found in APT, *Juhan Martínez Cabero, Vol. 1498* fol. 5v. Abravanel's perceptions on the state of affairs in Castile-Aragon are discussed by Benzion Netanyahu in his *Don Isaac Abravanel;* see, especially, pp. 46 and 276. Suárez Fernández in his *Judíos españoles en la edad media,* pp. 252–256, argues that Ferdinand and Isabella were at first perceived as protectors of the Jews, and that the expulsion had not been decided upon until much later. If his argument is correct, it lends support to Abravanel's perceptions. See also Maurice Kriegel, "La prise d'une décision: l'expulsion des juifs d'Espagne en 1492," *Revue historique* 260 (1978):49–90.

2. On the political situation in Navarre from 1479 through the death of Francisco Febo, again see Boissonade, *Histoire de la réunion,* pp. 16–32; Lacarra, *Historia política* 3:345–356; and Suárez Fernández, *Fernando. . . y Navarra,* pp. 92–105. Boissonade gives slightly different dates for Francisco's coronation; see Lacarra p. 352 and the footnotes thereto.

3. This document was found in the notarial archives of Tudela; see above chapter three and the discussion there. J. M. Lacarra, *Historia política* 3:353, is of the opinion that Francisco had definitely returned to Bearne by February 12. The document here was issued in the name of the king on February 4 in Sangüesa. It is highly probable that Francisco passed through this eastern Navarrese city on the way home to his French dominions.
   Not all of the provisions in this *privilegium,* of course, were positively oriented toward the Jews. For example, mention is made of an order by prince Carlos, the son of Juan II, decreed on 3 April 1444 in Tafalla that Jews must wear a sign on their clothing—the "Jewish badge." Nevertheless, the tenor of the document (i.e., the *privilegium*) and its very issuance by Francisco Febo was clearly a positive sign to the Jews.

4. Many historians view the year 1479 as a turning point for the Jews; see, inter alia, Hillgarth, *The Spanish Kingdoms* 2:481 and *passim,* and H. Beinart, *Conversos on Trial,* p. 4. Beinart, p. 34 observes, as do others, that the first tribunals were established in Seville and that within two years the expulsion from Andalusia was effected.

5. On the Inquisition in Navarre, see chapter four. The Corellan edict

is clearly connected with the struggle over the Inquisition. Kayserling, *Die Juden in Navarra,* pp. 104–105, connects the 1488 decree with the 1469 action of Leonor that required Pamplonese Jews to rebuild their *judería* and then return to it, whereas Amador de los Ríos, *Historia de los judíos,* p. 729 ties the decree to the 1482 Ordenamiento de Tafalla. On the latter, see note 11.

6. Four copies of the decree are extant. The original clearly is AMC, *Legajo 1* and it was signed by Johan and Catalina. At the bottom of the document is a statement that it was shown to the royal authorities on 26 March 1500, presumably as proof of the village's privileges.

Two copies of the edict were made by Fernando de Vacua; one is dated 7 August 1511, and is AGN, *Fondo de monasterios: Fitero,* Legajo 22, No. 273, which incidentally is covered by folios of the biblical book of Ezekiel in Hebrew. The second transcription is from 6 July 1512, and is filed in AGN, *Cámara de comptos, Documentos* Caj. 165 No. 16. According to Florencio Idoate, *Catálogo del Archivo General de Navarra* 48:385 there is a copy of 14 February 1502 in AGN, ibid., Caj. 165 No. 19, III.

7. For the Cortes of Toledo document, see F. Baer, *Die Juden* 2:346–347. Discussions of this source can be found in Baer's *History* 2:325, and Hillgarth, *Spanish Kingdoms* 2:441. Although the issues mentioned in the document were not new, this was the first time the laws were rigorously applied. Ferdinand and Isabella claimed that this action was prompted by requests of the *procuradores* of the municipalities, who complained that Christians were being harmed; see Suárez Fernández, *Judíos españoles,* pp. 263–264. The arguments employed in the Cortes decrees were later employed in the Castilian-Aragonese expulsion edict.

Now see H. Beinart, "The Separation in Living Quarters between Jews and Christians in Fifteenth Century Spain," (Hebrew) *Zion* 51 (1986):61–85 and, especially, pp. 70–71.

8. On the taxes collected in Corella, see chapter two. AMC, *Legajo 22,* 1491–92 contains a reference to the Jewish tax collectors aiding the impoverished municipality.

9. The 1488 Cortes declaration is in AGN, *Documentos* Caj. 165 No. 30 and in AGN, *Archivo del reino: sección de cuarteles y alcabalas* Leg. 1 Car. 12 (B); and of 1493 in AGN, *Documentos* Caj. 165 No. 59, Caj. 193 No. 42, *Registro* 516 fol. 56r, v, and AMT, Lib. 4 No. 6. AGN, Caj. 165 No. 60, though undated, is probably from 1490.

These documents are royal recapitulations of the demands of the Cortes. On Jews as tax collectors, see chapter two.

10. On this subject, see chapter five.

11. AGN, *Documentos* Caj. 164 No. 28(A). The document was published by Béatrice Leroy in her article "Le royaume de Navarre el les juifs aux XIVe et XVe siecles," pp. 291–292. Many historians, following the

mistake of José Yanguas y Miranda, *Diccionario* 1:520, claimed that this edict was published in Tafalla in 1482. Amador, *Historia*, p. 727, even called it the "Ordenamiento de Tafalla" and so did Baron, *Social and Religious* 11:406 who cites Amador. Yanguas erred because the document of the 1482 Tafalla Cortes meeting was the next paper in the archival box: Caj. 164 No. 29. Also, he connected Tafalla with the 1492 letter it sent to Tudela warning against the influx of the Castilian-Aragonese refugees. Indeed, Kayserling, *Die Juden*, p. 106, linked these two events and criticized Tafalla for its anti-Jewish attitudes. It should be noted that the Cortes of 1492 was convened in Estella.

This type of decree had been published at other times in the history of the Jews in Navarre. Zabalo Zabalegui, *La administración del reino de Navarra*, p. 219, note 988, cites an example in 1345, and AMT, Lib. 31 No. 40, dated in 1456, declared that the Tudelan Jews should not walk in front of the collegiate church of Santa María during Mass.

12. AGN, *Papeles sueltos*, Leg. 28 Car. 18(A), (B), and (C). Letters (B) and (C), if they are working drafts of the report, indicate that Jews were not singled out and indeed "personas eclesiásticas y religiosas" were included.

For these issues in Castile and Aragon during this period, see Suárez Fernández, *Documentos*, pp. 461–462, passim.

13. That Jews were in fact involved in lending money and grain is shown in chapter two.

14. AGN, *Papeles sueltos*, Leg. 28 Car. 18 (A). Gabriel also took notaries to task for drawing up fraudulent instruments that harmed the kingdom and the common good. Letter (C) focuses on usury in Tudela and the *merindad* of la Ribera and does not specifically mention Jews. It does report that people had left the kingdom because of inability to pay off their debts. Letter (B) talks of the farmers' need for seed grain, which caused them to borrow at the beginning of the year; on this, see chapter two. The document also laments the effects on the farmers and their families.

15. See chapter five.

16. AGN, *Documentos* Caj. 165 No. 80 fol. 40v dated 10 November 1494 in Pamplona.

17. On the investigation of Fray Miguel, see chapter four. On relations between Castile-Aragon and Navarre at this time, see Boissonade, *Histoire de la réunion*, pp. 100–20, Lacarra, *Historia política*, pp. 380–387, and Suárez Fernández, *Fernando . . . y Navarra*, pp. 166–173. It is tempting to hypothesize that Fray Miguel may have been related to Lope de Baquedano, one of the henchmen of the conde de Lerín. It was during these months in 1495 that Ferdinand was attempting to banish the conde from Navarre to pacify the kingdom, and this process may have included proceeding against many of the allies of the conde, as well.

An April investigation of coin clipping by Francisco Cambiador and a Jew named Dabit Alazar is in APT, *Martín Novallas, Cascante,* fols. 278r–284v. This document points up anti-Jewish sentiment in Navarrese society. During the trial, Alazar was typecast as ill-mannered, cheap, and a liar, and one witness testified that "since Dabit Alazar was a Jew, he did not want any truck with him."

18. AGN, *Documentos* Caj. 166 No. 16 fol. 7r. A brief summary of the anti-Jewish proclamation can be found in AGN, *Archivo del reino (cortes y diputación): sección de legislación general y contrafueros* Leg. 1 Car. 10 fol. 11r. According to Amador, *Historia,* pp. 730–731, Ferdinand's henchmen were influential at the Pamplona Cortes of 1496.

19. In order to avoid duplicity on the part of the Jews, the Cortes asked that loans should be made only as prescribed by ancient *fueros;* that is, with an attached seal. If the Jews did not comply, the parliamentarians proposed that half the principal be confiscated and given to the royal treasury, the other half to the injured party, and further requested a fine of 220 pounds to be paid by the guilty notary. The monarchs accepted the request of the three estates and ordered that loan contracts be of a kind allowed by the "fuero antigo."

The attaching of the seal is mentioned in the "fuero antigo" as a method for registering loans. The fee charged by the notary provided income for the royal treasury.

20. For the 1497 documents, see APT, *Pedro Latorre, Vol. 1492–1498* fols. 294r–295r, 304r, and 319r. M.S.: Gehuda Bendebut. Also check APT, *Pedro de Lesaca, Cortes, Vol. 1494–1523* fol. 178r. On reasons for the expulsion from Portugal, see note 30.

21. APT, *Latorre, Vol. 1498–1501* fols. 1v–2r. The price was eighty florins. On *majuelos,* see chapter two.

22. Ibid., fols. 13r–14r. See Baer, *History* 2:433 for parallel activities prior to the 1492 expulsion. The following articles in the journal *Sefarad* tell of financial (and travel) arrangements made by Jews in the kingdom of Aragon during those hectic weeks: Leopoldo Piles, "La expulsión de los judíos en Valencia. Repercusiones económicas," 15 (1955):89–101; José Cabezudo Astraín, "La expulsión de los judíos zaragozanos," ibid., pp. 103–136; idem, "La expulsión de los judíos en Ejea de los Caballeros," 30 (1970):349–363; Gonzalo Máximo Borrás Guales, "Liquidación de los bienes de los judíos expulsados de la aljama de Calatayud," 29 (1969):31–48; and Gabriel Secall Güell, "Noticias de judíos aragoneses en el momento de la expulsión," 42 (1982):103–112.

23. APT, *Latorre, Vol. 1498–1501* fol. 7r–v. Ms: Habran de la Rabiça. On New Christians during these days, see ibid., fols. 1v and 7r.

24. AGN, *Fondo de monasterios: Fitero,* Leg. 2 No. 37. For judaizers within religious orders in late fifteenth-century Castile, see H. Beinart,

"The Judaizing Movement in the Order of San Jeronimo in Castile," *Scripta Hierosolymitana* 7 (1961):167–192 and Albert A. Sicroff, "Clandestine Judaism in the Hieronymite Monastery of Nuestra Señora de Guadalupe," in I. A. Langnas and B. Sholod eds., *Studies in Honor of M. J. Bernadete* (New York, 1965), pp. 89–125 and idem, "The Jeronymite Monastery of Guadalupe in 14th and 15th Century Spain," in M. P. Hornik ed., *Collected Studies in Honor of Américo Castro's 8oth Year* (Oxford, 1965), pp. 397–422.

25. AGN, ibid., Leg. 36 No. 405, 1° cuerpo. This document was copied on 2 November 1532 from the register of the then-deceased notary Miguel Oliva. Jaco had said that Rui Díaz "guarda el sabado como judio." For similar phrases derived from Hebrew idioms that were used to describe *conversos'* activities, see Beinart, *Conversos,* pp. 275–277. Jaco's defense was based on the argument that he only said such statements through the "boca del diablo."

See H. C. Lea, *A History of the Inquisition of Spain* 1:255, note 1, for an incident in which Ferdinand of Aragon attempted to arrest a New Christian living in Fitero.

26. Already in May 1487 the Inquisition was attempting to gain a foothold in Fitero; see chapter four.

27. Many historians have confused the year of the Navarrese expulsion. Among them, Suárez Fernández, *Documentos,* p. 64, dated the event in 1499, whereas José María Lacarra, "El Desarollo urbano de las ciudades de Navarra y Aragón en la edad media," p. 16, and Yanguas y Miranda, *Diccionario histórico-político de Tudela,* p. 148, employed the year 1492. S. Rosanes, *Divrei yemei yisrael be-Togarmah* (Tel-Aviv, 1930) 1:265 used 1497.

Both APT, *Juhan Martínez Cabero, Vol. 1498* fol. 5v and AMT, Lib. 43 No. 11 refer clearly to the expulsion or banishment of the Jews. APT, *Latorre, Vol. 1498–1501* fol. 7r–v contains a reference to a Jew on March 6, and APT, *Miguel Martínez Cabero, Vol. 1498–1502* fol. 1r–v refers to the "former *aljama* of Tudela" on March 29. It is possible that the expulsion took place before March 17; see AGN, *Documentos* Caj. 166 No. 47 whereby houses in the former *judería* of Pamplona were leased in 1498 to a Christian. Idoate's comments, *Catálogo,* No. 993, on the problems of the dates listed in the document are apposite.

According to Juan Ignacio Fernández Marco, *Cascante, ciudad de la Ribera,* p. 338, who cites a now-lost document, the local synagogue was passed on to Christians for use as a church because the "banishment of the Jews has already been decreed." The document is said to be dated 16 January 1498.

28. Alesón's comments are in J. Moret and F. de Alesón, *Annales del reyno de Navarra,* Libro XXXV, chapter 4, pp. 136–137. The marginal

note indicates that Alesón—who wrote volume five, which contains book 35—followed a writer named Agramonte, the author of a *Historia de Navarra,* but this book cannot be found. Alesón also wrote that the expulsion took place again in the following year, that is 1499, but there is absolutely no corroborating evidence for his assertion.

Yosef ha-Kohen's remarks are found in *Emek ha-Bakha,* ed., M. Letteris, p. 102, and in his *Sefer Divrei ha-Yamim le-Malkhei Zarefat u-Malkhei Beit Ottoman ha-Togar,* Part One, p. 49b. Isaac Abravanel mentions the Navarrese expulsion as one of many that befell the Jews in his commentary on Ezekiel 20:34 in *Perush al Nevi'im Aharonim* (Jaffa and Jerusalem, 1956–57), p. 521. See also the second account in A. Marx, "The Expulsion of the Jews from Spain" in his *Studies in Jewish History and Booklore* (New York, 1944), p. 101 and p. 103 in translation. The dating there is incorrect.

29. AMT, Lib. 43 No. 11 clearly indicates that the expulsion was directly ordered by the Navarrese monarchs. There is no evidence that Juan de Lasalle (ms: Johan de la Sala), Bishop of Couserans (ms: Coserans), who was again named lieutenant governor of the kingdom in October 1497 and was politically connected to Ferdinand of Aragon, was responsible for the edict, pace Amador, pp. 730–731, and Baron, p. 243. On Juan de Lasalle during this period, see Lacarra, *Historia política,* p. 389. It should be added that the chroniclers all agree in placing the responsibility for this edict on Johan and Catalina.

The best accounts of the attempts to divide Navarre during the years 1494 through 1498 can be found in Boissonade, *Réunion,* pp. 100–133, and Suárez Fernández, *Fernando . . . y Navarra,* pp. 157–199.

30. The situation of Navarre during 1497 and 1498 is summarized clearly in Lacarra, *Historia política,* pp. 387–390. For examples of the increase of pressure from Ferdinand and Isabella on the kingdom, see A. de la Torre, *Documentos sobre relaciones internacionales de los reyes católicos,* Nos. 20, and 71 through 76. These documents are from February and March 1498. King Johan complained in September 1497 that Juan de Ribera, Ferdinand and Isabella's captain general of the frontier, was massing troops near Navarre; see L. Suárez Fernández, *Política internacional de Isabel la católica* (Valladolid, 1972) 5:200–201.

Political pressure from local Navarrese does not appear to have been the deciding factor in the expulsion edict. There is no evidence for the assertions by many historians that the hatred of the Jews was a prime cause. A sample of these writers include Yanguas y Miranda in his *Historia compendiada del reino de Navarra* (San Sebastian, 1832), p. 64 and M. Arigita y Lasa, *Los judíos en el pais vasco,* pp. 45–46, and most recently, in passing, Iñaki Reguera, *La Inquisición,* p. 179. Béatrice Leroy in her short précis entitled "Les juifs de Navarre du XIIe au XVe siècle," p. 493 is correct in identifying Navarre's fear of an invasion by the Catholic Monarchs, but she has no evidence to support her assertion that the Pope had threatened Johan and Catalina with excommunication.

Pimenta Ferro, *Os judeus,* p. 483, suggests that the expulsion edict in Portugal was a result of a combination of factors, domestic and peninsular. She too needs to explain the superficial paradox in Portuguese policy of allowing the entry of Castilian Jews in 1492 and their expulsion four years later. Her list of social factors in the issuance of the edict, many of them structural, leaves the question of the timing of the decree unexplained; see pp. 498–500. On structural reasons for expulsions of Jews, see Maurice Kriegel, "Mobilisation politique et modernisation organique. Les expulsions de juifs au bas moyen age," *Archives de sciences sociales des religions* 46 (1978):5–20, and just recently Sophia Menache, "On the expulsions of the Jews from England and France," (Hebrew) *Zion* 51 (1986):319–32.

31. Even if the Jews had been permitted to travel through the French dominions of Johan and Catalina, the exiles would have had to pass through Languedoc. Unlike in 1493—see chapter five above—there is no record of Ferdinand allowing the Jews to pass through Aragon. See Suárez Fernández, *Documentos . . . la expulsión,* pp. 534–535, wherein Ferdinand and Isabella in 1499 declared that only Jews who had been baptized or intended to do so could enter their kingdoms.

32. Gamil's account is found in a fragment of his volume of sermons titled *Keter Shem Tov,* and it was published by Toledano in the *Hebrew Union College Annual* 5 (1928):403–409. The *ketubbah* that Gamil signed · is numbered 3, labeled as "Documento hebreo no. 8," and is located in the Archivo Municipal de Tudela. José Luis Lacave has transcribed the document and will publish it and others in a forthcoming volume on Spanish *ketubbot.*

Gamil's business was located in "קשטילנוב," which perhaps is to be identified with Castellón de la Plana, near Valencia. For the Valencian Inquisition during those years, see Ricardo García Cárcel, *Orígenes de la inquisición española. El tribunal de Valencia, 1478–1530* (Barcelona, 1976), pp. 69–76. On Muslims leaving al-Andalus through 1499, see generally Hillgarth 2:389–390. Gamil was eighty-two years old when he published his work *Keter Shem Tov,* and his memory of some of the particulars may have been faulty. Interestingly, some Jews were converting to Islam as early as 1490, probably for reasons of safety; see Hillgarth 2:470.

33. Amador, *Historia,* pp. 730–731, misunderstood Yosef ha-Kohen when he wrote that the Navarrese Jews left for Provence and France. Yosef was referring to his own family and others who had left Navarre in 1493. H. C. Lea in his *A History of the Inquisition in Spain* 1:141, made the same mistake. Béatrice Leroy, "Le royaume," p. 406, follows Lea and Baron, *Social and Religious* 11:406, relies on Amador, and so they both

fell into the same error. Henry Léon in his *Histoire des juifs de Bayonne* (Paris, 1893), pp. 13 and 16 declares that Navarrese Jews were among the first Jews from the Iberian peninsula to arrive in southern France, although he admits that the archives have not preserved any trace of them. See also B. Leroy's conjectures in *The Jews of Navarre*, p. 147.

Rosanes, *Divrei Yemei Yisrael*, p. 267, without citing sources, states that a separate community of Navarrese Jewish exiles was established in Salonica. Yosef Hacker's dissertation, *The Jewish Community of Salonica from the Fifteenth to the Sixteenth Century* (The Hebrew University, Jerusalem, 1978) does not contain any reference to such a group. See also B. Leroy, "Recherches sur les juifs de Navarre à la fin du moyen age," p. 377, note 160.

It must be noted that the possession by a Jew of the family name Nabarro does not prove that the individual or his family left the kingdom circa 1498; they might have left before the expulsion as Jews, or even a century later as outwardly professing Christians.

34. Yosef ha-Kohen in his *Emek ha-Bakha,* and with a slight variation in the *Sefer Divrei ha-Yamim.* Yosef's family may have been well aware of the difficulties facing Navarrese Jews should they try to exit the kingdom and therefore wrote of his family being happy to leave the "iron cauldron for they feared for their lives." Alesón's statement about the conversions is in *Annales,* pp. 136–137.

Kayserling, *Die Juden,* p. 108, following Yosef ha-Kohen wrote that the Jews had no avenue for escape, although he was incorrect in asserting that the roads were barricaded.

35. The first account of the baptisms is from APT, *Martínez Cabero, Vol. 1498* fol. 5v. It is dated 21 September 1498. García Pérez, one of the witnesses to the baptism, was the *padrino* and Johana Deazpeleta the *madrina.* On others of the Paçagon family taking the name Berrozpe, see *Latorre, Vol. 1492–98* fol. 109v. For more on their family, see chapter five.

The second report on baptisms is from *Pedro de Lesaca, Cortes,* fols. 169v–170r, and the list is crammed onto the pages, earlier material apparently having been erased. Abram's sons were formerly named Salamon, Çebi, Çeaj, and Yuçef. Leonor was formerly named Orabuena. If this was her surname, she probably was a member of the Orabuena family, whose ancestor Juçe was chief rabbi of Navarre at the turn of the fifteenth century. Abram Orabuena, another scion of this famous Navarrese Jewish clan, *Sancho Ezquerro, Vol. 1480–1500* fols. 436v–437r, became Benedit Ferrandez.

On the Portuguese conversions, see Pimenta Ferro, pp. 483 and ff. It appears that in the late fifteenth century, other Jewish communities converted as well when faced with an edict of expulsion. See for example Eliyahu Ashtor, "Palermitan Jewry in the Fifteenth Century," *Hebrew*

Union College Annual 50 (1979):219–251 and especially the conclusion on p. 241. Much research still needs to be done on how many Jews converted, and how many chose exile, even on the Iberian mainland in Castile and Aragon. When Jewish historians go beyond looking for heroism (read exile) on the part of Jews and simply seek to describe human behavior in the face of these communal traumas, a more balanced history of the Jews' response to the expulsions will be written. It is interesting to add here that Provençal Jewry behaved in a similar fashion: In 1501, the majority converted.

36. AGN, *Archivo del reino: sección de negocios eclesiásticos* Leg. 1 Car. 21 contains a number of documents that were copied in the seventeenth century. Yanguas published parts of them in his *Diccionario* 1:520–522. Among these is a 1510 list of the 180 heads of New Christian families in Tudela and their payment of special tax. This figure of 180 is similar to the number of native and immigrant Jewish families in Tudela given above in chapter one, and supports the conclusion that almost the whole community converted. Florencio Idoate published the list of names in his *Rincones de la historia de Navarra* (Pamplona, 1954) 1:157–161. See the citations for Corella in note 38; there it simply states that there have been no receipts of taxes from the Jews "after the *conversion* [italics mine] of the Jews." A tax-related reference to the conversion of Jews of Viana is in AGN, *Registro* 537 fol. 18v.

Mercedes García Arenal, *Los moros*, pp. 132–133, recently published a document of 9 January 1517 (APT, *Pedro Copin de Lorenz*) wherein the viceroy of Navarre ordered that an inventory be made of all the property that was abandoned by the expelled Jews and Muslims. That the Muslims had been expelled the year before probably occasioned this decree. Still it indicates that some Jews—or after 1498, *conversos*—left the kingdom. Parenthetically, as García Arenal notes, p. 64, very little is known of the Muslim expulsion.

The document about Ossua's family is in AMT, Libro 43 No. 11. On Ossua's conversion, see AGN, *Registro* 519 fol. 38r, where it is stated that this 1497 report was first composed by "Mastre Ossua who at that time was a rabbi." Ossua's family was probably in the border town of Uxanavilla trying to leave the peninsula from a port on the Bay of Biscay. That was clearly the shortest route out. There is no indication how the information came to the attention of the government.

37. The document of March 29 appears in APT, *Miguel Martinez Cabero, Vol. 1498–1502* fols. 1r–2r. The August transaction is in *Juhan Martínez Cabero, Vol. 1494–1500, Segundo Cuaderno* fol. 122r.

Iñaki Reguera, *La Inquisición*, pp. 178–179 points out that very few cases of judaizers from Navarre are recorded in the 16th century, which convinces him that the conversions were generally sincere.

38. The Tudela document is in AMT, *Libro de cuentas*, fol. 220r. That

of Corella is in AGN, *Documentos* Caj. 166 No. 65 fol. 3r and from 1498–
1502 in ibid., *Registro* 519, passim. See chapter three, where the Jews were
described in 1498 as a people who paid their taxes above and beyond their
responsibilities.

39. On Viana, see AGN, *Registro* 537 fol. 18v. On Pamplona, generally, see AGN, *Documentos* Caj. 166 No. 63 and No. 47. The fate of the
synagogue (ms: *sinoga*) is told by AMP, 264(A), which has been published
by José Goñi Gaztambide in *Estudios de la edad media de la corona de
Aragón* 10 (1975):300–03. The Jewish cemetery in Pamplona is referred
to in *Registro* 541 Bis fol. 68r. On the synagogue in Cascante, see the
reference cited in note 27. Various tributes owed the king by the
synagogues and *almosnas* of Tudela, Cascante, Corella, Cintruénigo, Arguedas, Villafranca, Valtierra, and other places within the *merindad* of
Tudela were granted, AGN, *Documentos* Caj. 168 No. 37, by King Ferdinand (of Aragon, Navarre) on 18 February 1514 to Alonso Sanz de Berrozpe. Christians paid taxes on the former synagogue and charnel house
of Corellan Jews, *Registro* 519 fol. 55r.

Houses that belonged to a Jew from the erstwhile *judería* of Pamplona
were rented, AGN, *Documentos* Caj. 166 No. 47, by the royal authorities
to a Johan de San Pelay in May of 1498.

Compare Pimenta Ferro, p. 489, and the data on Portugal. On Muslim
communal and private property in Navarre after the Muslims' expulsion
in 1516, see documents 48 and 49 in García Arenal, pp. 130–132.

40. For the opposing argument that diaspora Jews possess an unde-
veloped political sense, see, among others, Isaac Abravanel, *Ma'ayenei ha-
Yeshuah,* Ma'ayan 8 Tamar 9, specifically pp. 349–350. Abravanel was
clearly troubled by this lack of political wisdom and leadership, which he
probably considered one of the causes of the many late fifteenth-century
expulsions. That he did see them as a pattern, see Y. Hacker, "New
Chroniclers on the Expulsion of the Jews from Spain. Its Causes and Results," (Hebrew) *Yitzhak F. Baer Memorial Volume, Zion* 49 (1979), particularly p. 201, note 1. At five hundred years distance, we can afford to
be more sympathetic to his generation. See Ismar Schorsch, "On the Political Judgment of the Jew," especially pp. 8–12, and Yosef H. Yerushalmi,
The Lisbon Massacre of 1506 and the Royal Image in the Shebet Yehudah
(Cincinnati, 1976).

Selected Bibliography

Alcalá Galve, Angel. *Los orígines de la inquisición en Aragón.* Saragossa?, n.d. [1984?].

Altadill, Julio. *Castillos medioevales de Navarra.* San Sebastián, 1936.

Amador de los Ríos, José. *Historia social, politica y religiosa de los judíos de España y Portugal.* Reprint edition. Madrid, 1960.

Arigita y Lasa, Mariano. *Los judíos en el país vasco.* 2nd. ed. Pamplona, 1908.

Ashtor, Eliyahu. *The Jews of Moslem Spain.* Translated by Aaron Klein and Jenny Machlowitz Klein. 3 vols. Philadelphia, 1979.

————. "Palermitan Jewry in the Fifteenth Century." *Hebrew Union College Annual* 50 (1979):219–251.

Atlas de Navarra. Pamplona, 1977.

Azcona, Tarsicio de. *Isabel la católica.* Madrid, 1964.

Baer, Yitzhak. *A History of the Jews in Christian Spain.* Translated by Louis Schoffman et al. 2 vols. Philadelphia, 1961.

————, Fritz, ed. *Die Juden im Christlichen Spanien.* Vol. 1. Part 1: *Aragonien und Navarra.* Part 11: *Kastilien/Inquisitionsakten.* Berlin, 1929 and 1936.

Baron, Salo W. *The Jewish Community.* 3 vols. Philadelphia, 1943.

————. *A Social and Religious History of the Jews.* 2nd. ed. Vols. 10 and 11. New York and London, 1965 and 1967.

Beinart, Haim. "The Converso Problem in 15th Century Spain" in R. D. Barnett, ed., *The Sephardi Heritage.* (London, 1971):425–456.

————. *Conversos on Trial.* Translated by Yael Guiladi. Jerusalem, 1981.

————. "The Expulsion of the Jews from Valmaseda." (Hebrew) *Zion* 46 (1981):39–51.

————. "Hispano-Jewish Society." In H. H. Ben-Sasson and S. Ettinger eds., *Jewish Society through the Ages.* (New York, 1971):220–238.

————. "Jewish Witnesses for the Prosecution of the Spanish Inquisition." In Wouter de Vos et al. eds., *Essays in Honour of Ben Beinart, Acta Juridica.* (Capetown, 1978):37–46.

————. "The Judaizing Movement in the Order of San Jeronimo in Castile." *Scripta Hierosolymitana* 7 (1961):167–192.

————. "The Separation in Living Quarters between Jews and Christians in Fifteenth Century Spain." (Hebrew) *Zion* 51 (1986):61–85.

————. *Trujillo. A Jewish Community in Extremadura on the Eve of the Expulsion from Spain.* Jerusalem, 1980.

Ben-Sasson, Haim Hillel. "The Generation of the Spanish Exiles on Its Fate." (Hebrew) *Zion* 26 (1961):23–42.

Ben-Zimra, Eliyahu. "Ha-Malshinut ve-ha-Mesirah be-Mishnatam shel Hakhmei Sefarad." In Meir Benayahu ed., *Studies in Memory of the Rishon Le-Zion R. Yitzhak Nissim.* (Jerusalem, 1984/1985) 1:297–321.

Boissonade, Prosper. *Histoire de la réunion de la Navarre à la Castille.* Paris, 1893.

Borrás Guales, Gonzalo Máximo. "Liquidación de los bienes de los judíos expulsados de la aljama de Calatayud." *Sefarad* 29 (1969):31–48.

Braudel, Fernand. *The Structures of Everyday Life.* New York, 1985.

Cabezudo Astraín, J. "La expulsión de los judíos en Ejea de los Caballeros." *Sefarad* 30 (1970):349–363.

————. "La expulsión de los judíos zaragozanos." *Sefarad* 15 (1955):103–136.

————. "Los conversos aragoneses según los procesos de la inquisición." *Sefarad* 18 (1958):272–282.

————. "Los conversos de Barbastro y el apellido 'Santángel'." *Sefarad* 23 (1963):265–284.

Cantera Burgos, Francisco. "Christian Spain." In Cecil Roth ed., *The World History of the Jewish People, The Dark Ages.* (Ramat Gan, 1966):359–381.

————. "Los judíos expulsados de San Martin de Valdeiglesias." In Iacob M. Hassan, ed., *Actas del I Simposio de Estudios Sefardíes.* (Madrid, 1970):23–32.

————. *Sinagogas españolas.* Madrid, 1955.

Caro Baroja, Julio. "Los judíos." In *Etnografía histórica de Navarra.* (Pamplona, 1971) 1:175–194.

Carpenter, Dwayne E. *Alfonso X and the Jews: An Edition of and Commentary on Siete Partidas 7.24 "De los judíos."* Berkeley and Los Angeles, 1986.

Carrasco Pérez, Juan. "Acerca del préstamo judío en Tudela a fines del siglo xiv." *Príncipe de Viana* 166–167 (1982):909–948.

————. "La actividad crediticia de los judíos en Pamplona" In *Minorités et marginaux en France meridionale et dans la peninsule ibérique (VIIe-XVIIIe siècles).* (Paris, 1986):221–263.

————. "La hacienda municipal de Tudela a fines de la Edad Media (1480–1521)." In Emilio Sáez, Cristina Segura Graíño and Margarita Cantera Montenegro eds., *La ciudad hispánica durante los siglos XIII al XVI.* [Actas del coloquio celebrado en la Rábida y Sevilla del 14 al 19 de septiembre de 1981] (Madrid, 1985) 2:1663–1697.

————. *La población de Navarra en el siglo xiv.* Pamplona, 1973.

———. "Los judíos de Viana y Laguardia (1350–1408): aspectos sociales y económicos." In *Vitoria en la edad media*. (Vitoria, 1982):419–447.

———. "Prestamistas judíos de Tudela a fines del siglo xiv (1382–1383)." *Miscelánea de estudios árabes y hebraicos* 29 (1980):87–141.

Clavería, Carlos. *Historia del reino de Navarra*. Pamplona, 1971.

Ciérvide Martinena, Ricardo. *Inventario de bienes de Olite [1496]*. Pamplona, n.d. [1979?].

De las Cacigas, I. "Tres cartas públicas de comanda." *Sefarad* 6 (1946):74–93.

De la Torre, Antonio. *Documentos sobre relaciones internacionales de los reyes católicos*. 6 vols. Barcelona, 1949–1966.

Desdevises du Dezert, G. *Don Carlos d'Aragon, prince de Viana*. Paris, 1889.

Edwards, John. "Jewish Testimony to the Spanish Inquisition: Teruel 1484–1487." *Revue des études juives* 143 (1984):333–350.

Elliot, J. H. *Imperial Spain 1469–1716*. London, 1963.

Emery, Richard. *The Jews of Perpignan in the Thirteenth Century*. New York, 1959.

Fernández Marco, Juan Ignacio. *Cascante, ciudad de la Ribera*. Vol. 1. Pamplona, 1978.

Fita, Fidel. "La inquisición española y el derecho internacional en 1487. Bula inédita de Inocencio VIII." *Boletín de la real academia de historia* 16 (1890):367–371.

García Arenal, Mercedes. "Los moros de Navarra en la baja edad media." In Mercedes García-Arenal and Béatrice Leroy, *Moros y judíos en Navarra en la baja edad media*. (Madrid, 1984):9–139.

García Cárcel, Ricardo. *Orígenes de la inquisición española. El tribunal de Valencia. 1478–1530*. Barcelona, 1976.

Goñi Gaztambide, José. "La formación intelectual de los navarros en la edad media, 1122–1500." *Estudios de la edad media de la corona de Aragón* 10 (1975):143–303.

Gonzalo Maeso, David. "Aportaciones a la historia de la judería de Soria." *Celtiberia* 56 (1978):153–168.

Graetz, Heinrich. *Geschichte der Juden*. Vol. 8. Leipzig, 1890.

Grayzel, Solomon. *The Church and the Jews in the Thirteenth Century*. Philadelphia, 1933.

Hacker, Joseph. "Some Letters on the Expulsion of the Jews from Spain and Sicily." (Hebrew) In E. Etkes and Y. Salmon, eds., *Studies in the History of Jewish Society in the Middle Ages Presented to Professor Jacob Katz*. (Jerusalem, 1980):64–97.

———. "The Jewish Community of Salonica from the Fifteenth to the Sixteenth Century." (Hebrew) A Hebrew University dissertation. Jerusalem, 1978.

———. "New Chronicles on the Expulsion of the Jews from Spain, Its

Causes and Results." (Hebrew) *Yitzhak F. Baer Memorial Volume. Zion* 44 (1979):201–228.

Haliczer, Stephen. "The Castilian Urban Patriciate and the Jewish Expulsions of 1480–92." *American Historical Review* 78 (1973):35–58.

———. "The Expulsion of the Jews and the Economic Development of Castile," in Josep M. Solá-Solé et al. eds., *Hispania Judaica, I: History* (Barcelona, n.d.):39–47.

Hamilton, E. J. *Money, Prices and Wages in Valencia, Aragon and Navarre. 1351–1500.* Cambridge, Mass., 1936.

Hillgarth, Jocelyn N. *The Spanish Kingdoms 1250–1516.* 2 vols. Oxford, 1976 and 1978.

Idoate, Florencio. *Rincones de la historia de Navarra.* 3 vols. Pamplona, 1954–1966.

Irurita Lusarreta, María Angeles. *El municipio de Pamplona en la edad media.* Pamplona, 1959.

Katz, Jacob. *Exclusiveness and Tolerance.* Oxford, 1961.

Kayserling, Meyer. *Geschichte der Juden in Portugal.* Leipzig, 1867.

———. "Das Handelshaus Ezmel in Ablitas." *Jahrbuch für Israeliten 5620.* Vienna (1859–60):40–44.

———. *Die Juden in Navarra, den Baskenlaendern und auf den Balearen.* Berlin, 1861.

Kriegel, Maurice. "La prise d'une décision: l'expulsion des juifs d'Espagne en 1492." *Revue historique* 260 (1978):49–90.

———. "Mobilisation politique et modernisation organique. Les expulsions de juifs au bas moyen age." *Archives de sciences sociales des religions* 46 (1978):5–20.

Lacarra, José María. "El desarrollo urbano de las ciudades de Navarra y Aragón en la edad media." *Pirineos* 6 (1950):5–34 and xi maps.

——— and A. J. Martín Duque eds., *Fueros de Navarra.* 2 vols. Pamplona, 1975.

———. *Historia política del reino de Navarra.* 3 vols. Pamplona, 1973.

Lacave, José Luis. "Importante hallazgo de documentos hebreos en Tudela." *Sefarad* 43 (1983):169–179.

———. "La carnicería de la aljama zaragozana a fines del siglo xv." *Sefarad* 35 (1975):3–35.

———. "Pleito judío por una herencia en aragonés y caracteres hebreos." *Sefarad* 30 (1970):325–337.

———. "Un interesante documento hebreo de Tudela." (to be published in the Haim Beinart Jubilee Volume.)

———. Translation of Y. Baer's "A History of the Jews in Christian Spain." *Historia de los judíos en la España cristiana.* 2 vols. Madrid, 1981.

Ladero Quesada, Miguel Angel. "Le nombre des juifs dans la Castille du XVème siecle." In *Proceedings of the Sixth World Congress of Jewish Studies* (Jerusalem, 1975) 2:45–52.

————. "Las juderías de Castilla según algunos 'servicios' fiscales del siglo xv." *Sefarad* 31 (1971):249–264.

————. "Los judíos castellanos del siglo xv en el arrendamiento de impuestos reales." *Cuadernos de Historia. Anexos de la revista Hispania* 6 (1975):417–439.

Lea, Henry Charles. *A History of the Inquisition of Spain*. 4 vols. New York, 1906–8.

Léon, Henry. *Histoire des juifs de Bayonne*. Paris, 1893.

Leroy, Béatrice. *The Jews of Navarre*. Jerusalem, 1985.

————. "La juiverie de Tudela aux XIIIe et XIVe siècles sous les soverains français de Navarre." *Archives juives* 9 (1972–3):1–10 and 15–18.

————. "Le royaume de Navarre et les juifs aux XIVe–XVe siècles: entre l'accueil et la tolérance." *Sefarad* 38 (1978):263–292.

————. "Les comptes d'Abraham Enxoep au début du XVe siècle." *Príncipe de Viana* 146–147 (1977):177–205.

————. "Les juifs de Navarre du XIIe au XVe siècle." *Revue des études juives* 138 (1979):491–493.

————. "Recherches sur les juifs de Navarre à la fin du moyen age." *Revue des études juives* 140 (1981):319–432.

Lindo, E. H. *History of the Jews of Spain and Portugal*. London, 1848.

Llorca, Bernardino. *Bulario pontificio de la inquisición española en su periodo constitucional. 1478–1525*. Vol. XV: Miscellanea Historiae Pontificiae. Rome, 1949.

Llorente, Juan Antonio. *Historia crítica de la inquisición de España*. 2 volumes. Barcelona, 1870.

Loeb, Isidore. "Les exilés d'Espagne en France." *Revue des études juives* 10 (1885):236–237.

————. "Un convoi d'exilés d'Espagne à Marseille en 1492." *Revue des études juives* 9 (1884):66–76.

Lopez, Robert S. and Raymond, Irving W. *Medieval Trade in the Mediterranean World*. New York and London, 1955.

López Elum, Pedro. "Datos sobre la usura en Navarra en los comienzos del siglo xiv." *Príncipe de Viana* 124–125 (1971):257–262.

————. "La depresión navarra en el siglo xv." *Príncipe de Viana* 126–127 (1972):151–168.

Lunenfeld, Marvin. *The Council of the Santa Hermandad*. Coral Gables, 1970.

Marín de la Salud, Jorge. *La moneda navarra y su documentación*. Madrid, 1975.

Marín Royo, Luis Maria. *Guía Tudelana*. Tudela, 1974.

Márquez Villanueva, F. "Conversos y cargos concejiles en el siglo xv." *Revista de archivos, bibliotecas y museos* 63 (1957):503–540.

Martinena Ruíz, Juan José. *La Pamplona de los burgos y su evolución urbana (siglos xii-xvi)*. Pamplona, 1974.

Marx, Alexander. "The Expulsion of the Jews from Spain." *Jewish Quar-*

terly Review, Old Series, 20 (1908):240–271 and reprinted in his *Studies in Jewish History and Booklore.* New York, 1944.

Menache, Sophia. "On the expulsions of the Jews from England and France." (Hebrew) *Zion* 51 (1986):319–332.

Mendoza, P. Fernando de. "Con los judíos de Estella." *Príncipe de Viana* 12 (1951):253–271.

Moret, José de and Alesón, Francisco de. *Annales del reyno de Navarra.* Reprint of the Pamplona 1766 edition. Vol. 5. Bilbao, 1969.

Motis Dolader, Miguel Angel. "Explotaciones agrarias de los judíos de Tarazona (Zaragoza) a fines del siglo xv." *Sefarad* 45 (1985):353–390.

Netanyahu, Benzion. *Don Isaac Abravanel, Statesman and Philosopher.* 2nd ed. Philadelphia, 1968.

———. *The Marranos of Spain.* 2d ed. New York, 1966.

Neuman, Abraham A. *The Jews in Spain.* 2 vols. Philadelphia, 1942.

Noonan, John T. Jr. *The Scholastic Analysis of Usury.* Cambridge, 1957.

Ozaki, Akio. "El régimen tributario y la vida económica de los mudéjares de Navarra." *Príncipe de Viana* 178 (1986):437–484.

Pavón Maldonado, Basilo. *Tudela, ciudad medieval: arte islámico y mudéjar.* Madrid, 1978.

Phillips, Carla Rahn. "Time and Duration: A Model for the Economy of Early Modern Spain." *American Historical Review* 92 (1987):531–562.

Piles, Leopoldo. "La expulsión de los judíos en Valencia. Repercusiones económicas." *Sefarad* 15 (1955):89–101.

Pimenta Ferro Tavares, Maria José. *Os judeus em Portugal no século xiv.* Lisbon, 1979.

———. *Os judeus em Portugal no século xv.* 2 vols. Lisbon, 1982.

Ramón Magdalena, J. "Estructura socio-económica de las aljamas castellonenses a finales del siglo xv." *Sefarad* 32 (1972):341–370.

Reguera, Iñaki. *La inquisición española en el país vasco.* San Sebastian, n.d. [1986?].

Romano, David. "Aljama frente a judería, call y sus sinónimos." *Sefarad* 39 (1979):347–354.

———. "Los judíos en los baños de Tortosa (siglos xiii-xiv)." *Sefarad* 40 (1980):57–64.

Rosanes, S. *Divrei yemei yisrael be-Togarmah.* Vol. 1. Tel-Aviv, 1930.

Ruíz Almansa, Javier. "La población de España en el siglo xvi." *Revista internacional de sociología* 3 (1943):115–138.

Ruíz Martín, F. "La población española al comienzo de los tiempos modernos." *Cuadernos de historia. Anexos a la revista Hispania* 1 (1967): 189–202.

Schorsch, Ismar. "On the Political Judgment of the Jew." *Leo Baeck Memorial Lecture* 20 (1976).

Secall Güell, Gabriel. "Noticias de judíos aragoneses en el momento de la expulsión." 42 (1982):103–112.

Sesma Muñoz, José Angel. *La diputación del reino de Aragón en la época de Fernando II (1479–1516)*. Saragossa, 1977.

Shatzmiller, Joseph. *Recherches sur la communauté juive de Manosque au moyen age*. Paris, 1973.

Sicroff, Albert A. "Clandestine Judaism in the Hieronymite Monastery of Nuestra Señora de Guadalupe." In I. A. Langnas and B. Sholod eds., *Studies in Honor of M. J. Bernadete*. (New York, 1965):89–125.

———. "The Jeronymite Monastery of Guadalupe in 14th and 15th Century Spain." In M. P. Hornik ed., *Collected Studies in Honor of Américo Castro's 80th Year*. (Oxford, 1965):397–422.

Soloveitchik, Haym. "Can Halakhic Texts Talk History." *Association for Jewish Studies Review* 3 (1978):152–196.

———. *Pawnbroking, A Study in the Inter-Relationship between Halakhah, Economic Activity and Communal Self-Image*. (Hebrew) Jerusalem, 1985.

———. "Pawnbroking: A Study in Ribbit and of the Halakhah in Exile." *Proceedings of the American Academy for Jewish Research* 38–39 (1970–1971):203–268.

Suárez Fernández, Luis. *Documentos acerca de la expulsión de los judíos*. Valladolid, 1964.

———. *Fernando el católico y Navarra*. Madrid, 1985.

———. *Judíos españoles en la edad media*. Madrid, 1980.

———. *Política internacional de Isabel la católica*. 5 vols. Valladolid, 1965–1972.

Toledano, Y. M. "Mi-Kitvei Yad." (Hebrew) *Hebrew Union College Annual* 5 (1928):403–409.

Vicens Vives, Jaime. *An Economic History of Spain*. Translated by Frances M. López Morillas. Princeton, 1969.

Wagner, Klaus. *Regesta de documentos del archivo de protocolos de Sevilla referentes a judíos y moros*. Salamanca, 1978.

Yanguas y Miranda, José. *Diccionario de antigüedades del reino de Navarra*. 3 vols. Reprint ed. Pamplona, 1964.

———. *Diccionario histórico-político de Tudela*. Reprint ed. Saragossa, 1828.

———. *Historia compendiada del reino de Navarra*. San Sebastian, 1832.

Yerushalmi, Yosef H. *The Lisbon Massacre of 1506 and the Royal Image in the Shebet Yehudah*. Cincinnati, 1976.

Zabalo Zabalegui, Javier. *La administración del reino de Navarra en el siglo xiv*. Pamplona, 1973.

Index

Designer: U.C. Press Staff
Compositor: Prestige Typography
Text: 10/12 Sabon
Display: Sabon
Printer: Braun-Brumfield, Inc.
Binder: Braun-Brumfield, Inc.